ITALIAN

Kathleen Speight
M.A., M.Litt., Dott.Lett.(Florence)

D0353427

TEACH YOURSELF BOOKS
Hodder and Stoughton

First printed 1943
Ninth impression 1981

Copyright © 1962 edition
Hodder and Stoughton Ltd.

This volume is published in the U.S.A. by David McKay Company Inc., 750 Third Avenue, New York, N.Y. 10017.

ISBN 0 340 27209 0

Printed in Great Britain
for Hodder and Stoughton Paperbacks,
a division of Hodder and Stoughton, Ltd.,
Mill Road, Dunton Green, Sevenoaks, Kent
(Editorial Office: 47 Bedford Square, London WC1 3DP
by Richard Clay (The Chaucer Press), Ltd., Bungay, Suffolk

PREFACE

THE title of this book explains itself: its purpose is to enable the reader to teach himself Italian without any help other than that which it provides. It is intended for those who do not know the language and while not being a formal grammar, all essential grammatical points are explained one by one in easy stages and illustrated by sentences; and anyone who works carefully through it should be able to read, write and speak Italian with a very considerable degree of success.

The study of Italian has, unhappily, been neglected in this country, which is a great pity, seeing how easy it is to acquire a working knowledge of the language, and considering the vast and interesting treasure house of literature which is open to him who learns how to unlock the door. *Teach Yourself Italian* aims at providing a key to that door, by giving the student the essentials of Italian, so that he may be in a position to enter and explore the treasure-house unaided. Being planned with an eye to the needs of the person intending or hoping to travel in Italy, the sentences and exercises are conversational in tone and practical, everyday things form their subject-matter; while the short extracts of Italian prose for translation give a hint of some of the many delights that await the visitor to that country and afford a glimpse—although a very brief one—of the character of its people.

It is hoped that the chapter on pronunciation will be found useful. It cannot be claimed that it will give the student a faultless Italian accent—that can only be acquired by contact with Italians—but it should at least prevent him from making many blunders, such as asking a waiter for roast dog (*cane* is the word for dog, and *carne* for meat); or talking about riding on cabbages (*càvoli*—pronounced cà-volee) when he means horses (*cavàlli*—pronounced cavàllee); or like a tall, thin, gaunt American lady who once caused much merriment in a Florentine tram by stressing the wrong syllable in a word: she wanted a ticket to Gràssina (stress on the Gràss)—a little village outside Florence—but what she said was: *Una, grassína* (grasséena), which means " One, small and fat ".

This book follows in the main the method of *Teach Yourself*

French and *Teach Yourself Spanish* published in the same series, and I am grateful to the author of those two books, Mr. Norman Scarlyn Wilson, for some very useful suggestions he made for this one. I should also like to thank my friend Dottoressa Antonietta Pettoello for very kindly reading some of the passages for translation, and Professor Bullock of Manchester University for reading through the proof.

KATHLEEN SPEIGHT

Manchester University
1943.

NOTE TO REVISED EDITION

In this revised edition the bibliography on pages 151–154 has again been brought up to date, as have also the Italian passages for translation, particularly as regards post-war hotel prices, etc. A comprehensive index has also been added, referring to both parts of the book, so that information on specific grammatical points may be found more readily.

KATHLEEN SPEIGHT

Manchester
1961.

INTRODUCTION

IN order to use this book to the best advantage the following points should be noted:

There are two parts: Part I contains most of the actual instruction and a series of exercises; and Part II is the key to the exercises in Part I and, in addition, it offers notes on any difficulties arising from them. The two parts should be used in conjunction. Study the lesson and then attempt the exercise *before* looking at Part II. Then turn to Part II and correct your effort. After the first three lessons the exercises marked (*a*) are always translation from Italian into English, and those marked (*b*) are translation the other way about: from English into Italian. Most benefit will be derived from the instruction if you do exercise (*a*) and *correct* it by means of Part II before you do exercise (*b*) for that lesson, and having corrected exercise (*a*), you will find (*b*) all the easier to do. Whenever uncertain how to express an English sentence in Italian, look back at previous lessons, where you will nearly always find a model from which to work.

It would be a good thing to revise after every *three* lessons; in fact, the lessons are so arranged that revision will be found most convenient after lessons 3, 9, 12, etc. When revising, turn back and again study each lesson in Part I; but for the exercises turn straight to the corresponding section in Part II, and do those sentences as exercises, using Part I as a key to correct them. In this way you will have done a fresh lot of exercises, as what was in the first place Italian–English is now English–Italian, and vice versa.

Memorize each new word and phrase as it appears. Try to remember the Italian word for the various things you see about you during the day, and get into the habit of repeating sentences in Italian over and over again. If you can get native help for the pronunciation, so much the better; if not, try to imitate the wireless. The oftener you repeat sentences over to yourself, the more quickly will you learn the language and the sooner will you begin to think in Italian. They need not be long nor difficult sentences; the shorter and simpler the better. "I get up", "I open the door", "I enter the room", and such like will do excellently to start with; when performing simple actions such as these, try to remember to say to yourself in Italian what you are doing.

The vocabulary at the end is Italian–English only, to give you the necessary help in translating from Italian to English, when you will be meeting new words. In translating from English into Italian you will be using words which you have already met—words which should therefore be in your memory; if they are not, they will usually be found without much trouble by consulting previous lessons.

Two words of advice and warning: First, use the key sensibly. Never turn to it until you have made some attempt at the exercise yourself. Always write down something *before* you see what the key says. Having to put right a wrong effort of your own is a hundred times more useful than merely copying down a correct version of someone else's, for in the latter case no impression is left on the mind. An Italian saying is very apt in this connection: *Sbagliando s'impara* ("By making mistakes one learns"); so don't be discouraged at the number of mistakes you make; correct them, and resolve not to make the same mistakes again. Secondly, while teaching yourself Italian, try to do some regularly each day. A short time, even only half an hour, each day will be far more beneficial than a huge spurt every now and then with long periods in between of no study at all. You cannot teach yourself a language by fits and starts; you must make up your mind to go slowly and steadily, always being sure of one lesson before passing on to the next, and you will soon surprise yourself with the progress you are making.

CONTENTS

		PAGE
	PREFACE	v
	INTRODUCTION	vii

PART I

LESSON

	ITALIAN PRONUNCIATION . . .	11
I.	INDEFINITE ARTICLE—GENDER . . .	19
II.	VERBS AND PRONOUNS	21
III.	DEFINITE ARTICLE—NUMBER . . .	24
IV.	MORE VERBS—THE POLITE PRONOUN .	27
V.	CONTRACTIONS OF WORDS—THE PARTITIVE .	31
VI.	THE PAST DEFINITE TENSE—POSITION OF ADJECTIVES	35
VII.	THE IMPERFECT TENSE—INVARIABLE NOUNS—DEMONSTRATIVE ADJECTIVES . . .	40
VIII.	POSSESSIVES—INTERROGATIVES . . .	44
IX.	THE FUTURE AND CONDITIONAL—NOUNS IN -IO	48
X.	COMPOUND TENSES OF VERBS . . .	52
XI.	CONJUNCTIVE PRONOUNS—THE IMPERATIVE .	57
XII.	CONJUNCTIVE PRONOUNS (CONTD.)—PRESENT PARTICIPLE	63
XIII.	DISJUNCTIVE PRONOUNS—MORE PLURALS .	67
XIV.	RELATIVE PRONOUNS—REFLEXIVE VERBS .	71
XV.	CONJUGATION OF REGULAR VERBS . .	76
XVI.	FIRST READING LESSON	82

LESSON   PAGE

XVII. IRREGULAR VERBS 85

XVIII. COMPARATIVES AND SUPERLATIVES . . . 90

XIX. NUMERALS 95

XX. NUMERALS (CONT.) 98

XXI. ADVERBS—ORTHOGRAPHIC CHANGES IN VERBS . 102

XXII. PASSIVE VOICE—IMPERSONAL VERBS—IDIOMATIC USE OF CERTAIN TENSES 107

XXIII. DEMONSTRATIVES (CONT.)—INDEFINITE ADJECTIVES AND PRONOUNS 111

XXIV. USE OF THE ARTICLES 116

XXV. SUFFIXES 120

XXVI. THE INFINITIVE 124

XXVII. PREPOSITIONS 129

XXVIII. THE SUBJUNCTIVE 135

XXIX. THE SUBJUNCTIVE (CONT.) 140

XXX. CONDITIONAL SENTENCES—NOTE ON *DOVERE* AND AUXILIARY VERBS 146

CONCLUSION 151

PART II

KEY TO EXERCISES AND TRANSLATIONS . . . 155

APPENDIX I. ADDITIONAL NOTES ON PRONUNCIATION, ACCENTS, SYLLABICATION . . . 212

II. LIST OF COMMON IRREGULAR VERBS . 214

III. VOCABULARY 221

INDEX 247

PART I

ITALIAN PRONUNCIATION

It is not easy to learn from a book how to pronounce a language; but Italian is simpler than some other languages to learn this way, for it is almost entirely phonetic: the same letter or combination of letters is nearly always used for the same sound. Therefore once we have become acquainted with the various sounds an Italian makes, and learnt which letters represent them, there will be little difficulty in pronouncing new words met in reading, or in spelling words heard spoken for the first time.

The following rules for pronunciation should be studied, and the words given as examples might be read aloud. It would be a good plan to read aloud the Italian words and sentences as we do each exercise. During the first few lessons this will involve some looking back to this preliminary chapter; but gradually there will be less looking back as the words become familiar. While teaching ourselves Italian we should make a point of hearing it spoken as much as possible. If we have no Italian acquaintances and no possibility of hearing lectures in Italian, there is always the wireless to fall back on. The news bulletins, talks and plays will seem rather difficult at first; but very soon we shall be able to distinguish words, then phrases, then whole sentences, and all the time we shall unconsciously be acquiring a correct intonation and a good accent.

Alphabet.—The Italian alphabet has twenty-one letters. These are the same as ours, except that there is no *j*, *k*, *w*, *x* or *y*.

Pronunciation of the Vowels.—The five vowel signs represent seven sounds which are pronounced approximately as follows:

a as *a* in *father*	carta = paper	sala = room
e as *a* in *mate* (called the close *e*)	mele = apples	vedere = to see
e as *e* in *pet* (called the open *e*)	bello = fine, beautiful	tenda = tent
i as *i* in *machine*	vini = wines	spilli = pins
o as *o* in *rope* (close *o*)	sole = sun	colore = colour

o as *o* in *soft* (open *o*)		porta = door		toro	= bull
u as *oo* in *moon*		fumo = smoke		luna	= moon

The following points should be noted:

1. Each vowel must be distinctly sounded, whatever its position in a word. In English unstressed vowels are often slurred; in Italian the unstressed vowels, although pronounced more rapidly and more lightly than the stressed ones, keep their pure sound.

2. They do not tend to become diphthongs, as in English. For instance, we pronounce the *a* in the word *mate* almost as *ay-ee*, and the *o* in rope is nearly *oh-oo*. The Englishman, when speaking Italian, must remember to avoid drawling the vowels.

3. The voice should be carried farther forward in the mouth when speaking Italian. The mouth should be opened well for the vowels *a*, *open e* and *open o*; in pronouncing *i* it should be nearly closed, with the lips drawn well back. The mouth, lips and jaw may be moved more than when speaking English; an Italian does not mind what sort of a face he is making so long as he produces clear and correct sounds. If we wish to speak his language correctly, we must try to imitate him.

Bearing these points in mind, let us return for a moment to the Italian words just given as examples and read them aloud. The consonants are more or less the same as in English, except that the *r* is strongly trilled, with the point of the tongue vibrating against the back of the top teeth. In each word the stress falls on the syllable next to the last:

carta	(cárr-tah)*	sala	(sáh-lah)
mele	(máy-lay)	vedere	(vay-dáy-rray)
bello	(béll-loh)	tenda	(tén-dah)
vini	(vée-nee)	spilli	(spée-lee)
sole	(sóh-lay)	colore	(coh-lóh-rray)
porta	(páwrr-tah)	toro	(táw-rroh)
fumo	(fóo-moh)	luna	(lóo-nah)

Stress in Pronunciation.—In Italian words one syllable is always more stressed than the others. The majority of words have the stress on the vowel in the syllable next to the last; but there are some which have the final vowel, and others which have the vowels in the third-last or fourth-last syllable,

* The division of words for pronunciation is not always syllabically correct. See Appendix, page 214. It will also be realized that these pronunciations in brackets can only be approximate.

stressed. When the *final vowel* is stressed it has a written accent to show that this is the case:

> virtú = virtue (pronounced veer-tóo)
> portò = he carried (pronounced pawrr-taw)
> città = town (pronounced chee-táh)

but there is normally no accent to indicate when the stress falls on the third-last or fourth-last syllables. To help the student, this book adopts the following device: words which have the stress on any syllable *before* the next to the last will have the vowel in that syllable printed in dark type, as: camera = bedroom (pronounced cáh-may-rah), sedici = sixteen (sáy-dee-chee). Therefore a word which has no written accent on its last vowel and no vowel printed in dark type will have the stress in the normal position: on the syllable next to the last.

Open and close *e* and *o*.—*E* and *o* each have two sounds: the open and the close. When these two vowels are in an unstressed position, they have the close sound; but when stressed, they may have either. It is important to distinguish between the open and close sounds, as important as, for example, our distinguishing between our words *pen* and *pain* and *not* and *note*. But, in writing, these sounds are not differentiated, so the student needs some guide to enable him to know when the vowel is open and when close. In this book we are adopting special printing in dark type to denote the OPEN sounds of *e* and *o*:

> bello   tenda   porta   toro

The CLOSE *e* and *o* in a stressed position will therefore be printed in ordinary printing.*

The special printing and the dark type will appear in the grammar rules and examples and in the vocabularies, but not in the exercises. In this way the student will be guided as to how to pronounce each new word as he comes across it, and at the same time, when doing the exercises, he will be getting used to reading Italian as it is normally written.

Pronunciation of Two or More Vowels.—*A*, *e* and *o* are called strong vowels, and *i* and *u* weak vowels. When two strong vowels come together we have what is called *hiatus*, and they are pronounced as two separate syllables:

---

* They may or may not be in dark type according to whether the stressed position is normal or not. See preceding paragraph.

soave = sweet, gentle (pronounced soh-áh-vay)
beato = happy (pronounced bay-áh-toh)

Hiatus also occurs when a strong and a weak vowel come
together and the weak one is stressed:

via   = road   (vée-ah)
pio   = pious   (pée-oh)
due   = two   (dóo-ay)
paura = fear   (pah-oó-rah)

When a strong and weak vowel come together and the strong
is stressed, they count as one syllable, the weak one being
lightly and rapidly pronounced, and this is called a diphthong:

piede = foot   (peeáy-day)
fiore = flower (feeóh-rray)
buono = good   (bwáw-noh)
guerra = war   (gwáy-rrah)
rauco = hoarse (ráh-oo-coh)

Two weak vowels together also form a diphthong:

guida = guide   (gwée-dah)
piú   = more   (like English word *pew*)

There are a few cases in which three vowels come together
and are pronounced as one syllable: this is called a triphthong.
The three vowel combinations used in Italian are: $iu\jmath$, $u\jmath i$, $i\varepsilon i$:

barcaiuolo = boatman (barr-cah-yoo-óll-loh)
suoi = his (masc. plural) (swóh-ee)
miei = my (masc. plural) (mee-áyee)

In pronouncing a triphthong, remember that the stress is
always on the strong vowel. You will have noticed that, when
making an effort to produce the three vowels as one syllable,
the first weak one almost loses vowel force and becomes a
consonant, the *i* has the force of English *y* and the *u* of our *w*.

Pronunciation of Consonants.—The sixteen consonant signs
are used to represent the following sounds: *b, d, f, l, m, n, p, q, t*
and *v* are pronounced as in English, except that *d, l, n* and *t*
are pronounced farther forward in the mouth, the tongue
pressing just behind the top teeth, instead of touching the roof
of the mouth;

c has two sounds. Followed by *e* or *i*, it is like the English
ch in *church*, otherwise it has the hard sound of *k*:

centro = centre (chén-trroh)
vicino = near (vee-chée-noh)
comprare = to buy (kohm-práh-rray)

g also has two sounds. Followed by *e* or *i*, it has the sound of *g* as in *general* or *j* as in *July*; otherwise it has the hard sound as in *go*:

gigante = giant (gee-gán-tay)
generale = general (jay-nay-rráh-lay)
gatto = cat (gáh-toh)

h is never sounded, and, except with *c* and *g* (see groups of consonants below), appears in only two or three words:

ha = he has (pronounced ah)

n followed by a hard *c*, hard *g* or *q* is like the English *n* in *ing*:

banca = bank (báng-ka)
lungo = long (lúng-goh)

r is always trilled with the point of the tongue against the upper teeth:

caro = dear (cáh-rroh)

s has two sounds: like *s* in *taste*, called unvoiced; and like *s* in *rose*, called voiced:

unvoiced: spillo = pin   casa = house
voiced: viso = face   smemorato = forgetful

z also has two sounds: unvoiced like a sharp *ts*; and voiced, which is pronounced *dz*:

unvoiced: *ts*: azione = action   zio = uncle
voiced: *dz*: romanzo = novel   mɛzzo = half

To help the student to determine whether to give the *s* and *z* the voiced or the unvoiced sound, the *voiced s* and *z* will in future be distinguished in the text and in the vocabularies by a small dot printed beneath them as: viṣo, romanẓo.

Double Consonants are pronounced as prolonged single ones. They always represent a single sound; never two different ones, as in the English *accept*:

accɛnto = accent (ah-chén-toh)
vacca = cow (váh-cah)

Groups of Consonants.—The following five groups each represent a single sound:

ch (used only before *e* and *i*) is pronounced as *k*:

> chiesa = church (keeáy-zah)*
> perché = because (pair-káy)

gh (only before *e* and *i*) is like the hard *g*:

> ghiaccio = ice (g [as in *gear*] eeáh-cho)

gl followed by *i* has a very liquid sound, as in the word *million*:

> figlio = son (féel-yo)

(There are a few exceptions to this rule when *g* and *l* are pronounced as separate letters; but these are mostly unusual words, with which we do not need to concern ourselves.)

gn is like the *ni* of our word *onion*:

> bagno = bath (báhn-yoh)

sc before *e* and *i* is like the English *sh*; before any other vowel or a consonant it is like *k*:

> uscire = to go out (oo-shée-rray)
> oscuro = dark (oh-skóo-rroh)

It would be a good plan to put these rules into practice by reading aloud and learning by heart the numbers from one to twenty. Here they are, with approximate English pronunciation. Note which syllable carries the stress in each word:

1.	uno (masc.)	oó-noh
	una (fem.)	oó-nah
2.	due	dóo-ay
3.	tre	tray
4.	quattro	kwát-trroh
5.	cinque	cheéng-kway
6.	sei	sáy-ee
7.	sette	sét-tay
8.	otto	áwt-toh
9.	nove	náw-vay
10.	dieci	deeáy-chee
11.	undici	oón-dee-chee

* It should be emphasized that these approximations in English are only *very* approximate. It is, for instance, not possible to indicate the "open" quality of the *ε* here.

12.	dodici	dóh-dee-chee
13.	tredici	tráy-dee-chee
14.	quattordici	kwat-tórr-dee-chee
15.	quindici	kwéen-dee-chee
16.	sedici	sáy-dee-chee
17.	diciassette	dee-cheeah-sét-tay
18.	diciotto	dee-cheeáwt-toh
19.	diciannove	dee-cheeah-náw-vay
20.	venti	váyn-tee

For those who would like more practice, here are the days and the months; a capital letter is not required in Italian:

Monday, etc.	lunedí	(loo-nay-dée)
	martedí	(mahrr-tay-dée)
	mercoledí	(mairr-coh-lay-dée)
	giovedí	(joh-vay-dée)
	venerdí	(vay-nayrr-dée)
	sabato	(sáh-bah-toh)
	domenica	(doh-máy-nee-cah)
January, etc.	gennaio	(jay-náhee-oh)
	febbraio	(fay-bráhee-oh)
	marzo	(máhrr-tso)
	aprile	(ah-prrée-lay)
	maggio	(máh-jeeoh)
	giugno	(jeeóon-yoh)
	luglio	(lóo-leeoh)
	agosto	(ah-góh-stoh)
	settembre	(say-tém-brray)
	ottobre	(oht-tóh-brray)
	novembre	(noh-vém-brray)
	dicembre	(dee-chém-brray)

Written Accents.*—It will be noticed in the paragraph on stress on page 13 that the examples had different accents over the final vowel. Those who have learnt French are familiar with the use of three accents: the acute (´), the grave (`) and the circumflex (ˆ). These accents are also used in Italian, but

* The use of the grave and acute accents is not uniform throughout Italy. Many writers always use the grave to denote the stressed vowel, irrespective of whether the sound may be open or close. Others differentiate only with the vowel E. The system here followed, if written accents are to indicate pronunciation as well as stress, is the most logical, and it has the authority of many of the chief publishers in Italy, as: Mondadori, Einaudi, S.E.I., Laterza, etc.

not to serve quite the same purpose. In Italian the acute and grave accents are stress marks. They are primarily used to indicate that the vowel over which they are placed is the one to be stressed, and only in the cases of the open and close *e* and *o* are they concerned with pronunciation, for then they are distinguishing signs as well as stress marks, the acute being used for the close sounds and the grave for the open. These two accents must not be placed over the other vowels just as one wishes: the acute is over *i* and *u*, and the grave over *a*. The third accent, the circumflex, is very rarely used, and has a different function: it denotes that a word has been abbreviated by the omission of a letter or syllable.

Examples:
Acute: lunedí; virtú; credé (he believed).
Grave: portò; onestà (honesty); caffè (coffee, café).
Circumflex: studî—studies (the plural of studio—study, a shortened form of studii, the accent denoting that one *i* has been omitted).

As we learn each new word we must note where the stress falls and remember that all words of more than one syllable which have the final vowel stressed must have the accent over that vowel.

The *acute* and *grave* accents are also used:

1. On certain words of one syllable to distinguish them from other words of the same spelling and pronunciation, but of different meaning:

ché	= because	che	= which, that, who (rel. pronoun)
dà	= he gives	da	= by, from
dí	= day	di	= of
è	= is	e	= and
là	= there	la	= the (fem. sing.)
lí	= there	li	= them (masc.)
né	= nor	ne	= of it
sé	= himself	se	= if
sí	= yes	si	= himself
tè	= tea	te	= thee

2. And on the following five short words:

ciò	= that, this
già	= already
giú	= down
piú	= more
può	= he can

Additional notes on pronunciation and syllabication are to be found in the Appendix, page 212.

Preliminary Exercise

1. Place the correct accent on each of the final vowels of the following words: virtu, porto, perche, mercoledi, crede, onesta, caffe, citta (town), sincerita (sincerity).

2. Pronounce the following words with a true Italian accent and *not* as we say them in English. Then turn to the Key to this Exercise, where you will find approximate pronunciations in English, from which to check your effort: arena, cupola, incognito, pianoforte, vermicelli, terra cotta, ultimatum, Galli-Curci, Marco Polo, Medici.

LESSON I

INDEFINITE ARTICLE—GENDER

WHEN learning the numbers from 1 to 20 you will have noticed that there are two words for "one": *uno* and *una*. *Uno* is used with persons and things of masculine gender and *una* with persons and things which are feminine. In English we have three genders: masculine, feminine and neuter, gender being equivalent to sex; a man is masculine, a cow feminine, an apple neuter. In Italian there is no neuter; therefore things, not only persons and animals, are also masculine and feminine.

Uno and *una* also mean *a* and *an*: *uno* for the masculine and *una* for the feminine: *uno zio* = an uncle; *una zia* = an aunt. In English we have two forms for the indefinite article: *a* for words beginning with a consonant and *an* for words beginning with a vowel: *a* man, *an* apple; and in Italian *uno* and *una* have different forms according to what letter comes at the beginning of the word which follows them. But in Italian the matter is a little more complicated:

Masculine		*Feminine*	
un	uno	una	un'
un ragazzo	= a boy	una ragazza	= a girl
un albero	= a tree	un'ora	= an hour
uno spillo	= a pin	una strada	= a street
uno zio	= an uncle	una zia	= an aunt

Of the two masculine forms, *un* is the more usual: *uno* is used only before words beginning with *s impure* (*s* followed by another consonant) and *z*; and of the feminine forms *una* is to be used before any consonant and *un'* before a word beginning with a vowel.

Look again at the nouns given as examples. You will see that all the masculine nouns end in -*o*, and all the feminines in -*a*. ALL ITALIAN NOUNS END IN A VOWEL: those in -*o* are masculine, except one: *mano* (hand), which is feminine. "A hand" is therefore *una mano*. Nouns ending in -*a* are mostly feminine. Before doing Exercise I, read through this vocabulary and decide the gender of the various nouns.

Vocabulary

(Words which have already appeared in the text are not included in these vocabularies.)

Maria	= Mary	hanno	= they have
Piero	= Peter		
donna	= woman	a	= at, to
figlia	= daughter	anche	= also
finestra	= window	che?, che cosa?	= what?, what thing?
fratello	= brother	chi?	= who?, whom?
libro	= book	dove?	= where? (dov'è? = where is?)
sbaglio	= mistake	ecco	= here is, here are, there is, there
sorella	= sister		are
specchio	= mirror	in	= in
uomo	= man		

Exercise 1

a. Supply the indefinite article in the blank spaces in the following sentences:

1. Maria è   donna e Piero è   uomo.
2. Maria e Piero hanno   casa.
3. Piero e Maria hanno   figlio e   figlia.
4. Chi ha   fratello? Maria ha   fratello e anche   sorella.
5. Ha Piero   zio? Sí, Piero ha   zio e anche   zia.
6. Dov'è   porta? E dov'è   finestra?
7. Chi ha   libro? Piero ha   libro? Che cosa ha Maria? Maria ha   specchio.
8. Dov'è   sbaglio? Ecco   sbaglio in   libro.

b. Translate the preceding sentences into English.

c. Translate into Italian:

1. Mary has a house and Peter has a house.
2. Peter has a son and * daughter.
3. Has Mary an aunt? Yes, Mary has an aunt and also an uncle.
4. Where is a mistake? Here is a mistake.
5. Who has a book? Mary has a book. Mary gives a book to Peter.
6. Mary has a brother and * sister.
7. What has Peter in one hand? Peter has a book in one hand.
8. Has Mary a mirror? Yes, Mary has a mirror.

LESSON II

VERBS AND PRONOUNS

I N Italian, changes in the meaning of words are often indicated by changes in their endings, particularly in the case of verbs. We met some verbs in the preliminary chapter. Among these were: *comprare*, *credere* and *uscire*. The Infinitive, which gives the general idea of the verb without saying who is doing the action or when it is done, is indicated in English by the word *to* and in Italian by the endings *-are*, *-ere* and *-ire*. Italian verbs are divided into three groups, called conjugations, according to these three infinitive endings. First conjugation verbs end in *-are*; second in *-ere* (some verbs in this conjugation have the stress on the infinitive ending: as *vedere*; others, like *credere*, have the stress on an earlier syllable), and the third in *-ire*. If we cut off these endings we have left what is known as the *stem*, the part of the verb which does not usually change: *compr-*, *cred-*, *usc-*, and it is to this part that other endings are added which denote the *person* (that is, *who* is doing the action) and the *tense* (that is, *when* it is taking place).

Let us take the first two conjugations and study their present indicative tense, using *comprare* and *credere* as models. The present indicative makes a plain statement about some action which is going on at the present time.

* Repeat article before each noun.

comprare, 1st conjugation   *credere*, 2nd conjugation

Sing.

1st person	compr-o *	I buy	cred-o	I believe
2nd ,,	compr-i	thou buyest	cred-i	thou believest
3rd ,,	compr-a	he buys	cred-e	he believes

Plur.

1st ,,	compr-iamo	we buy	cred-iamo	we believe
2nd ,,	compr-ate	you buy	cred-ete	you believe
3rd ,,	compr-ano	they buy	cred-ono	they believe

Note where the stress falls. It comes on the *stem* in all three persons singular and in the third person plural: COMPR-, and CRED-, and on the *ending* (the syllable next to the last) in the first and second persons plural: compriAMO, comprATE, crediAMO, credETE.

Note, in the second place, that where in English we have only three different endings: buy, buyest and buys; in Italian there are six, a different one for each person. In Italian, therefore, we always know which person is meant by the ending of the verb: *compriamo* is always *we* buy, for *-iamo* is the ending for *we*, and so no word for *we* is required. Normally no subject pronoun of a verb—I, thou, he, etc.—is necessary in Italian, and it is omitted.

And thirdly we must note that this present tense also translates the other two English present tenses: the emphatic: *I do buy*, and the continuous or progressive: *I am buying*.

Subject pronouns are sometimes required for emphasis or for clearness. In such a sentence as: "I am learning Italian and he is learning French", the pronouns are necessary to indicate the contrast between the two subjects. It would be useful, therefore, to learn these pronouns at this point, and we may then practise them while making ourselves familiar with the present indicative. They are as follows:

	Singular		*Plural*	
First person	†io	= I	noi	= we
Second ,,	tu	= thou	voi	= you
Third ,,	lui	= he	loro	= they (masc.)
	egli	= he	. . . . .	
	esso	= he, it	essi	= they (masc.)

* The division of words in these tables is made to help you to memorize the verb endings and is syllabically incorrect. For correct syllabication, see Appendix, page 214.

† Capital letter not required except at beginning of a sentence.

Third Person	lɛi = she	loro = they (fem.)
	ella = she	. . . . .
	essa = she, it	esse = they (fem.)

Third person pronouns may seem a little confusing, but they are really quite simple. *Egli* and *ella* are used only in writing, in literary style; never in conversation. They refer only to persons, not to things or animals. *Lui* and *lɛi* are used in conversation and in familiar or intimate style when writing; we shall use these mostly in this book: they are also only for persons. *Esso* and *essa* are used both in literary and conversational style and for things, animals and persons; but they are more often used for things than for persons. There is no plural of *egli* or *ella*, the plurals of *esso* and *essa* being used instead.

This all boils down to a simple solution: we shall use *lui* and *lɛi* mostly in this book with their plural *loro* when speaking of persons, and *esso* and *essa* when speaking of things. But at the same time we must know the literary forms; for although we may not aspire to write literary Italian, we may very easily feel bold enough to read some, and therefore we must be able to recognize these forms.

Interrogative Sentences.—In the first lesson we saw that in Italian one asks a question as we do in English, by inverting the order of the verb and its subject: *Ha Maria una zia?* But this inversion is not so frequent as in English; we might as well have said: *Maria ha una zia?* the question being indicated merely by the tone of voice. What Italian *never* does is employ an auxiliary (or helping) verb to form a question, as we do in English. "Does Mary speak Italian?" is: *Parla Maria italiano?* or *Maria parla italiano?*

Vocabulary

fɔglio = sheet of paper	guardare = to look at	con = with
inchiɔstro = ink	lɛggere (irreg.)* = to read	
lɛttera = letter	scrivere (irreg.)* = to write	mentre = while
penna = pen		ɔggi = today
tavola = table	trovare = to find	quando = when
	usare = to use	(pronounce:
	vendere = to sell	kwándoh)

* All verbs not regular will be so indicated in these vocabularies, and they are listed in the appendix, with their irregular parts shown. Take no notice of this "irreg." at present.

Exercise 2

a. Continue the following, throughout all persons, singular and plural:

> 1. Vendo una vacca e compro un gatto.
> 2. Mentre scrivo uso una penna, inchiostro e un foglio.
> 3. Quando leggo guardo un libro.

b. Continue the following through all the persons, including the subject pronouns in each case:

> Io parlo con Piero.

c. Translate into English:

> 1. Chi trova un libro? Io trovo un libro.
> 2. Maria e Piero parlano? Sí, parlano.
> 3. Scrive Maria una lettera a Piero?
> 4. Sí, e mentre lei scrive, io guardo un libro.
> 5. Che cosa compra Piero oggi?
> 6. Oggi Piero compra un libro.

d. Translate into Italian:

> 1. Where is a table?
> 2. She is selling a cow and buying a cat.
> 3. They are writing a letter to Mary.
> 4. While she reads I write.
> 5. What do you see? I see a woman and a man, a boy and a girl.
> 6. She is buying a mirror and I am buying a book.
> 7. Do Peter and Mary speak Italian? Yes, they speak Italian.
> 8. He is looking at Mary while she writes a letter.

LESSON III

DEFINITE ARTICLE—NUMBER

JUST as there are various forms of the indefinite article, according to its gender and to the initial letter of the word which follows it, so the definite article—translating "the"—has various forms in Italian:

Masculine

Singular: il	*Plural*: i
lo	gli
l'	gli, gl'

il libro	(the book)	i libri
lo studio	(the study)	gli studî
lo zio	(the uncle)	gli zii
l'insetto	(the insect)	gl'insetti
l'accento	(the accent)	gli accenti

From these examples it will be seen that *il*, plural *i*, is used before a masculine word beginning with a consonant (except *s impure* and *z*); that *lo*, plural *gli*, is used before masculine words beginning with *s impure* and *z*; that *l'* is used before a word beginning with a vowel, and its plural *gli* drops the *i* before another *i*.

It must be emphasized that it is the initial letter of the word *immediately* following the article which determines the form to be used. If any other word comes between the article and its noun, then it is this other word which determines the form of the article:

Example: il libro, l'altro libro (the other book), lo stesso libro (the same book).

Feminine

Singular: la
         l'

la porta
l'altra porta
l'entrata (the entrance)

Plural: le
      le, l'

le porte
le altre porte
l'entrate

The feminine forms are not so complicated. There is only one form for the singular: *la*, which becomes *l'* before a word beginning with a vowel; and one form for the plural: *le*, which becomes *l'* before another *e*.

Number.—By studying the endings of the nouns in the foregoing examples we can learn something about the formation of their plurals. In English we usually form the plural by adding *-s* or *-es* to the singular; but when we remember that we cannot say *sheeps*, *mouses* or *childs*, we realize that it is not so easy in English. In Italian, too, there are various ways of forming the plural. The first important rule is that nouns ending in *-o* form their plural by changing the *o* to *i*, and that *feminine* nouns ending in *-a* change the *a* to *e*. Words which go with or qualify the noun, such as *stesso* and *altro*, must also take the noun's gender and number. Adjectives which end in *-o* (there are some which end in *-e*) have a feminine form in *-a*, and they form their plural like the nouns in *-o* and *-a*:

| lo stesso libro | la stessa porta |
| gli stessi libri | le stesse porte |

il cappɛllo rosso = the red hat
i cappɛlli rossi = the red hats

la cravatta rossa = the red tie
le cravatte rosse = the red ties

Some adjectives precede their nouns, usually short ones of very common use; but more often they follow, as in the example just given. The student is advised to place them as he finds them in the examples, and if in any doubt, to put them *after* the noun to which they refer. An adjective must also agree in number and gender with its noun when it comes in a different part of the sentence:

Il cappɛllo ɛ̀ rosso, ma le cravatte sono gialle.—The hat is red, but the ties are yellow.

Vocabulary

calzino = sock	alto = tall, high	sono = are (they)
ɛrba = grass	aʒʒurro = blue	
giardino = garden	basso = low	molto = very, much
muro = wall	bellino = pretty	c'ɛ̀ = there is
tetto = roof	bɛllo = beautiful, fine, lovely	ci sono = there are
		non = not
	nuɔvo = new	
	piccolo = small	
	questo = this	

Exercise 3

a. Supply the definite article where missing in the following sentences:

1. Dov'è   donna?   donna è a casa.
2.   fratelli e   sorelle di Maria sono in città. Comprano   cappelli e   cravatte.
3.   zio di Pietro è alto, ma   zia è molto piccola.
4. Ecco   casa nuova.   Dov'è   entrata?
5.   tetto è rosso, e   muri sono gialli.
6. Questo muro è alto, ma   altro è basso.
7.   giardino è bellino;   erba è bella e ci sono molti alberi.
8. Piero guarda   zio, perché ha un cappello giallo, una cravatta azzurra e   calzini sono rossi.
9. Maria non è in casa; è in città e compra   specchi.

From the last sentence it will be seen that a sentence is made negative by placing *non* (not) before the verb. Note also that possession is expressed by the preposition *di* (of). Peter's uncle is tall = *Lo zio di Piero è alto*.

b. Translate into English the sentences in Exercise 3 (*a*). (Note that *a casa* or *in casa* means "at home").

c. Translate into Italian:

1. The trees are very high.
2. The new house has a red roof and yellow walls. It is in a very pretty garden.
3. The windows are very high, but the door is low.
4. Uncle is at home, but Aunt is in town. She is buying a hat. (Say: *the* uncle, *the* aunt.)
5. He is very tall, but Aunt is small.
6. This boy is buying a pen, but the other boy is buying socks and a tie.
7. The house has five doors and seventeen windows.
8. They are not writing the letters, they are looking at Peter's yellow hat and red socks.

LESSON IV

MORE VERBS—THE POLITE PRONOUN

VERBS of the third conjugation are divided into two groups according to whether they add *-isc* to their stem in certain persons of the present indicative, present subjunctive and imperative. We are now concerned only with the present indicative: and as the majority of verbs add the *-isc*, we will call these the first group, and those which do not, the second*. The present tense of verbs of the third conjugation is as follows:

1st group:	2nd group:
finire = to finish	*partire* = to depart
fin-isc-o	part-o
fin-isc-i	part-i
fin-isc-e	part-e
fin-iamo	part-iamo
fin-ite	part-ite
fin-isc-ono	part-ono

* Indication as to which group a verb belongs is to be found in the vocabularies.

The -*isc* is added in the first group throughout the singular and in the third person plural. Except for this addition of -*isc*, the verbs of both groups are exactly alike.

Note where the stress falls. Note also, in regard to group I, that in the first person singular and in the third person plural the *c* being followed by an *o* has the hard sound, but in the second and third persons singular it is soft (*finisco* is pronounced fee-née-skoh, *finisci* fee-née-shee).

The Polite Pronoun

We now come to an important point about the translation of "you". Italian has three different ways of saying *you*. In the verbs conjugated above we have used two forms: *tu* = thou, and *voi* = you; the third form is the same as the word for *she*: *lɛi*, but it is often spelt with a capital letter. Of these forms, *tu* is singular, and is used when speaking to a near relative, a very close friend or to a child; *voi*, besides being the plural of *tu*, is also used for the singular when speaking to acquaintances or to strangers; but as it carries with it a slight indication that the person to whom one is speaking is an inferior, or at any rate no better than oneself, the third form, *Lɛi* (originally from an expression meaning Your Grace, and which infers special courtesy towards the person addressed), is more generally used between persons not on intimate terms. *Lɛi* is the form we shall mostly use in this book, and if and when you go to Italy it is the form you should use when speaking to Italians.

Lɛi, although meaning *you*, is always third person; the verb used with it must be THIRD PERSON SINGULAR. The plural of *Lɛi* is *Loro* (the same form as the word for "they") and it requires the verb in the THIRD PERSON PLURAL.

While learning the present indicative of two more verbs, we might insert these pronouns for practice. These two verbs, *ɛssere* = to be and *avere* = to have, are called auxiliary verbs, for, like the corresponding English verbs, they help to form compound tenses; and as they do not conform to any of the models of the three conjugations, they are called irregular verbs.

Present Indicative

ɛssere = to be		*avere* = to have	
io sono	I am	io hɔ	I have
tu sɛi	{thou art {you are	tu hai	{thou hast {you have
lui, lɛi, esso, essa, ɛ	he, etc., is	lui, etc., ha	he, etc., has
Lɛi ɛ	you are	Lɛi ha	you have

noi siamo	we are	noi abbiamo	we have
voi siete	you are	voi avete	you have
loro sono	they are	loro hanno	they have
Loro sono	you are	Loro hanno	you have

The following sentences will help to clarify the uses of the three forms of address. We will translate the sentence *You are very tall* into Italian in three ways: first as if addressing a child, secondly a social equal or inferior, and thirdly as one would speak to a stranger; then we will put all three sentences into the plural:

Singular	Plural
Tu sei molto alto	Voi siete molto alti
Voi siete molto alto	Voi siete molto alti
Lei è molto alto	Loro sono molto alti

As *lei* and *loro* mean respectively *she* and *they* as well as *you*, it might be thought that confusion would arise. But one nearly always knows from the tone of the speaker's voice whether he is talking *to* you or *about* her; if there should be any doubt, this is overcome by adding *Signore* (Sir), *Signora* (Madam) or *Signorina* (Miss) when using the polite form. Note that these three words: *signore*, *signora* and *signorina*, also mean respectively: (1) "gentleman", "lady" and "young lady"; and (2) "Mr.", "Mrs." and "Miss". A capital letter is required in the latter case only when used in direct address, not otherwise

Nouns and Adjectives in -e.—Many Italian nouns end in *-e*, and some are masculine and some feminine. They form their plural by changing the *-e* to *-i* (except those ending in *-ie*: see page 42).

Singular	Plural
il padre = the father	i padri
la madre = the mother	le madri

Many adjectives also end in *-e*; they have the same form in the masculine and the feminine, and they form their plural in the same way as the nouns ending in *-e*: *L'albero è verde* = the tree is green; *Gli alberi sono verdi* = the trees are green.

Vocabulary

balcone (m.) = balcony
bambino = child
cucina = kitchen
parola = word

aprire (irreg.) (2nd group) = to open
capire (1st group) = to understand

piano = floor
  al pianterreno = on the
    ground floor
  al piano superiore = on
    the upper floor
sala da pranzo = dining
  room
salotto = drawing room
sedia = chair
soprabito = overcoat
stanza = room
terrazza = terrace

dormire (2nd group) = to sleep
preferire (1st group) = to prefer

comodo = comfortable
facile = easy
grande = large
spagnuolo = Spanish

troppo = too, too much

domani = tomorrow
per = for

Exercise 4 (a)

1. La madre apre la finestra mentre il bambino dorme.
2. Non capisco perché la signora parte oggi e non domani.
3. Capiamo questa parola ma non l'altra.
4. Questa casa ha dodici stanze.
5. La sala da pranzo ha una terrazza e le due stanze grandi hanno balconi.
6. La sala da pranzo e la terrazza sono belle, ma la cucina è troppo piccola.
7. Apriamo la finestra e vediamo il giardino.
8. Noi abbiamo un giardino molto bello.
9. Dov'è la sorella di Piero? È in cucina.
10. Aprono la porta e vedono la terrazza.
11. Il salotto non è piccolo e le sedie sono comode.
12. Il salotto è al pianterreno ma lo studio è al piano superiore.
13. Dove dormite voi, Maria e Lucia? Noi dormiamo in una camera al piano superiore.
14. Lei trova facile l'italiano,* Signorina?
15. Sì, trovo facile l'italiano. È facile anche lo spagnuolo; ma preferisco l'italiano.

Exercise 4 (b)

1. This chair is very comfortable, but I prefer the other.
2. I do not understand this word.
3. Do you understand this book?
4. Where are the young ladies? Are they leaving today?
5. Yes, they are leaving today. They are in the kitchen with Peter. (Say: *in kitchen*.)
6. Peter sleeps on the ground floor.

* A small letter, except when speaking of the people: Gl'Italiani = the Italians. The article is required, except after the verb parlare and certain prepositions (see page 117).

7. Mary's bedroom is on the upper floor.
8. Is Peter at home? No, he is in town.
9. Are Peter and Mary in town? Yes, they are buying apples.
10. Why are they leaving today? I do not understand why.
11. The kitchen is small, but the dining-room is large.
12. They are buying a new house with a garden.
13. We prefer a house in town.
14. Here is the study. Peter opens the door and we see Uncle. (Say: *the* uncle.) Uncle is sleeping.
15. While Uncle is sleeping, Aunt is in town. She is in town with Mary. They are buying ties, socks, hats and an overcoat for Uncle.

LESSON V

CONTRACTIONS OF WORDS—THE PARTITIVE

ITALIAN is a very melodious language It avoids harsh and ugly sounds and sounds that are difficult to pronounce. It cuts words short or runs them together, or sometimes changes their form so as to produce agreeable sounds and a pleasing and harmonious rhythm. Some examples of this we have already met in the different forms of the article, when, to avoid an ugly hiatus, *lo* and *la* become *l'* before a following vowel. Something of the same kind occurs when the definite article is preceded by certain prepositions, some of which we have met, such as *a*, *di* and *in*. These prepositions, together with one or two more when used with the definite article, often join with it and form one word. For example, *di* when followed by *il* becomes *del*, so avoiding the hiatus between *di—il*. Seven of the common prepositions are written together with the article, and they may be studied from this table:

	il	*i*	*lo*	*gli*	*la*	*le*	*l'*
a = to, at	al	ai	allo	agli	alla	alle	all'
con = with	col	coi	collo	cogli	colla	colle	coll'
	or con il	con i	con lo	con gli	con la	con le	con l'
da = by, from	dal	dai	dallo	dagli	dalla	dalle	dall'
di = of	del	dei	dello	degli	della	delle	dell'
in = in, into	nel	nei	nello	negli	nella	nelle	nell'
per = for	pel	pei	per lo	per gli	per la	per le	per l'
	or per il	per i					
su = on	sul	sui	sullo	sugli	sulla	sulle	sull'

Study the following sentences. After which, practise the prepositions and articles by taking some nouns that you already know, such as *libro, albero, zio, casa*, etc., and place the correct form of the preposition and article before them. That is: find out how to say *to the uncle, with the uncle, from the uncle*, etc. Then change your expressions from the singular to the plural. Your effort can always be checked by referring to the preceding table. Practise with every kind of noun—*i.e.*, one that begins with a consonant, one with a vowel, one with *s impure*, etc.

Maria è nel giardino ma lo zio è nello studio.
Pietro dà una mela all'uomo e un'arancia (orange) alla donna.
Pietro dà i calzini al ragazzo.
Lui dà i calzini allo stesso ragazzo.
Capisco le parole dello zio.
La cravatta è sulla tavola nella sala da pranzo.
Il cappello della zia è sulla sedia nell'altra camera.

Translation of "Some" and "Any".—There are different ways of saying *some* and *any* in Italian. One is to use the preposition *di* with the definite article (the partitive construction):

Còmpra del pane = He is buying some (of the) bread.
Ha delle rose rosse = He has some red roses.
Ha dei calzini gialli, per favore? = Have you any yellow socks, please?

Another way is the use of *alcuno* or *qualche*, both meaning *some* and *any*:

Hanno alcuni libri nuovi? Sí: hanno alcuni libri nuovi.
Hanno qualche libro nuovo? Sí: hanno qualche libro nuovo.
Have they any new books? Yes, they have some new books.

Alcuno, an adjective in *-o*, has a feminine form in *-a* and the two plurals *alcuni* and *alcune*; but *qualche* (pronounced kwahl-kay) *never* changes for gender, nor for number. Also it is curious that it must ALWAYS BE FOLLOWED BY ITS NOUN IN THE SINGULAR. *Qualche libro* therefore means either *some books* or *some book*.

Leggeva qualche libro = He was reading some book.
Compra qualche libro = He is buying some books.

Negative Sentences.—*Some* and *any* mean the same thing in English, but we use *some* in affirmative sentences and *any* in negative and interrogative sentences. In Italian the partitive construction is used in all three kinds of sentences:

> Ha del pane = He has some bread.
> Ha del pane? = Has he any bread?
> Non ha del pane = He hasn't any bread.*

There are other ways of translating *any* in a negative sentence. If *any* is followed by a word in the plural, it may simply be omitted:

> Non ha libri = He hasn't any books.

If *any* is followed by a noun in the singular, which has a plural, like book, garden, etc. (but *not* bread, flour, etc.), another word, *nessuno*, which means *no, not one*, is used. *Nessuno* has forms like the indefinite article *un*: *nessun, nessuno, nessuna* and *nessun'*:

> Non ha nessun libro = He hasn't any book.

In this last sentence *nessuno* is an adjective, qualifying *libro*, but it can also be used as a pronoun, meaning "nobody", "no one":

> Non vedo nessuno = I see nobody, I don't see anybody.

There are, you will notice, two negatives in the Italian sentence, *non* and *nessuno*, but together they convey a *single* negative idea, and not an affirmative as is the case in English. Two negatives, also conveying a single negative idea, are used with other words:

> Pietro non scrive mai lettere = Peter never writes letters.
> Maria non vede nulla = Mary doesn't see anything.
> Non capisce niente = He understands nothing.
> Non trovo né la borsa né il denaro = I don't find either the money or the purse.

From these sentences we learn that never is *non . . . mai*; nothing—*non . . . niente* or *non . . . nulla*; neither . . . nor—*non . . . né . . . né*. In each case the final word is a negative in itself, and may be used without *non* if it precedes the verb:

> Non scrive mai, *or* mai scrive = He never writes.
> Non vede nulla, *or* nulla vede = He sees nothing.

In the second version of the sentences, great emphasis is laid on the negative words *mai, niente*, etc.

* Also: *Non ha pane.*

Vocabulary

fazzoletto = handkerchief	bianco = white
fiume (m.) = river	pigro = lazy
guanto = glove	povero = poor
macchina = car	
ospite (m. & f.) = guest, host	cercare = to look for
scarpa = shoe	
tasca = pocket	poi = then

Exercise 5 (a)

1. Maria è nel giardino e la zia è nella sala da pranzo.
2. Giovanni (John) dà delle mele agli ospiti e poi parte per la città nella macchina dello zio.
3. Lo zio è coi bambini nel salotto.
4. Che cosa hai nella tasca, Piero? Ho due fazzoletti e una cravatta dello zio.
5. Dov'è Piero? È nello studio con la ragazza.
6. Le sedie della sala da pranzo sono sul balcone.
7. Guardano nello specchio. Che cosa vedono?
8. Vedono il cappello e i guanti della zia. Essi sono sulla tavola.
9. Dov'è il cappello giallo dello zio? Il cappello giallo dello zio è nel fiume.
10. Povero zio! Giovanni e Piero comprano un nuovo cappello per lo zio.
11. Non abbiamo del pane? Sí, è sulla tavola nella cucina.
12. Che cosa c'è nel fiume? Io non vedo niente.
13. Ha delle cravatte gialle, per favore?
14. No, Signore, ma ho qualche cravatta bianca e azzurra.
15. È molto pigro Giovanni! Non scrive mai a nessuno.

Exercise 5 (b)

1. Mary is in the study with Uncle. They are writing letters.
2. Peter is buying socks, handkerchiefs and ties from a boy in the street.
3. John is buying a hat and gloves from the same boy.
4. He is a very poor boy; he has no shoes.
5. What have you in the pocket? I have three handkerchiefs and a tie.
6. What do you see in the river, John? I don't see anything.
7. I am looking in the mirror. I see the three children with the cat.
8. Mary is looking for the cat in the garden.
9. Where is the bread? We have no bread.
10. The man in the drawing-room is John's brother.

11. Where is John's tie? It is on the table in the dining-room with Aunt's gloves (of *the* aunt).
12. I see neither the tie nor the gloves.
13. Haven't you any ink? Yes, it is on the table in the study.
14. This chair is for the guest. But it isn't very comfortable.
15. The book that you are looking for is in the study.

LESSON VI

PAST DEFINITE—POSITION OF ADJECTIVES

THREE past tenses in Italian correspond to the following English past tenses:

The Past Definite translates the English simple past tense (example: *I bought*), and the emphatic past (*I did buy*);

The Imperfect translates our imperfect (*I was buying*), and the habitual tense (*I used to buy*);

The Present Perfect, a compound tense, as the English tense it translates (*I have bought*).

These three tenses are used more or less as the English tenses mentioned above, except that we often substitute our simple past tense for the imperfect and the present perfect, while Italian is much more particular in using each of these tenses on the occasion for which it is meant, particularly in the written language; in conversation we may sometimes take liberties with the past definite and use the present perfect instead.

The Past Definite makes a statement about something which happened at a definite time in the past, without any connection with or reference to the present; it is a narrative or historic tense: I *bought* the book last week; They *caught* the thief when he was climbing through the window; Columbus *discovered* America. In Italian this tense is formed by adding certain endings to the stem, as will be seen from the following table:

1st Conj. *comprare*	2nd Conj. *vendere*	3rd Conj. *finire*
compr-ai = *I bought*, etc.	vend-ei (-ɛtti) = *I sold*, etc.	fin-ii = *I finished*, etc.
compr-asti	vend-esti	fin-isti
compr-ò	vend-é (ɛtte)	fin-í
compr-ammo	vend-emmo	fin-immo
compr-aste	vend-este	fin-iste
compr-arono	vend-erono (-ɛttero)	fin-irono

Note the following points about this tense:

1. In all regular verbs the third person singular has the stress on the final vowel, and *must* have the written accent. A stressed final *o* has always the open sound, therefore a *grave* accent is required; final *e*, with very few exceptions, is close, and requires the *acute*, and *i* always takes an acute. Therefore the first conjugation has a grave accent: *compr-ò*, and the second and third an acute: *vendé, finí*. This does not apply to verbs which are irregular in this tense, for in that case the final vowel of the third person is NOT stressed.

2. The stress is on the syllable next to the last in all the other persons with the exception of the third plural, where it falls on the third from the end.

3. If we take the three characteristic vowels: *a* for the first conjugation (*-are*), *e* for the second (*-ere*) and *i* for the third (*-ire*), we see that—with the exception of the third person singular of the first conjugation—the characteristic vowel appears throughout the tense in each case, otherwise the endings are the same for all three conjugations.

4. The second conjugation has alternative forms for the first and third persons singular and the third person plural. Some verbs do not have this alternative form, and many which *do*, prefer the form which is here given first, for this is the one most commonly used.

Past Definite of the Auxiliary Verbs

Essere = to be	*avere* = to have
fui = I was, etc.	ɛbbi = I had, etc.
fosti	avesti
fu	ɛbbe
fummo	avemmo
foste	aveste
furono	ɛbbero

Note that these two irregular verbs have *no* written accent on the third person singular; and in the pronunciation of the past definite of *avere* the initial *e* of the three irregular persons is an open *e*, while the *e* of the second syllable of the regular persons is a close *e*.

Position of Adjectives.—We have seen that adjectives generally follow the noun they qualify. An Italian says "a table round" = *una tavola rotonda*, "a carpet green" = *un tappeto verde*. But some adjectives usually precede their noun.

The commonest of these are: *bɛllo* = beautiful, *buɔno* = good, *grande* = big, *lungo* = long, *giɔvane* = young, *nuɔvo* = new, with their opposites: *brutto, cattivo, piccolo, brɛve, vɛcchio, antico*. All these adjectives *may* come after their noun; when they do, special stress is laid on the idea in the adjective: *è un brutto affare* = It's an ugly business; *è una ragazza brutta* = She's an *ugly* girl.

One or two adjectives, having both a literal and figurative meaning, change their meaning according to their position. When they precede the noun they may be taken in the figurative sense; when they follow they have the literal meaning:

Example: *pɔvero* = poor. Literal meaning "not rich":

è una famiglia pɔvera, il padre è disoccupato.
They are (it is) a poor family, the father is out of work.

and figurative meaning, "miserable", "unfortunate":

Pɔvero ragazzo, non ha né padre né madre.
Poor boy, he has neither father nor mother.

Another adjective, *grande*, sometimes has the figurative sense of "great" when preceding its noun: *Un grand'uɔmo* = a great man; but *Un uɔmo grande* = a big, therefore a tall, man.

Note that before a word beginning with a vowel, *grande* drops its final -*e*. Three adjectives: *bɛllo, buɔno* and *grande*, undergo certain changes when they precede the noun.* *Bɛllo* imitates the definite article *il* and *lo*:

> un bɛl concɛrto = a fine concert
> i bɛi teatri = the fine theatres
> un bɛllo spɛcchio = a beautiful mirror
> i bɛgli spɛcchi = the beautiful mirrors
> un bɛll'anɛllo = a lovely ring
> i bɛgli alberi = the beautiful trees
> una bɛlla donna = a beautiful woman
> una bɛll'idɛa = a fine idea
> due bɛlle rɔṣe rosse = two lovely red roses

* *Santo* (= saint) undergoes similar changes.

> San Giɔrgio, Sant'Antɔnio, Santo Stɛfano;
> Sant'Anna, Santa Caterina.

Buono, in the singular, has forms similar to those of the indefinite article *un, uno, una* and *un'*:

> un buon cavallo = a good horse
> un buon amico = a good friend (masc.)
> una buon'amica = a good friend (fem.)
> un buono stipendio = a good salary
> una buona cuoca = a good cook

Grande becomes *gran* before a masculine singular word beginning with a consonant (other than *s* impure or *z*), *grand'* before any singular word beginning with a vowel, and it keeps its full form before *s* impure and *z*:

> un gran fuoco = a big fire
> un grande sbaglio = a big mistake
> un grand'armadio = a large wardrobe
> una grand'anima = a great soul

These adjectives always have their full forms when they follow the noun they qualify and when they are separated from their noun by the verb *essere*:

> il gran fuoco but il fuoco è grande
> una buon'idea „ l'idea è buona

Note, too, that when any of these adjectives are qualified by an adverb such as "very" (= *molto*), they always follow their noun, and therefore have their full forms: a very large house = *una casa molto grande*.

Vocabulary

avvocato = lawyer
cartolina = postcard
dottore (m.) = doctor
francobollo = stamp
giorno = day
pacco = parcel
posta = post office
postino = postman
ricevuta = receipt
sala di scrittura = writing-room
settimana = week

raccomandato = registered

firmare = to sign
incontrare = to meet
offrire (irreg.) = to offer (2nd group)
perdere (irreg.) = to lose
portare = to bring, carry, wear
ricevere = to receive

fa = ago
ieri = yesterday
scorso = past, last (in expressions of time as "last week", etc.)

Exercise 6 (a)

1. Vendé i due bei cavalli la settimana scorsa.
2. Tre settimane fa perdetti un bell'anello nel giardino.
3. Due giorni fa ricevei una lettera raccomandata e un pacco e firmai una ricevuta.
4. La cuoca offrí del tè al postino.
5. La settimana scorsa il postino portò una bella rosa rossa per la cuoca.
6. Il postino ha un buono stipendio ma è di una famiglia molto povera.
7. Dove fu * la cuoca ieri? Fu * alla posta e incontrò il postino. È una buon'amica del postino.
8. Io fui * anche alla posta e all'entrata incontrai il dottore.
9. Il dottore è un buon amico dell'avvocato.
10. Poi incontrammo anche l'avvocato nella sala di scrittura.
11. Comprai dodici cartoline e venti francobolli; finii una lettera e poi fummo * a un caffè.
12. Il postino portò due cartoline dalla zia in America ieri.
13. È un bell'uomo il postino, e la cuoca non è brutta.

Exercise 6 (b)

1. I sold a fine ring yesterday and bought these books.
2. She lost a lovely ring three weeks ago.
3. Where did she lose the ring? In the garden.
4. Aunt received a registered parcel yesterday and she signed a receipt.
5. Mary went with cook (with *the* cook) to the post office. They bought stamps and some postcards.
6. Mary's brother is a very handsome man.
7. I received a long letter from Uncle yesterday and also two postcards and a large parcel.
8. Didn't you receive anything yesterday, Mr. Pazzi?
9. No, I didn't receive anything yesterday.
10. The theatres in this town are very fine.
11. Yes, we went to the theatre last week.
12. The lawyer received a postcard from the doctor yesterday.
13. Last year he bought a car, two horses, a cow and a house with a large garden; now he is very poor.

* The past definite of *essere* may be used to translate "went".

LESSON VII

IMPERFECT—INVARIABLE NOUNS—DEMONSTRATIVE ADJECTIVES

THE Imperfect expresses an incomplete or habitual action in the past. It states what was going on or what used to happen when something else also happened. It is also a descriptive tense. The difference between the imperfect and the past definite is seen in this sentence: They *caught* the thief when he *was climbing* through the window: *caught* is the single complete action in the past; *was climbing* is incomplete (the thief never finished his climbing, for they caught him before he got through the window). Again, in this sentence: "The thief *used to climb* through the window but one day they caught him," *used to climb* indicates habitual action: the thief found he could take what he wanted and then escape through the window, so he did this regularly—until they caught him, which put a stop to it, once and for all.

Read the following extract (referring to the translations for help as to its meaning) and note the use of the tenses in Italian. The verbs in the imperfect are all in italics. Note how the imperfect describes the scene, while the past definite carries on the narrative. The subject-matter of the piece is briefly: Renzo, a poor young peasant engaged to Lucia, a girl of his village, learns on his wedding morning that the priest refuses to marry them because of the threats of a rich and powerful lord who has his eye on Lucia. He is on his way to break the dreadful news to the bride, who, knowing nothing at all about it, is busy dressing for the wedding.

"Predominato da questi pensieri Renzo passò davanti alla sua casa che *era* posta nel mezzo del villaggio, e attraversatolo, si avviò a quella di Lucia che *stava* all'estremità opposta. *Aveva* quella casetta un piccolo cortile davanti, che la *separava* dalla via, ed *era* cinto con un muretto. Renzo entrò nel cortile, e intese un misto e continuo gridío che *veniva* da una stanza superiore. S'immaginò che sarebbero amiche e comari venute a far corteo a Lucia; e non si volle mostrare a quel mercato, con quella novella in corpo e sul volto. Una fanciulletta che si *trovava* nel cortile, gli corse incontro gridando: lo sposo! lo sposo!"

Literal translation. Predominated by these thoughts, Renzo passed in front of his own house, which was situated in the middle of the village, and having crossed it (the village) himself he directed to that of Lucia, which was standing at the end opposite. Had that little house a small yard in front, which it separated from the road, and it was surrounded with a little wall. Renzo entered into the yard, and heard a mixed and continuous shouting which was coming from a room upper. Himself he imagined that they would be the girl friends and neighbours come to make procession to Lucia; and not himself did he wish to show to that market, with that news in body and on the face. A little girl who herself was finding in the yard, to him ran against shouting: "The bridegroom, the bridegroom!"

Free translation. With these thoughts uppermost in his mind, Renzo went right past his own house, which was situated in the centre of the village and going straight on he directed his steps to Lucy's home, which stood at the opposite end. Her little house had a small yard in front, which separated it from the road and which was enclosed by a low wall. Renzo entered the yard and heard a continual hubbub and shouting coming from one of the upstairs rooms. He imagined that it must be Lucy's friends and neighbours who had come to attend her to church; and he didn't want to show himself to that noisy party with sadness in his heart and bad news written all over his face. But a little girl who was in the yard ran to meet him shouting "The bridegroom, the bridegroom!"

It would be useful to pick out the verbs which are in the past definite. Note those which are regular and the three of the second conjugation which are irregular: *intese* (intendere), *volle* (volere) and *corse* (correre). Then study the imperfects and notice their endings, which may be learnt from this table:

I bought	I sold	I finished
was buying	was selling	was finishing
used to buy	used to sell	used to finish
compr-avo	vend-evo	fin-ivo
compr-avi	vend-evi	fin-ivi
compr-ava	vend-eva	fin-iva
compr-avamo	vend-evamo	fin-ivamo
compr-avate	vend-evate	fin-ivate
compr-avano	vend-evano	fin-ivano

It will be noted (with satisfaction) that this tense is an easy one to learn, for, except for the characteristic vowel, the endings are the same for all three conjugations.

Another reason for being satisfied with this tense is that,

with the exception of *essere*, all verbs are regular: all other
Italian verbs are conjugated in the imperfect like one or other
of the models just given.

Imperfect of the Auxiliary Verbs

Essere	*avere*
ero = I was, was being, used to be	avevo = I had, was having, used to have
eri	avevi
era	aveva
eravamo	avevamo
eravate	avevate
erano	avevano

Note where the stress in pronunciation comes in both these
tables; and, with regard to *essere*, note that the initial *e* of the
singular and of the third person plural is an open *e*.

Invariable Nouns.—The nouns we have met so far ended in
-*a*, -*o* or -*e*; and they formed their plurals by changing the final
vowel: -*a* to -*e*; and -*o* and -*e* to -*i*. The greatest number of Italian
nouns end in one or other of these three vowels, but there are a
few which end in -*i* and -*u*, and a few words borrowed from
other languages which end in a consonant. None of these
nouns change for the plural, and the only indication as to
whether we are speaking of one or more than one is given by
the article used with them or by the context. A few other nouns
are also invariable in the plural: the complete list is as follows:

1. Those ending in -*i* (nearly all feminine): la crisi (crisis),
le crisi.

2. Those ending in -*u* (always accented on the final *u*,
and nearly all feminine): la virtú, le virtú.

3. Those ending in any accented vowel: la città, le
città; il caffè, i caffè.

4. Those ending in -*ie* (always feminine): la serie (series),
le serie.

5. Those ending in a consonant: il bar, i bar (where one
drinks!).

6. Words of one syllable, whatever their ending: il re
(king), i re.

7. Certain compound nouns formed by a noun + a verb:
il portacenere (ash-tray), i portacenere.

Demonstrative Adjectives.—We have met the word *questo*,
meaning "this". Like other adjectives ending in -*o*, *questo* has a

feminine form in -*a* and the two corresponding plurals: *questo libro, questa casa, questi cavalli, queste tavole*. When *questo* comes before a *singular* word beginning with a vowel, it elides the final vowel and becomes *quest'*: *quest'uomo, quest'aria* ("this air"), but *questi alberi*.

There are two words for "that": *codesto*, which refers to something near to the person addressed, and *quello*. *Codesto* changes for the feminine and the plural, just as *questo*, and, like *questo*, it drops its final vowel before a singular noun beginning with a vowel; but *quello* needs a little more attention, for, like *bello*, it has various changes:

> quel medico = that doctor
> quell'albero = that tree
> quello specchio = that mirror
> quei ragazzi = those boys
> quegli uccelli = those birds
> quegli stessi alberi = those same trees
> quella signorina = that young lady
> quelle donne = those women

Vocabulary

biblioteca = library	scaffale (m.) = book-shelf	andare (irreg.) = to go
carne (f.) = meat		
giornale (m.) = news-paper	scrivania = desk	
	storia = story, history	che! = what! what a!
lampada = lamp	tory	
legume (m.) = vege-table	volta = time, turn	
		tutto = whole (plural, = all)
libreria = bookshop	elegante = smart	
mattina = morning	ricco = rich	

Exercise 7 (a)

1. Quando era a * Firenze andava tutti i giorni alla biblioteca.
2. Dove andavate voi? Andavamo a un caffè in Via Torna-buoni.
3. Via Tornabuoni era una delle vie eleganti di quella città.
4. Incontrai l'avvocato in città ieri. Era in Via Tornabuoni e guardava i nuovi libri nella libreria.
5. Cercava quel libro sulla storia d'Italia che vedemmo a Roma la settimana scorsa.

* Before names of towns English "in" is usually *a* in Italian, unless the meaning within is emphasized.

6. Vede Lei quella vecchia * senza scarpe? Una volta era molto ricca ma ora è molto povera.
7. Stamattina (short for *questa mattina*) cercavo la cuoca. Dov'era? Non era in cucina?
8. No, era in città; comprava carne e legumi al mercato.
9. Ieri incontrai il fratello di Maria e il postino in città; parlavano con quella ragazza della libreria.
10. Che bello studio aveva il signor Pazzi! Era una stanza grande con un balcone e due finestre.
11. La scrivania era davanti al balcone e sulla tavola rotonda vicino alla porta c'era una bella lampada.
12. Aveva anche un bel tappeto verde e un grande scaffale con molti libri.

Exercise 7 (b)

1. Did she go to church every day when she was in Florence?
2. Yes, she used to go with Aunt every morning.
3. She used to write to John every week.
4. I was looking for Mary's brother. Where was he?
5. He was in the bookshop and he was talking to the lawyer.
6. The doctor entered while they were talking.
7. The lawyer was finishing a letter when they entered the study.
8. He was looking at the lawyer, who was near the desk.
9. They were looking for that newspaper which those women were reading.
10. Was cook at the market this morning, Mrs. Pazzi?
11. Yes, she was buying meat and vegetables, bread and wine.
12. Have they good wines at the market? No, they are not very good.

LESSON VIII

POSSESSIVES—INTERROGATIVES

FOLLOWING is a table of possessive adjectives and pronouns. Note that each word has four forms: masculine singular and plural and feminine singular and plural, and that the definite article is used with them; an Italian usually says *the* my hat and *the* mine = *il mio cappɛllo, il mio*. Note, too, that the same word is used for *my* and *mine*, etc.; for in Italian these words

* *Vecchio* is used as a noun as well as an adjective; in the masculine it means *old man*, in the feminine *old woman*.

may either be used with a noun or they may stand alone: they are both adjectives and pronouns.

Masculine		Feminine		
Singular	Plural	Singular	Plural	
il mio	i miɛi	la mia	le mie	my, mine
il tuo	i tuɔi	la tua	le tue	thy, thine your, yours
il suo	i suɔi	la sua	le sue	his, her, hers, its
il Suo (suo)	i Suɔi	la Sua	le Sue	your, yours
il nostro	i nostri	la nostra	le nostre	our, ours
il vostro	i vostri	la vostra	le vostre	your, yours
il loro	i loro	la loro	le loro	their, theirs
il Loro	i Loro	la Loro	le Loro	your, yours

An important difference between English and Italian possessive pronouns and adjectives is that in Italian the possessive word refers to the thing that is possessed, and not to the possessor:

il mio giardino = my garden   la mia casa = my house

These Italian forms would be the same whether the person referred to in the "my" were a man or a woman, *mio* agreeing with *giardino*, and *mia* with *casa*. Similarly if two men shared a car they would talk about *la nostra macchina*, as *macchina* is feminine.

il suo giardino = his, her or its garden, or your garden
la sua casa = his, her, its or your house

Note that *il suo* and *la sua* may refer to four persons; his, her, its and your (polite form, sometimes spelt with a capital letter). Usually one can tell which person is meant; but if there is any doubt, a phrase meaning *of him, of her*, etc. must be used instead of the possessive. The possessive normally refers to the subject of the sentence, therefore in such a sentence as: *Lui lɛgge il suo giornale*, *il suo* naturally refers to *lui*, so we know that it is his own newspaper. But should we wish to say: "He is reading *her* newspaper," the possessive cannot be used, and the sentence is written: *Lui lɛgge il giornale di lɛi*.

Using the definite article "the" with the possessive seems strange to us at first, but one quickly becomes used to it. There is one important occasion when it is not used, and that is when one is speaking of a near relative in the singular, such as mother, father, etc.: *mia madre, mio padre*. But when this near relative is qualified by an adjective, it *does* require the article;

and the article is also required if the possessive is *loro*, or if the relation is in the plural. Study these examples:

> mia madre = my mother
> il mio caro padre = my dear father
> mia sorella = my sister
> la mia piccola sorella = my little sister
> i miei fratelli = my brothers
> la loro sorella = their sister

Just as we can use the definite article before the possessive and say *the* my book, so we can use the indefinite article and say *a* my book (meaning: "one of my books"). And we can go farther, and say *that* my book, *two* my books, *many* my books and even *some* my books:

> un mio libro = one of my books
> quel mio libro = that book of mine
> due miei libri = two of my books
> molti miei libri = many of my books
> dei, *or* alcuni miei libri = some of my books

The "of" in the English phrase is therefore not translated in Italian; although one might say *uno dei miei libri*, this is not usual, the more concise form is preferred.

Interrogatives.—We have used some of the more common interrogative words: *Chi? Che?* or *Che cosa? Dove?* and *Perché?* (*Perché* also means "because": *Perché non compra un nuovo cappello? Perché non ho denaro.* = Why don't you buy a new hat? Because I've no money.) These words may be governed by prepositions: to whom?—*a chi?* by whom?—*da chi?* with what?—*con che?* and they are all invariable. Two other interrogative words change their endings: *quale?* = which? and *quanto?* = how much? *Quale* becomes *quali* in the plural; *quanto?* has the feminine *quanta?* and in the plural (when it means "how many?") *quanti?* and *quante?* Study the following interrogative sentences:

Chi c'è nella stanza da bagno? = Who is there in the bathroom?

Chi vedo nella cucina? = Whom do I see in the kitchen?

A chi scrive quella lunga lettera? = To whom are you writing that long letter?

Di chi parlate? = Of whom are you speaking?

Di chi è questo fazzoletto bianco? = Whose is this white handkerchief?

Che cosa vende? = What is he selling?

Per chi è quel gran pacco? = For whom is that large parcel?

Da chi è quel libro? = By whom is that book?

Che (or quale) libro compraste ieri? = What (which) book did you buy yesterday?

Quali porte sono aperte? = Which doors are open?

Quante chiese ci sono in questa città? = How many churches are there in this town?

Vocabulary

autorimessa = garage	bere (irreg.) = to drink
barba = beard	mangiare = to eat
baule (m.) = trunk	
bottiglia = bottle	sempre = always
vestito = dress (woman's)	qui = here
suit (man's)	

Exercise 8 (a)

1. Chi è quel signore? È un amico mio.
2. Scrivo a una mia amica a Roma.
3. Per chi è quel pacco raccomandato? È per mio padre.
4. Quanto pane c'è in cucina, Maria?
5. Non c'è pane. Quel ragazzo mangiò tutto il nostro pane ieri.
6. Perché non compra uno scaffale per i suoi libri?
7. Che buon vino! Bevono vino Loro tutti i giorni?
8. Quella loro cuoca è molto buona.
9. Che bel fuoco è quello! Sí, la cuoca ha sempre un bel fuoco.
10. Quanto vino beve quell'uomo al giorno? * Generalmente beve cinque o sei bottiglie al giorno.
11. Quell'armadio è per i miei vestiti e questo è per i suoi.
12. Qual'è il suo baule, Signorina? Questo qui è il mio, codesto è di mia madre e quello là è di quel signore dalla † barba.

* Note that an Italian says "How much do you drink *at the* day?" The definite article is also used in Italian where we would use the indefinite in such phrases as: two shillings *a* pound—due scellini *la* libbra.

† An idiomatic use of the preposition *da*. This preposition is used where we in English use "with" to denote a special characteristic in the appearance of someone: Il ragazzo dal naso lungo = the boy with the long nose; but: The coat with the yellow belt = l'abito con la cintura gialla.

Exercise 8 (b)

1. Who is that man with the beard? He is a friend of my father's.
2. My father and mother went to town yesterday. They met that friend of yours in the bookshop.
3. Whose is this trunk? It is my mother's.
4. How many books are there in that bookcase?
5. We have many good wines, sir; which do you prefer, white or red?
6. One of my friends bought that car yesterday. Which? That car there in the garage.
7. What is that old woman selling? She is selling handkerchiefs and socks.
8. Where do you buy your hats? That new hat of yours (translate either "that your hat new", or: "that your new hat") is very smart.
9. Which dress do you prefer? I prefer that blue one. (Omit "one".)
10. That green hat of his is very old. Didn't he buy a new one last week?
11. Many of my books are in my trunk.
12. How many trunks have you, sir? I have two trunks. This one is mine and that one there is also mine.

LESSON IX

FUTURE AND CONDITIONAL—NOUNS IN -*IO*

THE future and conditional, translating respectively "I shall" and "I should", are formed in Italian from the infinitive. They take the infinitive as a stem and add to it certain endings. Before adding the endings the final vowel of the infinitive is dropped, and the first conjugation makes a further alteration by changing the -*a* of the -*are* to -*e*.

I shall buy, etc.	I shall sell, etc.	I shall finish, etc.
comprer-ò	vender-ò	finir-ò
comprer-ai	vender-ai	finir-ai
comprer-à	vender-à	finir-à
comprer-emo	vender-emo	finir-emo
comprer-ete	vender-ete	finir-ete
comprer-anno	vender-anno	finir-anno

Note that the *first* and *third persons singular* of all three conjugations have the stress on the final vowel, and therefore must have the written accent. There are no irregularities in any future endings, so when we have learnt these endings we shall be able to form the future of any verb—with the exception of a few which have slightly irregular forms in their stem (as *andare* = to go, *andrò* = I shall go). The same applies to the endings of the conditional:

I should buy, etc.	I should sell, etc.	I should finish, etc.
comprer-ɛi	vender-ɛi	finir-ɛi
comprer-esti	vender-esti	finir-esti
comprer-ɛbbe	vender-ɛbbe	finir-ɛbbe
comprer-emmo	vender-emmo	finir-emmo
comprer-este	vender-este	finir-este
comprer-ɛbbero	vender-ɛbbero	finir-ɛbbero

Future of ɛssere and avere

I shall be, etc.	I shall have, etc.
sarò	avrò
sarai	avrai
sarà	avrà
saremo	avremo
sarete	avrete
saranno	avranno

Conditional of ɛssere and avere

I should be, etc.	I should have, etc.
sar-ɛi	avr-ɛi
sar-esti	avr-esti
sar-ɛbbe	avr-ɛbbe
sar-emmo	avr-emmo
sar-este	avr-este
sar-ɛbbero	avr-ɛbbero

Uses of the Future.—The future is used, as in English, to denote what is going to happen, and it is also used in some cases where we use the present. In the sentence "When I sell the horse I shall buy a cow", an Italian would say: "When I *shall* sell the horse I shall buy a cow"—*Quando venderò il cavallo comprerò una vacca*. Strictly speaking the Italian is more correct, for both actions are really future. Subordinate sentences of this kind are introduced by "if" (*se*) or by a word denoting time, such as "when" (*quando*). So when translating into Italian be on the lookout for subordinate clauses beginning with "if" or "when" in the present tense, followed by a main clause which has its verb in the future, and make both verbs future in Italian. The future is also used in Italian to denote probability: She may be a clever girl, but she doesn't seem so = *Sarà una ragazza intelligente, ma non sembra.*

We must add a word about our English "shall" and "will". The English future tense is: I shall buy, thou wilt buy, he will, we shall, you will, they will buy; but if we mix up the "shalls" and "wills", using *will* instead of *shall* and *shall* instead of *will*, these auxiliaries have a special meaning. "I will buy" means "I want to buy" or "I insist on buying", and "He shall buy" means "He must buy" or "He is to buy". These are therefore not the simple future and cannot be translated into Italian by the future tense, or the ideas of *want* and *must* will be lost. We shall learn later how to turn into Italian *shall* meaning *must* and *will* meaning *want* (pages 83, 147); for the moment remember that *shall* and *will* are not always the simple future, and that when translating the Italian future tense into English we must be sure to use the correct English word.

Uses of the Conditional.—The conditional, like English *should* and *would*, is used in direct speech after a verb of saying (also thinking and believing) in the past. It is the tense which in direct speech would be future: "He said he would write the letter"; what he actually said was in the future: "I shall write the letter". It is also used for the conclusion of a conditional sentence: If I had enough money, I should buy a car. These sentences are dealt with in a later lesson, page 146.

Italian also uses the conditional to express what is said on the authority of someone else. There is usually some word or phrase in the sentence to indicate that the person who is reporting what was said is not sure of the truth of the statement and disclaims responsibility for it. Such a sentence is: According to the judge, the girl is not guilty = *Secondo il giudice, la ragazza non sarebbe colpevole.*

Nouns ending in -io may present uncertainty in the formation of their plural, for sometimes they have double *i*, and sometimes they merely drop the *o* of the singular. This depends on what use the *i* has in the word: if the *i* is stressed, as in *mormorio* (murmur) and *rio* (brook) there are two *i*'s in the plural: *mormorii, rii*; if the *i* is pronounced as a separate syllable, but not stressed, the plural usually keeps one *i* only, but may have a circumflex accent to show the abbreviation: *studio, studî*; and lastly, if the *i* hardly counts as a letter, but is merely to influence the pronunciation of a preceding consonant, as in *figlio, viaggio* (journey), the plural is formed by dropping the final *o* of the singular: *figli, viaggi*. Adjectives follow the same rule: *il vestito grigio* (= the grey dress), *i vestiti grigi*; and in the feminine if the *i* is not accented in the singular, it disappears in the plural: *la sciarpa grigia* (= the grey scarf), *le sciarpe grige*.

Nouns ending in -*aio* (only a few) should be noted. They form their plural by dropping the final *o* of the singular: *cucchiaio* (= spoon), plural: *cucchiai*.

Useful Expressions of Time.—We have already met the word *ora* = hour (also meaning *now*). An Italian asks not "What *time* is it?" but "What *hour* is it?" or "What *hours* are they?" and the corresponding reply is equivalent to: "It is the one" (hour understood), "They are the three", etc.:

Che ora è?   } = What time is it?
Che ore sono?   }

è l'una = It is one o'clock (*ora* understood).
Sono le quattro meno un quarto = It is a quarter to four (quattro *ore* understood, *meno* = less).
Sono le undici e mezzo = It is half-past eleven.
Sono le cinque meno venti = It is twenty to five.
Sono le otto e dieci = It is ten minutes past eight.
È mezzanotte = It is midnight.
È mezzogiorno = It is midday.
A che ora? = At what time? Alle tre = At three o'clock.
Stamane, stamani or stamattina = This morning.
Stasera = This evening.
Stanotte = Last night.

Vocabulary

stazione (f.) = station	arrivare = to arrive
tempo = time, weather	mandare = to send
treno = train	prendere (irreg.) = to take
ancora = yet, still, again	sicuro = sure, certain
prima di = before	generalmente = generally

Exercise 9 (a)

1. Quando venderò la casa, comprerò una macchina.
2. A che ora arriverà il treno?
3. Arriverà alle cinque e mezzo. Avremo il tempo per prendere il tè prima di andare (translate: "going") alla stazione.
4. Prendiamo il tè alle cinque generalmente.

5. A che ora arriverà suo figlio, Signora? Arriverà col treno delle otto meno venti.
6. Quando partiranno? Giovanni partirà stasera a mezzanotte, ma i suoi fratelli partiranno domani mattina per Firenze.
7. Noi mangiamo all'una generalmente, ma domani mangeremo a mezzogiorno e mezzo e prenderemo il treno alle due.
8. Sono le undici e la cuoca è ancora al mercato.
9. Che cosa comprerà al mercato? Al mercato comprerà molte cose e parlerà con le sue amiche.
10. Secondo mio padre la cuoca sarebbe una donna intelligente, ma non sembra.
11. Sono sicuro che mio figlio non firmerebbe questa lettera.
12. I viaggi in treno non sono sempre comodi.

Exercise 9 (b)

1. What time is it? It is half-past three.
2. At what time does the train arrive? At a quarter to eight.
3. How many hats has that woman? She has nine, I think. (She *will* have.)
4. When we sell the horses we shall buy a car.
5. I am sure that my mother would not buy that hat.
6. We generally take tea at half-past four, but tomorrow we shall take tea at four o'clock before going to the station. (Before *to go*.)
7. The lawyer will send the letter to the judge tomorrow.
8. When will he arrive at home? Not before midnight.
9. This evening her four sons will be at home.
10. She bought a grey hat yesterday and tomorrow she's going to buy (she will buy) a grey scarf and grey gloves. (Say: a scarf and some gloves grey; "grey" being masculine plural.)
11. It is a quarter to four, and cook is still at the market.
12. According to Mrs. Pazzi, our cook is lazy.

LESSON X

COMPOUND TENSES

So far we have learnt only *Simple* tenses of verbs; now we come to *Compound* tenses, which are formed with the help of the auxiliary verbs, *avere* and *essere*. These tenses are formed with the past participle (the part of the verb which in English goes with "I have", "I had", *e.g.*, I had *spoken*) and the various tenses of the auxiliary. Five compound tenses correspond to the five simple tenses we already know:

1. Present Perfect (Present indicative of the auxiliary verb and the past participle), translates: I have spoken.
2. Past Perfect (Imperfect of the auxiliary and the past participle), translating: I had spoken.
3. Second Past Perfect (Past definite of the auxiliary and the past participle), also: I had spoken.
4. Future Perfect (Future of the auxiliary and past participle): I shall have spoken.
5. Conditional Perfect (Conditional of auxiliary and past participle): I should have spoken.

To be able to form the compound tenses we must know the past participles; here they are:

1st Conjugation	2nd Conjugation	3rd Conjugation
compr-ato (bought)	vend-uto (sold)	fin-ito (finished)

Auxiliary verbs

stato (been)   avuto (had)

The past participle of verbs of the first conjugation end in *-ato* (there is only one exception: *fatto* from *fare* = to make); those of the second in *-uto* (generally, but we shall come across some irregular endings); and the third (with a very few exceptions) in *-ito*.

A participle, as its name implies, participates in two parts of speech, it is partly a verb and partly an adjective. Sometimes it is more of a verb than an adjective—in this case its ending never varies; at other times it is more of an adjective, and then it changes like the adjectives ending in *-o*.

Some Italian verbs use *avere* to form their compound tenses and others *essere*. *Avere* is used by verbs which are *transitive*, that is by verbs which have a direct object, as for example the verb "to buy". In the sentence "I buy a house", "house" is the direct object of "buy"; "I have bought a house" is in Italian = *ho comprato una casa*. *Avere* is also used for a very few *intransitive* verbs * (verbs which cannot take an object), as "to sleep" (*dormire*): I have slept = *ho dormito*; but most intransitive verbs, such as *arrivare* = to arrive, *partire* = to depart, take *essere* as their helping verb: I have arrived = *sono*

* Noted in the vocabulary.

arrivato (literally "I *am* arrived"). *essere* is also used with reflexive verbs (see page 73), and it is the auxiliary used to form the passive voice (just as in English we use the verb "to be"): *e.g.*, active voice: I buy a house = *compro una casa*; passive voice: a house is bought by me = *una casa è comprata da me*. *essere* is also used to form its own compound tenses: an Italian says: *Sono stato* (lit. "I *am* been"); *ero stato* ("I *was* been"); *siamo stati* ("we *are* been").

Note in the last example, and in the example of the passive: *la casa è comprata*, that we have agreement of the past participle with the subject of the sentence. WHEN THE VERB IS CONJUGATED WITH *essere*, THE PAST PARTICIPLE AGREES WITH THE SUBJECT; WHEN THE VERB IS CONJUGATED WITH *avere*, THERE IS NO AGREEMENT BETWEEN THE LAST PARTICIPLE AND THE SUBJECT; the past participle then usually agrees with the direct object if it precedes the verb, but the writer may please himself. (See also page 61.)

Consider the two past participles in the following sentence, and you will realize why one agrees with the subject and the other does not: She has fallen and broken all the glasses = *è caduta e ha rotto tutti i bicchieri* (*caduta*, from *cadere* = to fall; *rotto*, from *rompere* (irreg.) = to break). "Fallen" indicates a state or condition; it is more of an adjective than a verb, and *cadere* is intransitive; therefore we have the auxiliary *essere* and agreement of the past participle with the subject. But "broken" is more of a verb than an adjective, it governs an object "glasses"; *rompere* is a transitive verb, conjugated with *avere*; therefore we have no agreement of the past participle with the subject. As the object follows the verb, there is no agreement at all; but in such a sentence as: "The glasses which she has broken", we might have agreement in Italian with the preceding direct object: *I bicchieri che lei ha rotto*, or *I bicchieri che lei ha rotti* (*bicchieri* is plural of *bicchiere*, masculine).

The following compound tenses should be completed in all persons, singular and plural; remember that the past participle must change for the feminine and for the plural when the verb is conjugated with *essere*:

Present Perfect

I have bought, etc. = ho comprato
I have sold, etc. = ho venduto
I have finished, etc. = ho finito
I have arrived, etc. = sono arrivato -a
I have fallen, etc. = sono caduto -a

I have departed, etc. = sono partito -a
I have been, etc. = sono stato -a
I have had, etc. = ho avuto

Past Perfect

I had bought = avevo comprato
I had sold = avevo venduto
I had finished = avevo finito
I had arrived = εro arrivato -a
I had fallen = εro caduto -a
I had departed = εro partito -a
I had been = εro stato -a
I had had = avevo avuto

Second Past Perfect

I had bought = εbbi comprato
I had sold = εbbi venduto
I had finished = εbbi finito
I had arrived = fui arrivato -a
I had fallen = fui caduto -a
I had departed = fui partito -a
I had been = fui stato -a
I had had = εbbi avuto

Future Perfect

I shall have bought = avrὸ comprato
I shall have sold = avrὸ venduto
I shall have finished = avrὸ finito
I shall have arrived = sarὸ arrivato -a
I shall have fallen = sarὸ caduto -a
I shall have departed = sarὸ partito -a
I shall have been = sarὸ stato -a
I shall have had = avrὸ avuto

Conditional Perfect

I should have bought = avrεi comprato
I should have sold = avrεi venduto
I should have finished = avrεi finito
I should have arrived = sarεi arrivato -a
I should have fallen = sarεi caduto -a
I should have departed = sarεi partito -a
I should have been = sarεi stato -a
I should have had = avrεi avuto

Uses of the Compound Tenses.—The *present perfect* states something which happened in the past that has reference to the present; it is often introduced by a word expressing time in the present: This morning I bought a new hat = *Stamane ho comprato un nuɔvo cappɛllo*; or it expresses something which happened in the past the effects of which are lasting into the present: He has seen that famous picture = *Ha veduto quel quadro famoso*. This tense is often used in conversation in place of the past definite when the event is not very remote past: Yesterday I went to the theatre = *Iɛri sono stato al teatro*. The *future perfect* and *conditional perfect* are used as in English (but see the lesson on the conditional sentences, page 146). The two *past perfects* denote, as in English, what had happened; but the *second past perfect* is used only after certain conjunctions of time in a subordinate clause which is followed by a main sentence which has its verb in the past definite. These conjunctions are: *quando* = when, *appena* = as soon as, *dopo che* = after, *subito che* = immediately after; *e.g., Appena ɛbbe finito la lɛttera, partì* = As soon as he had finished the letter, he left.

Vocabulary

camieriɛra = maid, waitress	aiutare = to help
coltɛllo = knife	apparecchiare = to lay (a table)
forchetta = fork	
piatto = plate	invitare = to invite
piattino = saucer	lavare = to wash
poliziɔtto = policeman	lasciare = to leave, to let
pranzo = dinner	pulire (1st group) = to clean, polish
tazza = cup	
vassɔio = tray	tornare = to return
	tardi = late

Exercise 10 (a)

1. Oggi abbiamo ospiti a pranzo.
2. La cuoca è andata al mercato per comprare carne e legumi e la cameriera ha lavato i piatti, le tazze e i bicchieri.
3. Maria aiuterà la donna ad apparecchiare e a pulire le forchette, i cucchiai e i coltelli.
4. Quando avrà aiutato la donna andrà alla stazione per incontrare gli ospiti.
5. La donna aveva lavato tutti i piatti ma non aveva pulito i coltelli.
6. Quando vedrà il dottore, avrà già venduto la macchina.

7. Appena ebbe rotto una tazza lasciò cadere anche una bottiglia.
8. Ha rotto tutte le cose che erano sul vassoio? Sí, tutte.
9. Erano stati alla casa del dottore quando incontrarono l'avvocato.
10. Saranno già arrivati quando Carlo tornerà a casa? Sí, saranno già in casa.
11. Sarà intelligente quella cameriera ma non sembra. Ha già rotto dodici piatti e due bicchieri. Ha lasciato cadere anche tre bottiglie e abbiamo perduto del buon vino.
12. A che ora è tornata la cuoca dal mercato oggi? È arrivata molto tardi a casa, credo. Avrà incontrato il postino per la via.

Exercise 10 (b)

1. We have invited Mr. and Mrs. Pazzi to dinner today.
2. The maid has already laid the table for twelve.
3. She had already cleaned the knives and forks when cook returned from the market.
4. Cook had been at the market a long time ("much time") because she had lost her purse.
5. As soon as she had lost her purse she spoke to the policeman ("with the policeman").
6. She also met the postman this morning.
7. There were many things on the tray: plates, glasses, cups and saucers.
8. Has she broken many things? Yes, two cups, three saucers and five plates.
9. As soon as she had laid the table the guests arrived.
10. Will he have seen Mary, do you think?
11. She lost her purse in the train this morning.
12. All my books were in that trunk that I have sent to Naples (say "all the my books").

LESSON XI

CONJUNCTIVE PRONOUNS—IMPERATIVE

THERE are two kinds of pronouns: *disjunctive* and *conjunctive*— emphatic and unemphatic. The pronouns we already know— the subjects of the verb—are emphatic pronouns; they are required only for emphasis, and they are also known as disjunctive pronouns—disjunctive or separated, for they may stand alone, independent of the verb: *Chi è la? io.* = Who is there? I. Disjunctive pronouns may also stand alone as objects of a preposition: *A chi dà quel denaro? a me.* = Who's he giving that money to? To me. In both sentences the pronoun is the most emphatic word.

But in sentences and phrases such as: He sees me; I find them; seeing us; to help you; the *object* pronouns (me, them, us, you) are not emphatic; they are very closely connected with the verb, and are almost joined to it, hence the name *conjunctive*. We shall deal with these pronouns first. They are always used in close connection with the verb; they cannot stand alone, and they are always direct, indirect or reflexive objects of a verb. (A verb is called reflexive when the object and the subject are the SAME person; in English the reflexive objects are myself, himself, etc.)

Conjunctive Personal Pronouns

Direct object	Indirect object	Reflexive object
mi = me	mi = to me	mi = myself
ti = thee, you	ti = to thee, to you	ti = thyself, yourself
lo = him, it (m.)	gli = to him, to it (m.)	si = himself, herself, itself, yourself
la = her, it (f.), you	le = to her, to it (f.), to you	
ci = us	ci = to us	ci = ourselves
vi = you	vi = to you	vi = yourself, yourselves
li = them, you (m.)	loro = to them, to you	si = themselves, yourselves
le = them, you (f.)		

The first and second persons singular and plural are the same for the three different kinds of objects. Learn carefully the forms of the third person which are used in the polite form of address. They may be seen more clearly from the following:

	Direct	Indirect	Reflexive
Addressing one person:	La = you	Le = to you	Si = yourself
Addressing more than one man, or men and women:	Li = you	Loro = to you	Si = yourselves
Addressing more than one woman:	Le = you	Loro = to you	Si = yourselves

Position of the Conjunctive Pronouns.—In English the conjunctive pronouns FOLLOW the verb; but in Italian they PRECEDE (except in certain cases which we shall learn later). An Italian says: *Lui la trovò* = He her found; *Lεi gli scriverà* = She to him will write. Study the following sentences:

Non lo capisco = I don't understand it.
Ci mandò la lεttera iεri = He sent us the letter yesterday.
Gli ho parlato = I have spoken to him.
Mi ha, *or* m'ha veduto = He has seen me.
L'ho finito = I have finished it.
Io mi lavo = I wash myself.
Noi ci laviamo = We wash ourselves, we wash one another.
Manderò loro la lεttera = I shall send them the letter.

And now the following points should be noted: Some conjunctive pronouns drop their final vowel before a word beginning with a vowel or an *h*; *lo* and *la* nearly always do so, and *mi*, *ti* and *si* quite often. The reflexive pronouns in the plural may mean *one another* and *each other* as well as *ourselves*, *themselves*, etc.; and one conjunctive pronoun (*loro*) always FOLLOWS the verb.

The conjunctive pronoun *ne* is a very useful one; it means "of it", "of them", "some of it", "some of them", "any of it", "any of them". It precedes the verb:

Ne avevo tre = I had three of them.
Ne ho molto = I have a lot of it.
Non ne abbiamo = We haven't any.

Ne is inserted in a sentence where we in English do not always need to say "of it". It always refers to something that has just been mentioned, and it must not be omitted when a number or an adjective of quantity comes after the verb, if the noun itself is not repeated.

The Imperative.—When asking or commanding anyone to do anything, we are using the imperative. A true imperative exists only in the second person (singular and plural); but when speaking to someone in the polite form in Italian it would be very rude to change suddenly to the second person to ask him to do something. Therefore a polite form of the imperative is supplied from the third persons singular and plural of the present subjunctive. A first person plural is also supplied from this tense, which translates the English: "Let us . . ." We have, therefore, five persons to learn as used for the imperative:

	1st conj.	2nd conj.
(tu)	compr-a = buy	vend-i = sell
(Lei)	compr-i = buy	vend-a = sell
(noi)	compr-iamo = let us buy	vend-iamo = let us sell
(voi)	compr-ate = buy	vend-ete = sell
(Loro)	compr-ino = buy	vend-ano = sell

	3rd conj. (1st group)	(2nd group)
(tu)	fin-isc-i = finish	part-i = depart
(Lei)	fin-isc-a = finish	part-a = depart
(noi)	fin-iamo = let us finish	part-iamo = let us depart
(voi)	fin-ite = finish	part-ite = depart
(Loro)	fin-isc-ano = finish	part-ano = depart

essere	*avere*
sii = be	abbi = have
sia = be	abbia = have
siamo = let us be	abbiamo = let us have
siate = be	abbiate = have
siano = be	abbiano = have

Imperative Negative

non comprare = don't buy
non compri = don't buy
non compriamo = don't let us buy
non comprate = don't buy
non comprino = don't buy

To form the imperative negative of the second person singular (*tu*), Italian uses the *infinitive*; the other persons remain the same as in the affirmative:

Compra quella macchina = Buy that car.
Non comprare quel fazzoletto = Don't buy that handkerchief.
Compri un bel fiore, signora = Buy a beautiful flower, lady.
Non compri quella carne = Don't buy that meat.

And now let us study a few sentences in the imperative which have conjunctive pronouns as objects instead of nouns:

Comprala = Buy it (referring to *macchina*).
Compratela = Buy it (referring to *macchina* but using *Voi*).
Lo compri, Signora = Buy it, lady.
Compriamolo = Let's buy it.
Parlate loro = Speak to them.

Non lo comprare⎫
Non lo comprate⎭ = Don't buy it.

Non la compri = Don't buy it (referring to *carne* (f.)).

Non lo compriamo = Don't let's buy it.

It will be seen that with the imperative *affirmative* conjunctive pronouns used with the *second person singular* and *first and second persons plural* FOLLOW the verb, and they are joined to it, forming one word. When they do this, the word does not change its stress; the same syllable carries the stress as was the case before the unemphatic pronoun was added; LORO, however, is *never* joined to the verb. The polite form of the imperative takes the conjunctive pronouns (except *loro*) BEFORE the verb, both in the negative and in the affirmative.

Three other forms of the verb have the conjunctive pronouns after them in the same way as the imperative affirmative: the infinitive, the past participle used without an auxiliary verb and the present participle (which corresponds to our form of the verb ending in *-ing*):

> Andava a vederla = he was going to see her.
> Parlandone loro = speaking of it to them.
> Parlatoci = (having) spoken to us.

Note that the infinitive loses its final vowel when it combines with the pronoun.

One more point about conjunctive pronouns. It has been noted that the past participle of a verb conjugated with *avere* may agree with a preceding direct object; * when that object is a conjunctive pronoun, the best writers always make the past participle agree with it. In fact, sometimes this agreement is necessary in the case of the third person singular pronoun to distinguish between *him* and *her*, as will be seen from these examples:

L'ho veduto al teatro = I saw *him* at the theatre.

L'abbiamo veduta per la strada = We saw *her* along the road.

Ci avrà veduti nel treno = He will have seen *us* on the train.

Hai comprato quella macchina? Sí, *l'*ho comprata = Have you bought that car? Yes, I have.

Vocabulary

albergo = hotel	facchino = porter
biglietto = ticket	finestrino = small window,
burro = butter	carriage window

* See page 54.

carrozza = carriage
prosciutto = ham
ristorante (m.) = restaurant
sala d'aspetto = waiting-room
salame (m.) (no plural) = sausage, sausage meat
salsiccia (pl. salsicce) = small sausage
valigia = suitcase

frutta = fruit
pronto = ready
un po' di = a little

addio = good-bye!
dappertutto = everywhere
finalmente = at last
forse = perhaps

Exercise 11 (a)

1. Ho perduto il mio baule, l'ha veduto Lei?
2. No, io ho perduto la valigia, l'ho cercata dappertutto ma non l'ho ancora trovata.
3. Il facchino non l'ha portata al treno?
4. No, l'avrà lasciata all'albergo.
5. Non è già nella carrozza? No, l'ho cercata nella carrozza, forse l'ho lasciata nella sala d'aspetto.
6. Ha comprato i biglietti, Signora? No, non li ho ancora comprati.
7. La cuoca ha portato il pane e burro e la frutta? Sí, li ha portati; ha portato anche del salame e un po' di prosciutto.
8. Dov'è quel facchino? Non l'hai trovato Giovanni? Ma il treno parte e noi partiremo senza bauli.
9. Ecco arriva il facchino. Eccolo: * Andiamo a incontrarlo. Ma ha delle rose rosse in mano! † [Note andare a—go to meet, translate "go and meet."]
10. Dio mio! rose rosse! Ma i bauli ! Dove sono? Dove sono i bauli? Eccoli, eccoli finalmente.
11. Ora siamo pronti. Ma dov'è Maria? Corri, corri Maria, il treno parte. Finalmente partiamo, addio, addio.
12. Ma per chi erano quelle rose rosse? Erano per la cuoca.
13. Povera cuoca ! Abbiamo perduto le sue belle rose rosse. Maria le ha lasciate cadere dal finestrino del treno.

Exercise 11 (b)

1. We have lost our suitcases. Have you seen them, porter?
2. No, madam, I have not seen them.
3. I have looked for them everywhere in the carriage.
4. Buy the tickets, please, John.

* Ecco takes the conjunctive pronouns after it.
† in mano. No possessive is necessary in Italian; we know it must be his own hand.

5. John and Mary, go and buy the tickets.
6. Have you any fruit? No, I haven't any.
7. Shall I go and buy some fruit? Yes, go * and buy fruit and a little ham.
8. Does she sell sausage too? Yes, she does.
9. Let us buy some fruit, bread and butter and a little ham.
10. Have you brought the sausages, too? Yes, here they are.
11. Why has he not brought the trunk? He has left it in the restaurant.
12. Shall we go and look for it?
13. No, children, stay here; you will miss the train. (Stay = remain.)

LESSON XII

CONJUNCTIVE PRONOUNS (*CONTD.*)—PRESENT PARTICIPLE

IN the preceding lesson each sentence contained only a single conjunctive pronoun; but two often come together, as direct and indirect objects of the same verb: He gives it to me. In Italian the indirect pronoun comes before the direct, and both pronouns either precede or follow the verb, according to the rules we have just learnt: *Lui me lo dà* = He to me it gives. But it will be said: There is a mistake: *me* should be *mi*. No, there is no mistake; for indirect pronouns change their form slightly when followed by the direct *lo, la, li, le* and *ne*:

Me lo danno = They give it to me (danno, from *dare* = to give, irreg.).
Te li danno = They give them to you.
Se lo dà = He gives it to himself.
Glielo daremo = We shall give it to him.
Glielo daremmo = We should give it to her.
Parlatecene = Speak to us of it.
Parlandovene = Speaking of it to you.
Parlatogliene = (Having) spoken to him of it.
Va' a dargliene = Go and give him some.
Lo daremo loro = We shall give it to them.

Note that *loro*, as before, always follows the verb. From the preceding we may learn that: before the direct pronouns *lo, la, li, le* and *ne*, the indirect change as follows: *mi, ti, si, ci* and *vi*

* *andare* has an irregular second person singular imperative—*va'*.

change the final *i* to *e*; and *gli* and *le* become *glie* and are written as one word with the following pronoun: *glielo* = it (masc.) to him, or to her, or to you (polite form); *glieli* = them (masc.) to him, or to her or to you; *gliene* = some to him, some to her, some to you.

Conjunctive Adverbs.—You will have noticed that *ci* (= us) is the same word as *ci* (= there, in the phrases "there is", *c' è*, etc.). *Ci* is both a pronoun and an adverb. *Vi*, too, means "there" as well as "you": *vi è* = there is; and *ne*, besides being a pronoun (= of it, some), is also an adverb meaning "thence". These three conjunctive adverbs are used to denote a place already mentioned when no special emphasis is required, and they precede or follow the verb, according to the rules given for the pronouns; *ci* and *vi*, as adverbs, also change to *ce* and *ve* when followed by *lo, la, li, le* or *ne*:

Vi andò ieri = He went there yesterday.
Spera di arrivarci alle due = He hopes to arrive there at two.
Ne arrivano oggi = They are arriving from there today.

Present Participle.—The forms for the three conjugations and the auxiliary verbs are as follows:

Compr-ando = buying	vend-endo = selling
fin-endo = finishing	essendo = being　　avendo = having

Perfect Participle

avendo comprato = having bought
avendo venduto = having sold
avendo finito = having finished
essendo stato = having been　　　avendo avuto = having had

The endings *-ando* and *-endo* correspond to the English ending *-ing*; but we cannot always use the Italian present participle for every occasion when English uses *-ing*, for the present participle in Italian is more truly a verb, and cannot be used as a noun or an adjective. In the sentence: "On opening the drawer she saw the box", the word "opening" is a verb, describing an action; therefore this can be rendered in Italian by a word in *-endo*: *Aprendo il cassetto vide la scatola* (the preposition "on" is not required). But in "I like riding" or "She spoke without hesitating", the word in *-ing* is more of a noun than a verb; while in phrases like "boiling water", "following chapter", the words in *-ing* are adjectives. In neither of these cases does Italian use a present participle; the way to render them will be dealt with later (Lesson XXVI, page 124, and Lesson XIX, Part II, page 183). For the moment we will concern ourselves only with the Italian present participle (remember that it never changes its endings); it is used in the following cases:

1. When it is preceded by one of the following prepositions (which are not translated in Italian): "by", "in", "on", "through":

Combattendo vinciamo = Through fighting we win.

2. Instead of a subordinate clause of time, cause or condition, which is introduced in English by "as", "while", "since", "if" (none of these words being translated into Italian, for they are understood in the present participle):

Camminando per Via Tornabuoni incontrai il dentista = As I was walking down Tornabuoni Road I met the dentist.
Andando per quella strada non la vedremo = If we go that way we shan't see her.

When the present participle is so used, however, it always agrees with the subject of the main sentence. For instance, the present participle could not be used in this sentence: "As I was walking down Tornabuoni Road a policeman stopped me"; this would be in Italian: *Mentre camminavo per via Tornabuoni un poliziotto mi fermo*.

3. It forms the progressive tenses with the verb *stare* (to stand, to be) as an auxiliary. There are two progressive or continuous tenses: the present, formed by the present indicative of *stare* and the present participle; and the past, formed by the imperfect of *stare* and the present participle:

> Sto leggendo = I am reading.
> Stavano dormendo = They were sleeping.

It should be noted that these two tenses are specially emphatic in Italian; they lay particular stress on the continuity of the action; we have seen that our continuous present and past tenses can often be rendered by the Italian ordinary present and imperfect respectively. There are no other progressive tenses in Italian; our other continuous tenses are usually rendered in Italian by the simple tense: "I shall be going" = *andro*.

Vocabulary

autobus (m.) = bus
cantonata = corner
farmacia = chemist
mancia = tip
passaporto = passport
piazza = square

aspettare = to wait for
domandare = to ask for

a piedi = on foot (piede (m.) = foot)
volentieri = willingly, gladly

Exercise 12 (a)

1. Uscendo dalla posta, incontrai il dentista.
2. Signora, dov'è la farmacia per favore? Ce n'è una alla cantonata, Signorina: eccola.
3. Mentre attraversava la piazza, un poliziotto lo fermò e gli domandò il passaporto. (Note the construction with *domandare*: to ask something *to* someone.)
4. Che belle rose rosse! Datemene una, per favore.
5. Non sono le mie; sono della cuoca, ma ve ne darò una molto volentieri.
6. Parlandogliene, perdette l'autobus e andò a casa a piedi.
7. Non c'è autobus, prendiamo una carrozza. Vedi, ce n'è una nella piazza, che aspetta.
8. Mentre apriva la scatola tutti la guardavano.
9. Sono stati a Firenze Loro? Sí, Signore, ne arriviamo ora.
10. È stata a Milano Lei, Signora? Sí, Signore, ci sono stata.
11. Aspettami, aspettami. Ma non aspettiamo nessuno. Il treno parte. Hai dato la mancia al facchino? Sí, gliel'ho data.
12. Ci hanno dato i biglietti? Sí, ce li hanno dati. E ha avuto la mancia il facchino? Sí, l'ha avuta.

Exercise 12 (b)

1. When coming out of the church they met the dentist and the doctor.
2. There was a large box in that drawer. Has she found it?
3. Yes, she has given it to him.
4. Why doesn't she give it to me? She has already given it to them.
5. While walking along Tornabuoni Road, Cook met the postman.
6. She has lost her passport. Have you seen it?
7. No, but the porter has found it; he will give it to her.
8. Give him some; but I haven't any more. (The polite form of the imperative, *i.e.*, the present subjunctive of *dare* is irregular: *dia*.)

9. Where is that famous church? At the corner. Don't you see it?
10. Has the dentist given you a receipt? Yes, he has given it to me.
11. Have you bought the tickets? Yes, I have bought them, and I have given them to Mary.
12. Has he given them to you? I have given them to him. Why didn't you (*voi*) give them to them? Because he hadn't given any to us. And why hadn't he given any to you? Because he hadn't any.

LESSON XIII

DISJUNCTIVE PRONOUNS—MORE PLURALS

WE know the disjunctive pronouns as subjects of the verb; as objects of the verb they have these forms:

	Singular	Plural
First person	me = me	noi = us
Second ,,	te = thee, you	voi = you
Third ,,	lui = him	loro = them (m. and f.)
	lɛi = her	
	esso = him, it	essi = them (m.)
	essa = her, it	esse = them (f.)
	Lɛi = you	Loro = you
	se = himself, herself, itself	se = themselves

With the exception of the first and second persons singular, the disjunctive or emphatic pronouns as subjects and as objects are the same; and again *lui*, *lɛi* and *loro* are used only for persons, *esso*, *essa*, etc., may refer to things and to animals.

The most common use of disjunctive pronouns is after a preposition:

Il mɛdico ɛ con lei = The doctor is with her.
Il bambino cammina da sé ora = The baby walks by himself now.

They are also used after "than" (= *di*) with a comparative:

Giovanni ɛ piú alto di me = John is taller (more tall) than I.

When a verb has two pronoun *direct* objects, disjunctives are required:

Ho veduto te e lui in città stamane = I saw you and him in town this morning and with two pronoun *indirect* objects:

Ne dò a lui e a lɛi = I'm giving some to him and to her

Sometimes when special emphasis is laid on the pronoun, a disjunctive is used:

Lo darò a lui = I'll give it to *him*;

and again when two objects are contrasted:

Lo darò a lui ma non a lɛi = I'll give it to him, but not to her.

In such phrases as the following the emphatic pronoun is required:

Felice lui ma povero me! = Happy he, but poor me!

and lastly, when the pronoun stands alone in the predicate:

Se io fossi te = If I were you (fossi = past subjunctive of ɛssere).

More Plurals.—The nouns ending in -*a* we have learnt so far have all been feminine. But there are a few in -*a* which are masculine, and they form their plural by changing the -*a* to -*i*. They mostly end in -*ma*, -*ta*, -*ca* and -*ga*:

Singular	Plural
il telegramma (the telegram)	i telegrammi
il poɛta (the poet)	i poɛti

Some words ending in -*a* may be either masculine or feminine, and then they have two plural forms. The most usual are nouns ending in -*ista*:

Singular	Plural
il pianista (m.) (the pianist)	i pianisti
la pianista (f.) (the pianist)	le pianiste
l'artista (m.) (the artist)	gli artisti
l'artista (f.) (the artist)	le artiste

Slight irregularities are found in the formation of the plural of nouns and adjectives ending in -*co*, -*go*, -*ca*, -*ga*, -*cia* and -*gia*:

-co and **-go.**—Words which have the stress on the syllable before the last add an *h* to keep the hard sound in the plural:

Singular	Plural
fuoco (fire)	fuochi
antico (ancient)	antichi
lago (lake)	laghi
albɛrgo (hotel)	albɛrghi

but if the stress is on a syllable before the next to the last, they do not keep the hard sound in the plural:

Singular	Plural
mɛdico (doctor)	mɛdici
monaco (monk)	monaci
magnifico (magnificent)	magnifici

There are, however, a few exceptions to this rule. The following should be remembered: *amico* (= friend), *nemico* (= enemy), *porco* (= pig), *grɛco* (= Greek), which, although having the next to the last syllable stressed, form their plurals in *-ci*: *amici, nemici, porci, grɛci*; and *carico* (= laden or load), with the stress on the *a*, puts in an *h* in the plural to keep the hard sound: *carichi*.

-ca and -ga.—Nouns and adjectives keep the hard sound of the *c* and *g* in the plural:

Singular	Plural
la barca (the boat)	le barche
il duca (the duke)	i duchi
lunga (long)	lunghe
magnifica (magnificent)	magnifiche

Note that an adjective ending in *-co* in the masculine and *-ca* in the feminine may preserve the hard sound in the feminine plural and not in the masculine:

Singular	Plural
il cavallo magnifico	i cavalli magnifici
la statua magnifica	le statue magnifiche

Note, too, the word for friend in both genders:

Singular	Plural
amico	amici
amica	amiche

-cia and -gia.—In a previous lesson (page 51) we noted that the word *grigio* became *grige* in the feminine plural. Like *grigia*, nouns and adjectives ending in *-cia* and *-gia* drop the *i* before the ending *-e* of the plural, provided the *i* is not stressed:

	Singular	Plural
	la guancia = the cheek	le guance
	la pioggia = the rain	le piogge
	la spiaggia = the shore	le spiagge
but	la farmacia = the chemist's	le farmacie
	la bugia = the lie	le bugie

There are a few exceptions to this rule, usually words which have a vowel immediately preceding the *-cia* or *-gia*: *valigia* (= suitcase), *valigie*.

Irregular Nouns.—A few masculine nouns ending in *-o* have an irregular plural in *-a* which is feminine. Some of the commonest are:

Singular	Plural
il braccio = the arm	le braccia
il ciglio = the eyelash	le ciglia
il dito = finger	le dita
il frutto = fruit	le frutta
(also la frutta = fruit, collectively)	
il ginocchio = the knee	le ginocchia
il labbro = the lip	le labbra
il lenzuolo = the sheet	le lenzuola
il muro = wall	le mura or i muri
il membro = limb, member	le membra (limbs), i membri (members of society, club, etc.)
il miglio = mile	le miglia
l'osso = bone	le ossa
il paio = pair	le paia
l'uovo = egg	le uova

The following have irregular plurals: *il bue* (= ox), *i buoi*; *l'uomo* (= man), *gli uomini*; and *la moglie* (= wife), *le mogli*.

Vocabulary

acqua = water
asciugamano (m.) = towel
capelli = hair (m. plur.)
pesce (m.) = fish
portamonete (m.) = purse
porto = port

alpino = alpine
calmo = calm
fortunato = happy, fortunate

Exercise 13 (a)

1. Non lo date a lui, datelo a lei.
2. Ho incontrato lei in città oggi ma non lui.
3. Avete veduto il lago voi? Sí, ci siamo andati oggi. L'acqua era molto calma, e c'erano molte barche.
4. Queste lenzuola sono molto vecchie, non sono per l'ospite, cerchiamone delle nuove.
5. Questo telegramma è per te, non è per me.
6. Le barche arrivarono al porto cariche di pesce.

7. Non sono aperte le farmacie oggi? Sí, Signora, sono aperte.
8. Ha già imparato a scrivere la bambina? Sí, ha scritto una lettera da sè. (*scritto* irreg. past participle of *scrivere*.)
9. Il duca ha una lunga barba bianca e i capelli bianchi. È vecchio ma sua moglie è piú vecchia di lui.
10. La vecchia stava dormendo; aveva ancora quel libro in mano e sulle ginocchia c'era il gatto che dormiva anch'esso.
11. I membri del club alpino di Torino sono arrivati oggi.
12. Che ragazza è quella! Ha perduto ieri due paia di guanti nel treno; e oggi in cucina ha lasciato cadere sei uova.
13. Mi dia un asciugamano pulito, per favore.

Exercise 13 (b)

1. Give it to me, not to him.
2. Those two men with the oxen will arrive tomorrow.
3. I met them in town this morning, but I did not see her.
4. That book was written by him.
5. This letter is for me, not for him.
6. Bring me those sheets, please. Here they are.
7. Those boats were laden with fish when they arrived at the port.
8. How many eggs have you bought?
9. That old man is very smart; he has a clean shirt every day.
10. That old woman has twenty pairs of shoes.
11. Lucky she! She had left her purse in the train, and the porter found it.
12. I have lost two new pairs of socks. I had them with me last week when I was carrying all those eggs from town. I have probably left them in the bus.
13. He was going to see her when I met him.

LESSON XIV

RELATIVE PRONOUNS—REFLEXIVE VERBS

WE have often used the relative pronoun *che*; it is the commonest, and it translates "who", "whom", "which" and "that". It is invariable, used as subject or object of a verb and for persons and for things. It cannot be left out of a sentence, as such words are in English:

Il libro che è sulla scrivania = The book which is on the desk.
I dolci che abbiamo mangiati = The sweets we have eaten.

Il giornale che ho trovato nel treno = The newspaper I found
  in the train.

Che is not used when the relative is an indirect object or
when it is governed by a preposition: then we have another
form, also invariable and also used for persons and for things:
cui.

La signora a cui mandiamo il pacco = The lady to whom we
  are sending the parcel.
Il film di cui parlo = The film of which I am speaking.
Il poeta da cui era scritta questa poesia = The poet by whom
  this poem was written.

A third relative pronoun, also referring to persons and
things, but which is variable, is *il quale* (fem. *la quale*; plurals:
i quali, le quali). This may be used in place of either *che* or *cui*,
and when it is governed by a preposition, this preposition and
article join together: *del quale* = of whom, whose. Note, too,
that it agrees in gender and number with the noun coming
before it, to which it refers. *Il quale* is not used very often, but
it is sometimes necessary, to avoid ambiguity, as in this sentence: *La moglie del dottore, la quale mi mandò quella lettera* =
The doctor's wife, who sent me that letter. Had we used *che*
it would presumably have been the doctor, not his wife, who
had sent the letter, for *che* usually refers to the noun immediately preceding it; but if it had been the doctor, and not
his wife, it would still have been better to use *il quale*, to be
quite sure of not being misunderstood.

Del quale is one way of translating whose; but it is not the
most usual. A commoner word is *cui* (invariable). It is preceded by the article (*il, i, la, le*) which agrees with the noun
which follows *cui*:

Quel ristorante, i cui piatti sono famosi = That restaurant,
  whose dishes are celebrated.
Il fornaio, il cui pane è molto buono = That baker, whose
  bread is very good.
Quella signora, il cui indirizzo ho perduto = That lady,
  whose address I have lost.

Had we used *del quale* in these sentences, it would have agreed
with the preceding noun in each case: *Quel ristorante del quale i
piatti . . . Quella signora della quale ho perduto l'indirizzo. . . .*

Other relative pronouns are: "he who", "him who" = *chi*
(invariable) and *colui che* (fem. *colei che*, plural both genders:
coloro che).

Chi dorme non piglia pesci = He who sleeps doesn't catch fish. (Italian version of "The early bird . . .")

Coloro che hanno tegole di vetro non tirino sassi al vicino = Those who have glass roofs (lit. tiles) let them not throw stones at their neighbour.

Colei che entrerà per quella porta è la pianista famosa = She who will come in by that door is the famous pianist.

"That which" or "what" is *quel che, quello che* or *ciò che*:

Prendermo quel che troveremo = We shall take what we find.

(It should be noted that in a sentence such as: It is I who have left the door open, Italian does not use the impersonal construction *it is*; instead we have: *I am I who have* . . . = Sono io che ho lasciato aperta la porta. Similarly: "Who is there? It is I", is in Italian: *Chi c'è? Sono io*: "It is we" = *Siamo noi*; "It is you" = *Siete voi*, etc.).

Reflexive Verbs.—A verb is reflexive when its subject and object are the same person: I wash myself = *Io mi lavo*. The present indicative of a reflexive verb is as follows:

Lavarsi (1st conj.), *to wash oneself*

mi lavo = I wash myself, etc.

ti lavi	
si lava (lui)	ci laviamo
si lava (lei)	vi lavate
	si lavano

All reflexive verbs are conjugated with *essere*; the present perfect of *alzarsi* (= to get up) is therefore:

mi sono alzato -a = I have got up, etc.
ti sei alzato -a
si è alzato -a
ci siamo alzati -e
vi siete alzati -e
si sono alzati -e

Some verbs are reflexive in Italian which are not so in English. You will always be able to recognize a reflexive verb in the vocabulary, for its infinitive will have the reflexive pronoun -*si* joined to it. One or two reflexive verbs are followed by the preposition *di*, instead of the direct object as in English; such a verb is *ricordarsi* = to remember. I remember that day = *Io mi ricordo di quel giorno*, and I remember it = *me ne ricordo* (*ne* = of it). For practice let us conjugate the past definite of this verb with *it* as an object:

> me ne ricoardai = I remembered it, etc.
> te ne ricordasti
> se ne ricordò
> ce ne ricordammo
> ve ne ricordaste
> se ne ricordarono

Italian uses reflexive verbs in some cases where English has a different construction: In the first place, instead of the possessive "my", "your", "his", etc., when speaking of clothes and of parts of the body (when we know from the context whose clothes or whose body is being referred to):

> Lui si mette il capotto = He is putting on his overcoat (lit.: He to himself puts on the overcoat).
> Povero Pinocchio! Si toccò il naso. Era lungo quasi un metro = Poor Pinocchio! He touched his nose! It was almost a yard long.

Secondly, when a verb in English is in the passive without any agent expressed, the third person singular or plural of the reflexive is used in Italian. This will be seen more clearly from the examples:

> Si parla inglese = English is spoken (lit.: English speaks itself).
> Molte storie si narravano = Many stories were told (lit.: Many stories were telling themselves).

In neither of the above sentences have we any agent expressed: we do not know by whom English is spoken nor by whom the stories were told; had an agent been expressed, the passive would have been used in Italian as in English (see pages 54 and 107).

Thirdly, the third person singular of the reflexive is also used to translate English impersonal sentences beginning "one", "you", "they", etc., meaning people in general:

> Qui si vede bene = The light is good here, or You see well here (lit.: Here itself it sees well).
> Come si sta bene sulla spiaggia! = How lovely it is on the beach! (lit.: How it stands itself well on the beach!).
> Sí, qui si è contenti, Signora = Yes, here one is happy, madam.

Note the last example, where we have a singular verb and pronoun, and a plural adjective which goes with them. This is a peculiarity of the verbs *essere*, *restare* (= to stay), *rimanere*, *diventare* (= to become), *divenire* (= to become), which may take the following adjective in the *plural* when the verb is *singular* with this reflexive construction standing for "one", "we", meaning people in general.

One brief admonition before we do the exercises. In English "myself", "himself", etc., are not always reflexive; they are sometimes used to give emphasis to another pronoun, as: "I will give it to him myself". Here "myself" merely emphasizes the "I", and is not the object of a verb as in: "I am buying myself a pair of shoes". This last sentence is reflexive in Italian, as in English: *Mi compro un paio di scarpe*; but in the first sentence "myself" is rendered in Italian by the word *stesso*: *Io stesso glielo darò* (*stesso* has fem. *stessa*, and the two plurals *stessi*, *stesse*). Note that *stesso* immediately follows the pronoun with which it is used, and if it is put at the end of the sentence for further emphasis, this pronoun must be repeated: *Io glielo darò, io stesso*.

Vocabulary

caldo (adj. and noun) = warm, hot	chiamarsi = to call oneself (come si chiama = what is your name?)
faccia = face	
montagna = mountain	lavorare = to work
professore (m.) = professor	pagare = to pay for
università = university	passare = to pass
veduta = view	scusare = to excuse
come! = what!	presto = early
	prossimo = next

Exercise 14 (a)

1. Mangeremo a pranzo il pesce che abbiamo pigliato stamane.
2. La signorina con cui parlavo ieri è mia sorella.—È una bella ragazza! Come si chiama?
3. Lo studio in cui lavoro è molto comodo. È una stanza grande con tre finestre, dalle quali ho una bella veduta del lago e delle montagne.
4. L'uomo a cui ha venduto la macchina è partito. Come! Partito! E non me l'ha ancora pagata (*pagare* takes a direct object: he has not yet paid it to me).
5. Come si chiama questa piazza? La piazza per cui passiamo ora è piazza Vittorio Emanuele.
6. Il signore, la cui figlia abbiamo veduta in città stamane, è professore d'università (supply in English "a" professor).

7. La figlia del dottore, alla quale Lei ha scritto oggi, è un'amica mia.
8. A che ora si alza Lei la mattina, Signora? Io mi alzo presto, generalmente alle sei; ma mia sorella è pigra e si alza molto tardi.
9. Che bel sole! Come si sta bene qui al caldo!
10. Sí, qui sulla spiaggia si è sempre contenti.
11. Scusi, Signora, la signorina il cui anello si perdette sulla spiaggia è alla porta.
12. Ti ricordi di quel bel giorno sulla spiaggia l'anno scorso? E come! Me ne ricordo molto bene.

Exercise 14 (b)

1. That woman to whom you were speaking is Cook's sister.
2. That book of which you were speaking is not in the library.
3. The girl from whom I have received this letter will arrive next week.
4. That man who has bought your car has already left for Italy (*the* Italy).
5. The cook whose dishes were so famous has left that restaurant. (Cook may also be masculine—*il cuoco.*)
6. What time does your father get up? He generally gets up at eight, but yesterday he got up at seven, and left by the eight o'clock train for Rome.
7. He was putting on his overcoat when his sister arrived.
8. That girl hasn't washed herself! What hands! and what a face!
9. Excuse me, sir. What is the name of this square?
10. The street I am looking for is near to this square.
11. Did you remember that book? Yes, I went to that bookshop where they speak English.
12. Is Uncle going already? Yes, he's putting on his hat. Where are those new gloves I bought for him? Here they are; he never remembers them.

LESSON XV

CONJUGATION OF REGULAR VERBS

As we are nearly half-way through this little book, it would be well to look back for a moment over what we have learnt, and revise particularly any points which seemed difficult or any rules which we do not seem to remember easily. It would be a good plan to look over the exercises and see which mistakes have been the most frequent; and also to turn back to tables and lists and run through some of them again. It is very likely that the conjunctive and disjunctive pronouns would benefit by a little revision. But probably it will be verbs that need the most attention; so it will be profitable at this point to show in tabular form the conjugations of the three types of regular verbs. The tenses we have already learnt are shown here together, where the different endings of the conjugations may be compared, and the tenses of the subjunctive mood—which we have not yet studied—are here also; they will be useful for reference later.

When studying the formation of the various tenses, the following points should be remembered:

1. The future and conditional are formed by adding the given endings to a shortened form of the infinitive (the first conjugation changing its *-a* to *-e*): *comprer-*, *vender-*, *finir-*.

2. All other parts of the verb are formed by adding certain endings to the stem: *compr-*, *vend-*, *fin-*.

3. The characteristic vowels, *-a*, *-e* and *-i*, mark the only difference between the three conjugations in the second person plural of the present indicative, in the whole imperfect indicative and imperfect subjunctive tenses, and in all persons of the past definite except the third singular.

4. The first person plural ending *-iamo* is the same for the present indicative, present subjunctive and imperative of all three conjugations.

5. Three persons only in each conjugation have a written accent: the first and third persons singular of the future (always a *grave*); and the third person singular of the past definite (*grave* on the final *-ò* of the first conjugation and *acute* on the final *-é* and *-ì* of the other two).

CONJUGATION OF REGULAR VERBS
SIMPLE TENSES

I	II	III
	Infinitive	
compr-are = to buy	vend-ere = to sell	fin-ire = to finish
	Present Participle	
compr-ando = buy-ing	vend-endo = sell-ing	fin-endo = finish-ing
	Past Participle	
compr-ato = bought	vend-uto = sold	fin-ito = finished

Indicative Mood

I	II	III

Present

I buy, do buy, am buying	I sell, do sell, am selling	I finish, do finish, am finishing
compr-o	vend-o	fin-isc-o *
compr-i	vend-i	fin-isc-i
compr-a	vend-e	fin-isc-e
compr-iamo	vend-iamo	fin-iamo
compr-ate	vend-ete	fin-ite
compr-ano	vend-ono	fin-isc-ono

* Verbs of tne second group of the third conjugation: part-o, parti-, part-e, part-ono; see page 27.

Imperfect

I was buying, used to buy	I was selling, used to sell	I was finishing, used to finish
compr-avo	vend-evo	fin-ivo
compr-avi	vend-evi	fin-ivi
compr-ava	vend-eva	fin-iva
compr-avamo	vend-evamo	fin-ivamo
compr-avate	vend-evate	fin-ivate
compr-avano	vend-evano	fin-ivano

Past Definite

I bought	I sold	I finished
compr-ai	vend-ei (-ɛtti)	fin-ii
compr-asti	vend-esti	fin-isti
compr-ò	vend-é (-ɛtte)	fin-í
compr-ammo	vend-emmo	fin-immo
compr-aste	vend-este	fin-iste
compr-arono	vend-erono (-ɛttero)	fin-irono

Future

I shall buy	I shall sell	I shall finish
comprer-ò	vender-ò	finir-ò
comprer-ai	vender-ai	finir-ai
comprer-à	vender-à	finir-à
comprer-emo	vender-emo	finir-emo
comprer-ete	vender-ete	finir-ete
comprer-anno	vender-anno	finir-anno

Subjunctive Mood

I	II	III

Present

(that) I (may) buy	(that) I (may) sell	(that) I (may) finish
compr-i	vend-a	fin-isc-a *
compr-i	vend-a	fin-isc-a
compr-i	vend-a	fin-isc-a
compri-amo	vend-iamo	fin-iamo
compr-iate	vend-iate	fin-iate
cɔmpr-ino	vɛnd-ano	fin-isc-ano

* Verbs of the second group: part-a, part-a, part-a, part-ano.

Imperfect

(that) I (might) buy	(that) I (might) sell	(that) I (might) finish
compr-assi	vend-essi	fin-issi
compr-assi	vend-essi	fin-issi
compr-asse	vend-esse	fin-isse
compr-assimo	vend-essimo	fin-issimo
compr-aste	vend-este	fin-iste
compr-assero	vend-essero	fin-issero

Conditional Mood

I should buy	I should sell	I should finish
comprer-ɛi	vender-ɛi	finir-ɛi
comprer-esti	vender-esti	finir-esti
comprer-ɛbbe	vender-ɛbbe	finir-ɛbbe
comprer-emmo	vender-emmo	finir-emmo
comprer-este	vender-este	finir-este
comprer-ɛbbero	vender-ɛbbero	finir-ɛbbero

Imperative

Buy	Sell	Finish
compr-a	vend-i	fin-isc-i *
compr-ate	vend-ete	fin-ite

* Verbs of the second group: part-i.

COMPOUND TENSES

parlare = to speak	partire = to depart
(conjugated with *avere*)	(conjugated with *ɛssere*)

Perfect Infinitive

avere parlato = to have   ɛssere partito = to have de-
  spoken   parted

Perfect Participle

avɛndo parlato = having   essɛndo partito = having de-
  spoken   parted

Indicative Mood
Present Perfect

ho parlato = I have spoken   sono partito = I have de-
                                       parted

Past Perfect

avevo parlato = I had spoken   ɛro partito = I had departed

Second Past Perfect

bbi parlato = I had spoken   fui partito = I had departed

Future Perfect

avrɔ̀ parlato = I shall have   sarɔ̀ partito = I shall have
  spoken   departed

Subjunctive Mood
Present Perfect

abbia parlato = I (may) have   sia partito = I (may) have
  spoken   departed

Past Perfect

avessi parlato = I (might) have   fossi partito = I (might) have
  spoken   departed

Conditional Mood
Perfect

avrɛi parlato = I should have   sarɛi partito = I should have
  spoken   departed

Before doing the following exercise we should give ourselves
some verb drill by taking, one after another, the stem of
several verbs we know and substituting them for *compr-, vend-*
or *fin-* (according to which conjugation they belong) in all the
forms and tenses in the preceding table. The more often we do

this, the better, and when choosing verbs we must be sure not to take any marked "irregular" in the vocabularies.

Vocabulary

grazie = thanks
letto = bed
minuto = minute
momento = moment
notte (f.) = night
occhiali (m. pl.) = spectacles
polizia = police
sera = evening
telefono = telephone
occupato = engaged, busy

piacere (irreg.) = to please
telefonare = to telephone
viaggiare = to travel

male = badly
naturalmente = of course
neppure = not even
proprio = just
sotto = under, beneath

Exercise 15 (a)

1. L'uomo di cui parliamo è stato qui stamane. Non l'hai veduto, Zio?
2. Naturalmente lo zio non l'ha veduto, perché era a letto.
3. Ma a che ora si alza tuo zio?—Mai prima delle dieci.
4. E tu? A che ora ti sei alzato stamane?—Ma se io non sono neppure andato a letto? Ho viaggiato in treno tutta la notte, e ho dormito molto male.
5. Che cosa sta cercando, Signore? I miei occhiali; mi sono caduti dal naso proprio in questo momento. Povero me, non vedo niente.
6. Lasci fare a me, Signore, li cercherò * io (*lasci fare* = let to do; that is: "leave it to me").
7. Eccoli, eccoli, li ho trovati; erano sotto quella sedia. Grazie Signorina.
8. Ho comprato questo vestito quando ero a Milano la settimana scorsa, Le piace? (lit.: does it please you?).
9. Sí, mi piace molto; quel colore Le sta molto bene. (*Stare bene* = to suit; also: "to be well" (of health).)
10. La casa aveva un piccolo giardino davanti, che la separava dalla via, dove lavorava ogni sera quel vecchio dalla barba bianca.
11. È arrivato l'avvocato? No, arriverà col treno delle sette e mezzo. Andremo a incontrarlo alla stazione.
12. Appena che ebbe finito la lettera, chiamò Giovanni per telefono, ma il numero era occupato.

* Verbs of the first conjugation in -*care* insert *h* after the *c* whenever it precedes -*e* or -*i*.

Exercise 15 (b)

1. I don't like Mary's new dress. Where did she buy it?
2. That colour doesn't suit her; I prefer the dress she had last year.
3. Aunt is always losing her spectacles. She never remembers where she has left them.
4. Last Monday she was looking for them for hours, and they were on her nose all the time. (Say: to her they were standing on the nose.)
5. Are we near Florence, please? Yes, we shall be there in five minutes.
6. The lady of whom you are speaking has just left. Yes, I met her as I came in.
7. This isn't a very comfortable bed. How is yours?
8. Did you sleep well, sir? No, I slept very badly.
9. I am leaving for Florence this evening.
10. I shall travel in the train all night and arrive there at six o'clock in the morning. (Say: of the morning.)
11. Whose is that overcoat? Is it yours or his?
12. As soon as the professor had finished the letter, the lawyer telephoned the police.

LESSON XVI

FIRST READING LESSON

IT is now time to attempt the translation of continuous Italian prose. So far we have done only sentences containing words and phrases already learnt; now we must be prepared to meet strange words and look them up in the vocabulary. We shall often find that we can guess the meaning of new words and get the hang of a sentence before referring to the vocabulary. Each new word should be memorized as we look it up, so that we do not have to waste time looking up the same word twice. Those who have studied a foreign language have had experience of dictionaries, and know that they do not give every single word we meet, particularly in the case of verbs, for only the infinitive is given, not the various parts. For instance, take the word *pɔsso* in the first sentence of the piece we are going to translate on page 84; we may guess that it must mean "can I". But we shall not find *pɔsso* in any dictionary, as it is part of an irregular verb, *potere*. We shall often meet verbs whose infinitives we do not know; if the verbs are regular, the infinitive is easily found, for the verb-ending tells us to which conjugation it belongs; but if they are irregular, the thing to do is to turn to the list of irregular verbs in the Appendix, page 214. Suppose we are hunting down *pɔsso*, then looking through all the verbs beginning with *pɔ-*, we shall soon find *potere* ("to be able"), with its irregular tenses, among which *pɔsso* stands out as the first person singular of the present indicative: our guess, "I can" or "can I" was correct.

Translation may be done in two ways: literal or free. A literal translation gives the meaning of the Italian, word for word, in English, and this results in English which reads very awkwardly—sometimes it will hardly make sense. A free translation is one which considers the meaning of the Italian sentence as a whole and then expresses that meaning in good English. When making our own translation it would be better to be rather literal at first, and not trouble too much about the sound of the English; after a little practice we shall soon be able to make our translation freer and pay more attention to the English style.

Before doing the translation we might learn some tenses of three of the irregular verbs which occur in it: *dovere*, *potere* and *volere*. These verbs are very often in use, for besides being main verbs—when they mean, respectively, "to owe", "to be able" and "to wish"—they are also used as a kind of auxiliary before an infinitive, when they have these meanings:

dovere = to be obliged to, to have to, must, ought;
potere = to be able (the idea of capability), can, could; and (the idea of possibility), may, might;
volere = to be willing, to want, will, would.

Each verb has an irregular present indicative:

dovere	*potere*	*volere*
I must, am obliged to, have to	I can, may, am able	I want, will, am willing
dɛvo or dɛbbo	pɔsso	vɔglio
dɛvi	puɔi	vuɔi
dɛve	puɔ	vuɔle
dobbiamo	possiamo	vogliamo
dovete	potete	volete
dɛvono or dɛbbono	pɔssono	vɔgliono

Note that *vuɔle* may drop its final *-e* before words beginning with a vowel or a consonant (except *s* impure): *vuɔl andare*, *vuɔl rimanere*, but *vuɔle studiare*.

Note, too, that each verb has a shortened infinitive stem to which the future and conditional endings are added: *dovrò, potrò, vorrò; dovrei, potrei, vorrei*.

Translation I

—Buon giorno, Signore, in che còsa posso servirla? *—mi domandò l'impiegato quando entrai nell'ufficio del turismo italiano a Londra.

Non risposi subito, perché, sebbene † avessi studiato l'italiano, non l'avevo mai parlato, e la parole non mi venivano prontamente alle labbra. Ma, contento dell'occasione di esercitarmi nella lingua prima del mio viaggio in Italia, gli dissi in italiano, un po' timidamente:

—Buon giorno. Avrei bisogno di qualche informazione. Vorrei andare in Italia per le vacanze quest'estate, ma ho poco tempo e denaro a mia disposizione.

—è la prima vòlta che va ‡ in Italia, Signore?—

—Sí, non ci sono mai stato.—

—Ho capito. Ma, prima di tutto, mi dica, ha il passaporto in regola?—

—Sí, è in regola. Vengo or ora dall'ufficio passaporti e il console italiano m'ha detto che non è necessario un visto speciale.—

—Benissimo. Allora, quali città vorrebbe visitare? Lei s'interessa di arte? Dunque vorrà vedere Firenze, forse anche Pisa e Signa o Venezia? O ha l'intenzione di andare a Roma a visitare le antichità? Oppure di fare un giro per i laghi? O forse preferisce fermarsi in qualche stazione balneare? o in qualche luogo di villeggiatura in montagna? Agl'Inglesi piacciono molto le bellezze naturali, lo so; e in Italia ci sono tanti bei posti . . . quali sono i Suoi progetti, Signore?—

—Lei mi dovrebbe consigliare. Di arte non me ne intendo molto, debbo confessarlo, e ben poco di antichità romane. Desideravo soprattutto visitare Firenze dove era nata mia madre, e forse altre città di Toscana, e mi piacerebbe moltissimo veder Venezia se c'è tempo e se il viaggio non costa troppo. Roma è un po' troppo lontana; sarà per un'altra vòlta.—

---

* The same punctuation marks are used in Italian as in English except that in Italian a dash is generally employed to denote conversation instead of quotation marks.

† *sebbene* (= although) is followed by the subjunctive.

‡ *va*—look up *andare* (irreg.).

When you have translated literally the foregoing passage, compare your version with the two in Part II, page 174, and after you have studied the notes given there, you will do the following exercise without much difficulty.

Vocabulary

gruccia (f.) = clothes-hanger   spesso = often
mare (m.) = sea
musica = music

Exercise 16

1. Where is he going for his holidays this summer?
2. He will go to Italy if the journey does not cost too much.
3. Does he speak Italian? Yes, he speaks it very well; he was born in Rome.
4. Do you want to go to the theatre today or tomorrow?
5. Tomorrow, please. I can't go today because Uncle arrives this evening and I shall have to go and meet him.
6. Good morning, madam. What can I do for you?
7. I should like to see some scarves, please.
8. Certainly, madam (say: very willingly). What colour would you like?
9. He often goes to the concert, but he is no judge of music.
10. When will you have finished with that book? I shall need it for next week. (Note: aver bisogno *di*.)
11. *We* are going to the sea this year for our holidays; and *you*, aren't you going? (Supply "there".)
12. No, this year we are going to spend our holidays in the mountains.
13. I need a coat-hanger. Can you give me one?
14. I am very thirsty ("I have much thirst"). Give me a glass of water, please.

LESSON XVII

IRREGULAR VERBS

IRREGULAR verbs are apt to worry people, for they seem to herald a long list of tiresome tenses to be learnt, when it would have been so much kinder of these verbs if they had made an effort to conform to the types we already know. A list of irregular verbs in an Italian grammar does seem rather long, as often between 200 and 300 verbs are given; but many of these are rare, and others are compounds from a shorter irregular verb conjugated like them. There are about fifty irregular verbs which must be learnt; but of these many are not original or unique—they have similarities with other irregular verbs: similarities which, if not of such a kind as to allow of the verbs being grouped together, are at any rate helpful when we have to commit them to memory. There is, too, the consoling thought that only one verb—*essere*—is irregular in all its tenses, and other irregular verbs—with the exception of four: *dare* (= to give), *fare* (= to do, to make), *stare* (= to stand, to be), and *dire* (= to say)—are *always* regular in certain parts. Therefore of the fifty or so which we must learn as we work through this book, we shall often be learning only a few parts, probably one tense only—the past definite—which will be irregular.

The parts which are always regular (except in *essere* and the four verbs just mentioned) are: the present participle, imperfect indicative, imperfect subjunctive, second person plural of the present indicative and of the imperative, and the second person singular and the first and second persons plural of the past definite. These will be seen from the conjugation of *porre* (= to put) which follows. The parts always regular are shown in italics; the changeable parts in ordinary printing.

Infinitive and Participles

Porre	*ponendo*	posto

Indicative Mood

Present	Imperfect	Past definite	Future
pongo	*ponevo*	posi	porrò
poni	*ponevi*	*ponesti*	porrai
pone	*poneva*	pose	porrà
poniamo	*ponevamo*	*ponemmo*	porremo
ponete	*ponevate*	*poneste*	porrete
pongono	*ponevano*	posero	porranno

Subjunctive Mood		Conditional	Imperative
Present	Imperfect (Past)		
ponga	*ponessi*	porrei	
ponga	*ponessi*	porresti	poni
ponga	*ponesse*	porrebbe	
poniamo	*ponessimo*	porremmo	
poniate	*poneste*	porreste	*ponete*
pongano	*ponessero*	porrebbero	

Note that the infinitive of this verb *porre* is irregular, as it is a contracted form of *ponere*. In verbs with a contracted infinitive the present participle keeps the regular stem, in this case *pon-*. *Condurre* (= to lead) from *conducere* is a similar verb: it has *conducendo* for the present participle and *conducevo* is the imperfect. *Fare* and *dire* are contracted from *facere* and *dicere* respectively, and they have changed their conjugations: if you remember these points, the irregularities become more understandable.

The following notes may be of help in learning irregular verbs:

Future and Conditional.—The only irregularity is the contracted form of the infinitive to which the usual endings are added. The contracted form is always given in the list in the Appendix; where there is no form given, these tenses are quite regular.

Imperative.—The same form as the present indicative, except in the following verbs: three which have a form like the present subjunctive—*avere* (*abbi, abbiate*), *sapere* (*sappi, sappiate*) and *volere* (*vogli, vogliate*)—and five which have an irregular singular —*andare* (*va'*), *dare* (*da'*), *fare* (*fa'*), *stare* (*sta'*) and *dire* (*di'*).*

Past Definite.—The tense which is most frequently irregular, but only in three persons: first and third persons singular and third plural. The irregular endings are the SAME for all irregular verbs: first singular, *-i*; third singular, *-e*; and third plural, *-ero*. When given the first person singular of this tense, you can form the other two irregular persons by changing the *-i* to *-e* for the third singular, and adding *-ro* to the third singular to form the third plural.

Example: Porre: posi, pose, posero.

Except in the three verbs *essere, dare* and *stare*, the other persons of this tense are always regular.

Examples of the past definite:

Sapere = to know	*Fare* = to make
(stem *sap-*)	(stem *fac-*)
Past def. *sɛppi*	Past def. *feci*
sɛppi	feci
sapesti	facesti
sɛppe	fece
sapemmo	facemmo
sapeste	faceste
sɛppero	fecero

* Conjunctive pronouns, except *gli*, double their initial consonant when added to any form of a verb ending in an accented vowel. These irregular imperatives are such forms:

dammi = give me   *fàllo* = do it   *dillo* = say it

Decidere = to decide	*Vedere* = to see
(stem *decid-*)	(stem *ved-*)
Past def. *decisi*	Past def. *vidi*
decisi	vidi
decidesti	vedesti
decise	vide
decidemmo	vedemmo
decideste	vedeste
decisero	videro

The majority of verbs of the second conjugation are irregular only in this tense and the past participle. It would be a good plan to practise with some more verbs, such as *chiudere, giungere, leggere, mettere, rimanere* and *scendere*. Look up their past definite tense (first person) in the Appendix, and then continue the whole tense, as in the examples above; at the same time note their past participles.

Translation II

—Bene, Signore. Lei decide dunque per Firenze,—continuò l'impiegato, mentre apriva un cassetto e tirava fuori diversi fogli e libri e un'enorme carta geografica.

—E sarebbe possibile andare a Firenze—chiesi,—passando per Genova e Pisa, e poi tornare per un'altra strada?—

—Possibilissimo.—

—Che direbbe se andassi * da Firenze a Venezia, poi da Venezia a Milano, e nel viaggio di ritorno facessi * un giro per i laghi? So che il biglietto di andata e ritorno è più a buon mercato; ma con quel giro, dovrei spendere molto di più?—

—No, no. Ecco qui la cosa che fa per lei; un biglietto circolare turistico, valevole per 45 giorni; e le conviene, perché le dà una riduzione del cinquanta per cento, purché si fermi in Italia per un periodo di almeno dodici giorni.—

—Va proprio bene per me, perché mi fermerò almeno due settimane, forse anche tre.—

—Vediamo un po' la carta geografica per fissare più precisamente il suo itinerario. Dunque, partendo da Londra la mattina presto, lei arriva a Parigi la sera verso le sei. Lì avrà il tempo di mangiare prima di ripartire col rapido Parigi-Roma: proprio la sua strada: Modane-Torino-Genova-Pisa. È un ottimo treno. Arriva alla frontiera italiana all'alba, e a Pisa nel pomeriggio. E col biglietto circolare lei può fermarsi quando e

* A condition uncertain in the future; this use of the subjunctive is explained on page 146.

dove vuole, e può viaggiare con qualsiasi treno: quindi lasciar
Pisa quando vuole e fermarsi a Firenze quanto le pare, naturalmente sempre nel termine dei quarantacinque giorni.—

—Capisco.—

—Dopo Firenze il suo percorso è questo: Bologna, Venezia,
Milano e poi Como e Lugano dove prenderà il direttissimo per
Parigi. Così entra in Italia per il passo del Moncenisio ed esce
per il San Gottardo. Va bene così?—

—Grazie, va benissimo. Vorrebbe prepararmi il biglietto?
Partirò venerdí prossimo e viaggerò in seconda.—

—Ecco fatto. Questo è il biglietto; e qui c'è anche un libro
che forse le sarà utile: "Annuario alberghi d'Italia", e una
rivista turistica con altre indicazioni interessanti.—

—Ben gentile, mille grazie.—

—Niente, Signore prego. Buon viaggio e buon divertimento.—

Learn, from the Appendix, the irregular verbs *andare* and
dare and then do the following exercise:

Vocabulary

cane (m.) = dog	marino = of the sea; blu
cinema (m.), cinematografo =	marino = navy blue
cinema	scuro = dark
colletto = collar	terzo = third
striscia = stripe	solo = alone, only

Exercise 17

1. As he was speaking he opened a drawer and took out a
   large map.
2. Couldn't you come with us to the cinema? They say there
   is a very good film.
3. A return ticket to London, please—second class. Must I buy
   a ticket for the dog, too? Yes, madam, the dog must have
   a ticket.
4. He didn't want to come and talk to you yesterday; today
   he is glad to. (Say: to do it.)
5. Did you put Uncle's collars in this drawer? No, he put
   them there himself.
6. Have you ever been to London, madam? Yes, I have been
   there many times.
7. Has he not arrived yet? No, Mary went to meet him, but
   she came back alone.
8. Perhaps he has gone by another road? Yes, it is possible.

9. Yesterday he got up at seven o'clock, but remained in his room reading (say: to read = *a leggere*) the newspaper, and only came down at ten for his coffee. (Say: for to take his coffee.)

10. Give me the map a moment, please; I want to look for Siena.

11. Good morning. I want a tie to wear with this suit. I have just the thing for you, sir. This navy blue with yellow stripe will go very well with the dark green of your suit.

12. You ought to buy a circular ticket. It is the cheapest; and you can stop where and when you like and for as long as you like.

LESSON XVIII

COMPARATIVES AND SUPERLATIVES

WHEN we wish to compare two persons or two things, we use the comparative. In English we form the comparative by adding a suffix -*y* or -*er* to the adjective, or by putting the words "more" or "less" in front of it: great, greater; beautiful, more beautiful. Italian uses the second way, and puts the words *più* (= more) and *meno* (= less) before the adjective.

Il poliziotto è più intelligente della cuoca = The policeman is cleverer than the cook.

Il poliziotto è meno furbo del postino = The policeman is less cunning than the postman.

The translation of "than" into Italian may present difficulty: it is *di* or *che*. *Di* before a noun (as in the above sentences), before a pronoun and before a number:

Tu sei più alto di me = You are taller than I.

Hai delle mele? Sí, ne ho più di dieci = Have you any apples? Yes, I've more than ten.

But if two nouns which are both subjects or objects of the same verb are compared, "than" is *che*:

C'erano più signori che signore = There were more gentlemen than ladies.

"Than" is *che* before all other parts of speech:

Before an adjective:

La ragazza è piú bella che intelligente = The girl is more beautiful than clever.

Before an adverb:

Meglio tardi che mai = Better late than never.

Before an infinitive:

Lui ama piú leggere che scrivere = He likes reading better than writing.

Before a preposition:

C'è piú acqua nel bicchiere che nella bottiglia = There's more water in the glass than in the bottle.

If "than" is preceded by *piuttosto* (= rather), it is also *che*:

Piuttosto la morte che il disonore = Rather death than dishonour.

And, finally, if "than" introduces a whole clause, it is either *di quel* or *che non*, and is followed by the subjunctive if implying uncertainty.*

La lezione è piú facile che non si pensi = The lesson is easier than one thinks.

In English we also compare things by "as . . . as" and "so . . . as". In Italian *cosí . . . come* and *tanto . . . quanto* both mean "as . . . as" and "so . . . as" (our "so . . . as" is simply the negative form of "as . . . as", and the two Italian expressions may be either affirmative or negative):

Lui è tanto alto quanto lei = He is as tall as she.
Il postino non è cosí ricco come il poliziotto = The postman is not so rich as the policeman.
Non parla l'inglese tanto bene quanto l'italiano = He doesn't speak English as well as Italian.

The first part of the comparison *cosí* and *tanto* may be omitted:

Lui è alto quanto lei.

In all these sentences *tanto* and *quanto* are adverbs; but they may also be adjectives, qualifying nouns, and in this case they mean: "as much as", "as many as", "so much as", "so many as":—

* See page 143, clause type no. 7.

Ho tanto denaro quanto Lɛi = I have as much money as
you.

Non ho scritto tante lɛttere quante Lɛi = I have not written
so many letters as you.

In Italian there are two superlatives: the relative, a comparison of more than two things, as in English, and the absolute,
which has no corresponding form in English and which we must
translate by "very" or "exceedingly". The relative superlative
is formed by placing the definite article before the comparatives *piú* and *meno*:

Questa torre ɛ̀ la piú alta della città = This tower is the
highest in the town.

Questa ɛ̀ la piú alta torre ⎫ = ⎧This is the highest (or
Questa ɛ̀ la torre piú alta ⎭   ⎩ higher) tower.

Note.—1. There is no difference in form between the comparative with the definite article and the relative superlative,
but the meaning is always clear, for the speaker always knows
whether he is comparing one thing with another or one thing
with many others.

2. When the superlative follows a noun which already has a
definite article, no other article is required (see the third
sentence).

3. After the superlative "in" is rendered by *di*.

We have already met the absolute superlative in the words
benissimo and *possibilissimo*. It is formed by adding *-issimo* to
the adjective or adverb after the last vowel has been dropped.

Lui ɛ̀ poverissimo = He is extremely poor.

A word ending in *-co* or *-go* preserves the hard sound of the *c* or *g*
before the ending *-issimo* by inserting an *h*: *ricco, ricchissimo*;
and five adjectives ending in *-re* or *-ro* have an irregular ending
in *-ɛrrimo* instead of *-issimo*:

acre = sour	acɛrrimo
cɛlebre = famous	celebɛrrimo
integro = righteous	integɛrrimo
misero = wretched	misɛrrimo
salubre = healthful	salubɛrrimo

To finish our lesson on the comparison we must learn the
following irregular comparisons:

Positive	Comparative	Rel. Superlative	Abs. Superlative
buono = good	migliore	il migliore	ottimo
cattivo = bad	peggiore	il peggiore	pessimo
grande = big	maggiore	il maggiore	massimo
piccolo = small	minore	il minore	minimo
alto = tall	superiore	il superiore	supremo
basso = low	inferiore	l'inferiore	infimo

These six adjectives also have the regular comparatives and superlatives. Slight differences of meaning in regular and irregular forms should be noted: *piú grande* and *piú piccolo* mean "larger" and "smaller", and *maggiore* and *minore* usually "older" and "younger"; *piú alto* and *piú basso* have the literal meaning "higher" and "lower", while *superiore* and *inferiore* the figurative: "superior" and "inferior" (although they, too, may have the literal sense).

Study the two irregular verbs *fare* and *stare*.

Translation III

Di solito non dormo bene in treno: ma forse perché questa volta ero stanco o avevo mangiato troppo bene al ristorante della stazione di Parigi (ci si mangia divinamente, ma si paga anche, profumatamente); o forse perché ero tutto solo nello scompartimento e mi ero potuto sdraiare sui cuscini come in un letto; il fatto sta che, tolte le scarpe, la cravatta e la giacchetta, appena posi il capo sul guanciale—noleggiato per cento franchi alla stazione,— m'addormentai profondamente e continuai a dormire come un ghiro tutta la notte.

Mi svegliai che era già giorno; il treno andava rallentando e finalmente si fermò. Guardando fuori del finestrino vidi sul marciapiede di una stazione intermedia un piccolo gruppo d'impiegati della ferrovia, facchini e soldati, con due carabinieri e diverse altre guardie, che ridevano e scherzavano fra di loro, con l'aria di non far nessum caso di noi e del nostro treno. Ma un fischio acuto emesso dal rapido Parigi—Roma sciolse quel gruppo. Uno di loro, il capostazione (lo si riconosceva dal berretto rosso) andò a parlare col macchinista, mentre tutti gli altri, sempre parlando e ridendo, salirono sul treno. L'orologio della stazione segnava le cinque. Soltanto le cinque del mattino e già faceva caldo e c'era un bel sole, un cielo azzurro e sereno e l'aria era cosí mite e dolce! Tirai fuori l'orologio per regolarlo, ma in quel momento, qualcuno aprí bruscamente la porta del mio scompartimento, e gridò con una voce rauca ma forte: —Signori, la dogana italiana, preparino il bagaglio.— Tre uomini in uniforme mi stavano davanti sulla porta.

Vocabulary

carrozza-letti = sleeping-car
orologio = clock
orologio da tasca = watch
passeggiata = walk

fare una passeggiata = to go for a walk
fare male (followed by *a*) = to hurt, harm, pain
presentare = to introduce, to present

Exercise 18

1. Good morning, sir. And how are you today? Thank you, today I am not very well; I am very tired.

2. Did you sleep well in the train yesterday? Yes, thanks, I slept very well indeed. I travelled in a sleeping-car. (I *have* travelled . . .)

3. Is the food good at that restaurant where you went yesterday? Yes, it is very good, but a bit dear. (Say: "Does one eat well at . . .")

4. Are you going to the station already? But the train only arrives at ten.

5. We have had a very good journey. (Say: "We have made . . .") There was nobody in our compartment, and we slept very well.

6. What lovely weather it is! Shall we go for a walk along the beach?

7. He closed the door and windows of the compartment, took off his tie, jacket and shoes, put his money, passport and watch under the pillow, and having stretched himself out on the seat, he fell asleep in a moment.

8. Where are you getting out, madam? I am getting out at Florence; I got in the train at Paris.

9. You are taller than I; but John is taller than you.

10. Who is the cleverest in that family? The cook; she's cleverer than you think.

11. That is the richest man in town! Is he a friend of yours? Will you introduce me to him?

12. I have not as much money as he, but I have more than you.

13. I do not want to go for a walk; my foot hurts (to me hurts the foot).

LESSON XIX

NUMERALS

WE have learnt the cardinal numbers up to 20. After refreshing our memory (pp. 16–17), we may continue with the following:

21 = ventuno		50 = cinquanta	
22 = ventidue		60 = sessanta	
23 = ventitré		70 = settanta	
24 = ventiquattro		80 = ottanta	
25 = venticinque		90 = novanta	
26 = ventisei		100 = cento	
27 = ventisette		101 = cento uno or centuno	
28 = ventotto		102 = cento due or centodue	
29 = ventinove		180 = cento ottanta	
30 = trenta		200 = duecento or dugento	
31 = trentuno		1,000 = mille	
32 = trentadue		2,000 = due mila	
38 = trentotto		100,000 = cento mila	
40 = quaranta		1,000,000 = un milione	

Note the following points:

1. *Venti, trenta,* etc., drop the final vowel when combining with *uno* and *otto.*
2. The accent is used on the final *e* of any number ending in *-tre* except *tre* itself: *cinquantatré.*
3. When a noun immediately follows *ventuno* and compounds of *-uno,* it must be in the singular, unless preceded by an adjective: *quarantuna lira* (= 41 lire); *trentun cavallo* (= 31 horses); but *trentun buoni cavalli.*
4. Eleven hundred, twelve hundred, etc., are always translated one thousand one hundred, one thousand two hundred, etc.; *mille novecento* = nineteen hundred.
5. No article is required before *cento* and *mille.*
6. *Milione* is a noun, and has the preposition *di* before the noun to which it refers:

    tre milioni di tonnellate = three million tons.

7. In compound numbers no conjunction is required:

    eighteen hundred and eighty six = mille ottocento ottantasei.

Dates are expressed as follows: the article *il* with the cardinal number (except for the 1st of the month, when *primo* (= first) is used), then the month, then the year. Never translate *on*:

il tre giugno mille novecento trentanove = on the 3rd of June, 1939.

If the month is not mentioned, the article is used with the year: 1494 = *il* 1494 (*mille quattrocento novantaquattro*); in 1910 = *nel* 1910. We might look back a moment to page 17 to revise the days and the months; and also learn the seasons: spring, etc. *la primavera, l'estate, l'autunno, l'inverno.* Note that a capital letter is not required for the days, nor for the months, nor the seasons:

Qual' è la data di oggi? Oggi è lunedí il 28 aprile = What is the date today? Today is Monday the 28th April.

Age is expressed by the verb *avere*:

Quanti anni hai? (lit.: How many years have you?) = How old are you?
Ho dodici anni (lit.: I have twelve years) = I am twelve.

The word for birthday is either *giorno natalizio* or *compleanno*, the second word being the more usual. This means the day on which one finishes one's year, from the verb *compiere* = to fulfil, to complete, and *anno* = year. This verb is also used to express age:

Il tre luglio compirà venticinque anni = On the third of July he'll be twenty-five.
Ha compiuto vent'anni il sedici del mese scorso = He was twenty on the 16th of last month.

Measurements are expressed by the verb *essere*, but the adjective comes before the measurement:

La torre è alta sessanta piedi = The tower is 60 feet high.

If the measurement is expressed by a noun: "The tower is 60 feet in height", the Italian equivalent is: *La torre è dell'altezza di 60 piedi*, or *La torre ha l'altezza di 60 piedi*, or again: *è di 60 piedi di altezza*. Long is *lungo*; wide = *largo*, deep = *profondo*, thick = *spesso*; and the nouns corresponding to these adjectives are: *lunghezza, larghezza, profondità* and *spessore* (m.).

Study the irregular verbs *dovere, potere* and *volere* (all tenses).

Translation IV

—Lei,— mi chiese il più vicino dei tre, —Ha spedito il bagaglio?—

—No, l'ho tutto qui,— risposi prontamente, tirando giù dalla rete la mia unica valigia. Siccome ero venuto in Italia per poco tempo, non avevo bisogno di bauli.

—Ha soltanto bagaglio a mano questo signore,— allora due dei doganieri se ne andarono, senza dubbio a cercare altre vittime, mentre il terzo, rimasto solo con me, riprese:

—Ha qualchecosa da dichiarare, Signore?—

—No, niente.—

—Proprio niente? Niente tabacco, sigarette, sigari, cioccolata. . . .— una pausa —. . . articoli di seta? . . . profumi?—

Abbozzai un sorriso.

—Ma che, diamine; che cosa me ne farei io, di profumi?—

Eh, Signore, non si sa mai! Non si sa mai! Un regalino per qualche amica italiana forse?— suggerì; poi, con un grosso pezzo di gesso bianco segnò qualche sua linea misteriosa sulla mia valigia.

—No, Signore, lasci stare,— disse, quando io feci per aprirla. —Non importa.—

—Mille grazie,— risposi io, contento di non dover aprire la valigia e mettere tutto in disordine.

—Viene a passare le vacanze in Italia, non è vero? Bene. Bravo. Si diverta! Buon giorno.— E se ne andò finalmente anche lui.

Ma appena fuori nel corridoio, fece un passo indietro e, tutto sorridente, s'affacciò ancora una volta alla porta dicendo:

—E buona fortuna . . . a quel profumo!—

Ascoltando quel burlone d'un doganiere non mi ero accorto che il treno era di nuovo in moto, e con sorpresa, guardando fuori del finestrino, vidi che già si passava velocemente fra alte montagne. Mi accomodai nel mio posto d'angolo a contemplar il paesaggio. La strada ferrata, fiancheggiata da una parte e dall'altra da precipizî rocciosi, seguiva il corso di un torrente; uno di quei tanti corsi d'acqua che, sorgendo dalle Alpi si rovesciano in cascatelle giù per i ripidi declivi delle lunghe valli strette per sboccare in quelli più grandi, tributarî del Po. Questo era un torrente impetuoso; ogni tanto s'udiva lo scroscio delle sue acque al di sopra del rumore del treno; e ci scorreva allato, come se volesse dire: —Arriverò io prima di voi.—

Vocabulary

capra = goat
carbone (m.) = coal
contadino -a = peasant
metro quadrato = sq. metre

mondo = world
pecora = sheep
superficie (f.) = surface, area
scoprire (irreg.) = to discover

Exercise 19

1. Have you sent three trunks or four for that gentleman with the beard?
2. Three only; I shall have to forward the other tomorrow.
3. There was once upon a time (*c'era una volta*) a peasant woman who had a hundred sheep, twenty-eight cows, fifty-five pigs, nineteen goats, a dog and a cat, and she was very happy.
4. What is the date today? It is the 4th of July 1940.
5. In what year did Columbus * discover America? In 1492, wasn't it? (Say: is it not true?)
6. How old are you, child? I shall be six next Monday, miss.
7. When is your birthday? On the 9th of May.
8. Have my luggage taken up to my room immediately, please.
9. Six million tons of coal pass through this port every week (through = *per*).
10. The largest church in the world is St. Peter's at Rome; it has an area of 15,160 square metres, and its dome is more than 130 metres high. (Say: *the* dome.)

LESSON XX

NUMERALS (*CONTD.*)

Ordinal Numbers

1st = primo	13th = tredicesimo
2nd = secondo	14th = quattordicesimo
3rd = terzo	15th = quindicesimo
4th = quarto	20th = ventesimo
5th = quinto	21st = ventunesimo
6th = sesto	22nd = ventiduesimo
7th = settimo	30th = trentesimo
8th = ottavo	101st = centesimo primo
9th = nono	102nd = centesimo secondo

* Without any article.

10th = dęcimo
11th = undicęsimo or dęcimo primo
12th = dodicęsimo or dęcimo secondo

111th = centundicęsimo
1000th = millęsimo
2000th = duemillęsimo

Note the following:

1. After the first ten ordinal numbers the others can be formed by dropping the last vowel of the cardinal number and adding -ęsimo. But the last vowel of 23, 33, etc., being stressed, it is kept: *ventitréęsimo* = 23rd.

2. After the first ten there is a second form: *dęcimo primo* (lit.: 10th 1st, *i.e.*, 11th) which may be used for any number: *ventęsimo tęrzo* = 23rd.

3. Ordinal numbers are adjectives, and agree as such: *la seconda lezione*.

4. They are used, without any article, after names of rulers and the words chapter, volume, canto, book, etc.: *Carlo quinto* = Charles the fifth; *Capitolo quarto* = the fourth chapter.

5. The ordinal number is used for the *first* of the month in dates: *il primo maggio* = on the first of May.

6. It is used when speaking of centuries: *Il sęcolo quarto* = the 4th century. After the 10th century (*il sęcolo dęcimo*) the form *dęcimo primo*, etc., is employed rather than *undicęsimo*. But from the 13th century onwards it is more usual to find the following expressions, instead of the ordinal numbers:

13th century = il duecęnto
14th ,, = il trecęnto
15th ,, = il quattrocęnto
16th ,, = il cinquecęnto

17th century = il seicęnto
18th ,, = il settecęnto
19th ,, = l'ottocęnto
20th ,, = il novecęnto

Collective Numerals.—Study the following: *un paio* = a pair (irregular plural: *due paia*); *una dozzina* = a dozen, *una decina* = about ten, *una quindicina* = about fifteen, *una ventina* = a score, *una trentina* = about thirty (forty, fifty, etc., have in Italian a corresponding collective number formed with the ending -*ina*); *un centinaio* = about 100, un *migliaio* = about 1000 (the last two have irregular plurals: *centinaia* = hundreds, *migliaia* = thousands). Note that all these words are nouns, and therefore require *di* before the following noun: *un paio di scarpe, una cinquantina di persone.*

Fractions are expressed as in English, a cardinal for the numerator and an ordinal for the denominator: *due quinti* = two-fifths. Half (noun) is *la metà*, (adjective) *męzzo*.

Useful Phrases of Time

Fra un'ora = In an hour.

Il mio orologio fa le cinque e mezzo = It is 5.30 by my watch.

Il mio orologio va bene = My watch is right.

Quest'orologio è avanti e quello è indietro = This watch is fast and that is slow.

Il mio orologio va avanti cinque minuti al giorno = My watch gains five minutes a day.

Quell'orologio rimane indietro dieci minuti al giorno = That clock loses ten minutes a day.

oggi a otto = today week, oggi a quindici = today fortnight.

Una settimana fa = A week ago.

Domani a quindici = Tomorrow fortnight.

Una quindicina di giorni = A fortnight.

Suonano le undici (*ore*, "hours", is understood) = Eleven is striking.

L'orologio batte le undici = The clock is striking eleven.

è un'uomo sulla cinquantina = He is a man nearing fifty.

Sapere and *Conoscere*. Both these verbs mean "to know"; but *conoscere* means to know in the sense of "being acquainted with", and *sapere* "to know a fact", and also "to know how to":

Conosci quella signorina dai capelli biondi? = Do you know that young lady with the fair hair?

Lui conosce l'Italia molto bene, c'è stato diverse volte = He knows Italy very well, he's been there many times.

Sa parlare bene italiano? = Can he speak Italian well?

Sa Lei chi è quella signora, per favore? = Do you know who that lady is, please?

Sa che Giovanni è tornato? = Do you know that John has come back?

Study the following irregular verbs: *conoscere, crescere, morire, nascere* and *sapere*.

Translation V

Ora la valle si allargava: montagne nude e rocciose davano luogo a colline coperte di pini e di abeti; poi queste alla pianura coi suoi vigneti, con le case coloniche, e i campi biondi di grano e di granturco già maturo. Ciò che mi sorprendeva di più era il poco terreno tenuto a pascolo; quasi tutto era coltivato: un succedersi di campi gialli, svariati qua e là dalle ombre degli

ulivi e di loppi, coi loro festoni di viti. M'interessava molto la
coltivazione della vite. I tralci si arrampicavano su per il
tronco e per i rami di alberi bassi, quali i loppi e gli olmi, e
penzolavano in bei festoni da un albero all'altro; di sotto
cresceva qualche pianta verde, che non potevo distinguere
bene. —Dev'essere molto fertile questo terreno,— pensai, —E
la gente lo vuol sfruttare il piú possibile.— Ma quanto diverso
questo paesaggio dal nostro! Da principio i colori e la luce mi
sembravano troppo forti; sentivo la mancanza del bel verde dei
pascoli inglesi. —E dove sono le vacche?—pensai. —Ah,
eccole.— In lontananza ce n'erano due bianche; e mi alzai per
vedere meglio; ma mi maravigliai che, invece di stare tranquillamente a ruminare, le due bestie lavorassero. —Ma che
vacche!— Erano due enormi buoi aggiogati a un carro carico
di fieno. —Allora il bue s'adopra qui come animale da soma,—
pensai; —E anche il mulo!— perché, passando vicino a
un'autostrada, vidi parecchi carri tirati da muli; e non tardarono ad apparire automobili, autobus, case alte e fabbriche.
Ci s'avvicinava a qualche grande città.

—Giornali, riviste, Domenica del Corriere!— Aprii il finestrino, e, chiamato il giornalaio, comprai un giornale per
trentacinque lire e una rivista per centocinquanta. era ancora
presto, ma nella stazione c'era molta gente. —Forse vanno già
a lavorare,— pensai, ricordandomi che in Italia si comincia il
lavoro piú presto che da noi, perché col gran caldo che fa nei
mesi estivi hanno bisogno di riposarsi durante il giorno. Cosí
molti negozi e uffici sono aperti dalle otto al mezzogiorno, e poi
chiudono per riaprire solamente alle tre o alle quattro, e
rimangono aperti la sera fino alle otto, e in alcuni casi, anche piú
tardi. Le ore dei pasti sono quindi alquanto diverse che da noi.
Si può dire che gl'Italiani mangiano due volte al giorno:
pranzano all'una e cenano alle otto. I piú non mangiano la
mattina presto; la loro prima colazione consiste di caffè e latte
e nient'altro; ma mangiano bene al pranzo e alla cena. Ciò non
toglie però che vadano spessissimo ai caffè, tanto di mattino che
di sera, come io venni a sapere piú tardi.

Vocabulary

chilometro = kilometre
domanda = question
est = east
ovest = west
persona = person
Adriatico = Adriatic

produrre (irreg.) = to produce
stare (irreg.) per = to be about to,
   to be going to

improvvisamente = suddenly
magro = thin

Exercise 20

1. That gentleman has received three trunks, but not the fourth.
2. The river Po is the longest river in Italy; it is more than 600 km. long.
3. It rises in the Piedmontese Alps, crosses a very fertile plain, and, flowing from west to east, it has its mouth in the Adriatic Sea.
4. Petrarch (say: *the* Petrarch, *il Petrarca*) was born in 1304 and died in 1374; he was only seventeen in 1321 when Dante (without article) died. Dante was born in 1265.
5. Do you know who that lady is? No, sir. You are the third person who has asked me that question. (Say: the third person to make me that question.)
6. Have you bought me two dozen eggs? No, I couldn't buy two dozen; I got only about twenty. (Say: *found* about twenty.)
7. How much does your watch gain in a day? It doesn't gain; it loses ten minutes a day.
8. What was yesterday's date? It was the 10th of June, 1941.
9. The year begins on the 1st of January and finishes on the 31st of December.
10. Henry VIII had six wives; but not all at the same time.
11. What a lovely vineyard! Yes, it produces thousands and thousands of bottles of wine a year.
12. It was striking twelve a year ago this evening, and I was just about to go to bed, when suddenly the door of my room was opened, and that tall thin man stood before me.

LESSON XXI

ADVERBS—ORTHOGRAPHIC CHANGES IN VERBS

WE are already familiar with every kind of adverb, for we have used the following:

Adverbs of manner: come, già, molto, così, bene, quasi;
Adverbs of place: dove, vi, ci, davanti, dappertutto, lí, là;
Adverbs of time: quando, sempre, oggi, mai;
Adverbs of quantity: molto, tanto, troppo, poco, soltanto;
Adverbs of affirmation and negation: sí, no, non;
Adverbial expressions: appena, di solito, da principio.

Position of Adverbs.—Looking back over the previous exercises, we see that unless the adverb begins a clause, it is generally placed immediately after the verb—with the exception of *non*, which always precedes a verb. When the verb is a compound tense, the adverb nearly always follows the past participle, with the exception of the following: (1) the conjunctive adverbs *vi* and *ci*, which precede both parts of the verb; and (2) *già, mai, piú, sɛmpre* and sometimes *ancora*, which may come *between* both parts of the verb:

Non l'ho mai veduto = I have never seen it.
Ha sɛmpre parlato cosí = He has always spoken like that.

Having gathered together these few points, we may add the following:

Adverbs of Place.—*Qui* and *qua*, both meaning "here", refer to something near the person who speaks: *costí* and *costà*, "there", to something near the person addressed, and *lí* and *là*, "there", to something far away from both. (Note the connection between these and the three demonstrative adjectives: *questo, codesto* and *quello*, see page 43.)

Adverbs of Quantity.—*Solo*, besides being an adjective meaning "only", "alone", is also an adverb meaning "only", used in place of *soltanto* or *solamente*. "Only" can also be rendered by *non* before the verb and *che* after it:

Non ne abbiamo che due = We have only two.

Adverbs of Manner are also formed by adding *-mente* to the feminine singular of an adjective or a participle (as we add "-ly": slow, slowly):

fortunato = lucky   fortunatamente = luckily
felice = happy   felicemente = happily
decișo = decided (resolute)   decișamente = decidedly (resolutely)

Adjectives ending in *-le* or *-re*, preceded by a vowel, drop the final vowel before adding *-mente*: *regolare* = regular, *regolarmente*. When the *-le* and *-re* are preceded by a consonant, they keep the final vowel in the ordinary way: *acre* = harsh, *acremente* = harshly.

The form in *-mente* should not be used too often, from the point of view of style and the unpleasant sound many "-mente's" will produce. Instead a phrase such as *in un mɔdo* or *in una manièra* ("in a way", "in a manner") is used with an adjective: *in un modo corraggioso* = courageously; or else *con* with a noun: *con corraggio.*

To avoid too often a recurrence of long words in *-mente*, an adjective (masculine singular form) is sometimes used instead of an adverb:

> Parlare chiaro = to speak distinctly
> Parlare forte = to speak loudly
> Parlare piano = to speak softly
> Andar diritto = to walk straight on
> Guardare fisso = to stare fixedly
> Veder chiaro = to see clearly

Comparison of Adverbs.—Adverbs are compared like adjectives:

> Lui corre piú rapidamente di me = He runs faster than I.
> Ma lei corre il piú rapidamente di tutti = But she runs the
>   fastest of all.

There is also an absolute superlative of adverbs, which is not very much used: *-mente* is added to the feminine singular superlative of the adjective: *ricco, ricchissimo, ricchissimamente.*

Four adverbs have irregular comparatives and superlatives:

Positive	Comparative	Rel. Superlative	Abs. Superlative
bene = well	meglio	il meglio	ottimamente / benissimo
male = badly	peggio	il peggio	pessimamente / malissimo
molto = very	piú	il piú	moltissimo
poco = little	meno	il meno	pochissimo

Orthographic Changes in Certain Verbs.—Certain letters— *c* and *g*, for example—vary in their pronunciation according to the vowel which follows them. This must be remembered when dealing with certain verbs. A verb like *cercare*, for example, which has the hard *c* in the infinitive, must add an *h* to its stem before endings which begin with *e* or *i*, if it is to preserve this hard sound. Thus the present indicative becomes: *cerco, cerchi, cerca, cerchiamo, cercate, cercano*, and the future *cercherò*, etc. The same thing happens in verbs ending in *-gare*: *paghi, paghiamo, pagherò*. The rule is therefore that verbs ending in *-care* and *-gare* insert an *h* after the *c* and *g* whenever these letters come before *e* and *i*. Verbs in *-ciare* and *-giare* drop the *i* before an *e* or another *i*:

lasciare = to let, leave lasci, lasciamo, lasceremo
mangiare = to eat mangi, mangiamo, mangeremo

while verbs in -*iare* drop the *i* before another *i* only:

pigliare = to catch: pigli, pigliamo; but: piglieremo.

All these verbs are first conjugation verbs. Other conjugations are not so particular about the preservation of the sound of the infinitive; look up, for example, the present indicative of l*e*ggere, which has the soft sound in four persons and the hard sound in two. The *only* orthographic change in verbs of the second conjugation is this: verbs in -*cere* or -*gere* insert an *i* before the *u* of the past participle: *piacere* = to please, *piaciuto* = pleased. There are no such changes in the third conjugation.

Study these irregular verbs: *rimanere, vedere, venire* and *vivere.*

Translation VI

—In carr*o*zza, Signori, in carr*o*zza!— e di nu*o*vo si partí. Questa v*o*lta non *e*ro piú solo. Due u*o*mini, uno giovane, l'altro sulla cinquantina v*e*nnero a sedersi nel mio scompartimento. Il piú v*e*cchio, di colorito molto scuro, aveva gli *o*cchi e i cap*e*lli neri; il giovane invece, con cap*e*lli biondi e *o*cchi az*z*urri, poteva *e*ssere inglese. Erano commessi viaggiatori, a quanto sembrava, e parl*a*vano ad alta voce e animatamente; ma s*e*mpre in piemont*e*se, dialetto cosí div*e*rso dall'italiano, che io non li potei capire. L*e*ssi un p*o*' il giornale; non c'*e*ra ni*e*nte di speciale e in p*o*co piú di due ore eravamo a G*e*nova.

—Gelati, biscotti, caram*e*lle, uva fresca, cestini da vi*a*ggio!— Mi affacciai al finestrino. Che rumore! Che f*o*lla! G*e*nte che saliva; g*e*nte che scendeva; g*e*nte venuta a salutare chi arrivava o a dare gli *u*ltimi addii a chi partiva; e nella calca facchini con bag*a*gli sulle spalle, fac*e*ntisi * avanti a f*o*rza di spinte, non meno dei giornalai, dei gelati*e*ri e dei venditori di dolci e di b*i*bite. Finalmente riuscii a richiamare l'attenzione di uno di questi e a comprare un cestino, molto a bu*o*n mercato, in verità, perché lo pagai solo 500 lire, e dentro c'*e*ra un piatto di maccheroni caldi, due fettone di vit*e*llo arr*o*sto, prosciutto, form*a*ggio, frutta, biscotti, due panini e perfino un fiaschettino di vino rosso. Avevo una fame da lupi; ma *e*ra ancora un p*o*' pr*e*sto per far colazione.

—Bu*o*n appetito, Signore,—mi disse con un sorriso colui che occupava il posto di f*a*ccia (il tr*e*no *e*ra oramai compl*e*to e n*e*l

* Verbal adjective from *farsi.*

mio scompartimento non c'erano piú posti liberi). —Grazie, altrettanto,—risposi, vedendo che cominciava a mangiare anche lui. Facevano altrettanto i miei altri compagni di viaggio, alcuni dei quali, indovinando che ero forestiere, m'indicavano tutto ciò che potesse interessarmi. —Questo è il golfo della Spezia, dove morí affogato il poeta Shelley;— mi dissero. In distanza biancheggiavano le montagne di Carrara con le famose cavé di marmo. Piú tardi, mentre si passava per una bella pineta, mi chiesero se amassi la musica e mi dissero che lí c'era la casa e la tomba del compositore Giacomo Puccini.

Vocabulary

pollo = chicken	mancare = to lack
radio (f.) = wireless	trasmettere (irreg.) = to transmit
	voltarsi = to turn
calvo = bald	
corto = short	a destra = to the right
grasso = fat	cortesemente = politely
	fino a = as far as, up to

Exercise 21

1. Do not take any notice of what she says; she has always spoken like that.
2. Yesterday he was a bit better, but today he is worse. Have they called a doctor?
3. Which is the shortest way to the station, please? (Say: for to go to . . .)
4. Keep straight on, sir, as far as the church, and there you turn to the right, and you will find the station opposite.
5. Speak quietly; can't you see that they are listening to us? (If you use progressive tense, put pronoun object before the auxiliary.)
6. What time do you have breakfast? At eight, usually; but I don't take much—only coffee and milk.
7. What time do they have lunch here? Generally at one o'clock, sir. Good! there's only ten minutes more. (Say: lack only ten minutes.) I'm ravenous.
8. Did you have a good meal on the train? Yes, very, thank you. I bought a luncheon basket, and in it there were so many good things: chicken, ham, biscuits, cheese and fruit.
9. There were so many people, and there wasn't a place empty (free). But a gentleman there near the door got up saying very politely: "Take this seat, madam, please."

10. Another traveller came and sat down in my compartment. He was a man nearing sixty, small and fat, bald and with a white beard (say: *the* white beard).

11. Didn't the boys come with you to the theatre? No, they remained at home; they wanted to hear the wireless; they were broadcasting a good concert from the Scala.

12. What did you do yesterday? Nothing in particular. I stayed at home.

LESSON XXII

PASSIVE VOICE—IMPERSONAL VERBS—IDIOMATIC USE OF CERTAIN TENSES

Passive Voice.—We have noted that the auxiliary of the passive voice is *essere*: *La casa è comprata da me* = "The house is bought by me", and if the verb is in a compound tense, we have the compound tense of *essere*: *La casa è stata comprata da me* = "The house has been bought by me", both past participles therefore agreeing with the subject. Instead of *essere* the following verbs are sometimes used as auxiliaries in the SIMPLE tenses of the passive voice: *venire, rimanere, restare* and *andare*. *Andare* implies a special meaning of duty or obligation:

I ladri vennero arrestati dal poliziotto = The thieves were arrested by the policeman.

Quella chiave non va toccata = That key must not be touched.

Impersonal Verbs.—A verb without a definite subject is impersonal. A real impersonal verb is one which is used only in the third person singular. The following are the most frequently met: *piove* = it rains, *nevica* = it snows, *tuona* = it thunders, *lampeggia* = it lightens, *grandina* = it hails, *gela* = it freezes.

But there are many other verbs which are used impersonally. The most common are:

bisogna = it is necessary   basta = it is enough
conviene = it is profitable   pare, sembra = it seems
ci vuole = it is necessary   succede = it happens
(ci—"there" = "for that", "for it")

    mi piace = I like it (lit.: it pleases me)
    mi dispiace = I am sorry (lit.: it displeases me)
    mi preme: = I am anxious (lit.: it presses me)
    mi riesce = I succeed, I can (lit.: it succeeds to me)

There are also some impersonal expressions formed by *fare*, *ɛssere* and one or two other verbs:

fa caldo = it is hot	fa freddo = it is cold
fa bɛl tɛmpo = it is fine	fa cattivo tɛmpo = it is bad
che tɛmpo fa? = what sort	weather
of weather is it?	c'ɛ della nɛbbia = it is foggy
tira vɛnto = it is windy	ɛ umido = it is damp
(tirare = to pull, also =	vale la pena = it is worth while
to throw)	(lit.: it is worth the trouble;
	(valere = to be worth))

Note that in all these expressions the pronoun "it" is always understood in the verb.

When these impersonal expressions are followed by an infinitive there is no intervening preposition, except in the case of the verbs *parere* and *sembrare*, which may be used with or without the preposition *di* and the verbs *piacere* and *dispiacere* which take *di*:

Bisogna vederlo subito = It is necessary to see him at once.
Mi dispiace di doverle dire = I am sorry to have to tell you.
Mi pare di vedere del fumo laggiú = I think I see smoke down there.

In the above Italian sentences there is no personal subject in the dependent clause; when there is, this clause has its verb in the subjunctive:

Bisogna vederlo   BUT   Bisogna che *io* lo veda = *I* must see him.
Mi dispiace di non ɛssere venuto piú prɛsto = I am sorry not to have come sooner   BUT   Mi dispiace che *lui* non sia venuto piú prɛsto = I am sorry that *he* didn't come sooner.

Auxiliary Verbs with Impersonals.—Compound tenses of impersonal verbs are formed with *ɛssere* in the case of true impersonal verbs: *ɛ piovuto* = it has rained; and also when an intransitive verb is used impersonally: *ɛ succɛsso* = it has happened; but *avere* is used when a transitive verb forms the impersonal expression: *Ha tirato vɛnto tutta la nɔtte* = It has blown wind all night.

It would be helpful at this point to list the common verbs which take the auxiliary *ɛssere* (excluding the impersonals mentioned above). This will be revision, as most of these verbs have already been used in the exercises. Note, too, that they are marked, both in the list of irregular verbs in the Appendix when irregular, *and* in the vocabulary as taking *ɛssere*:

andare	morire	salire
arrivare	nascere	scendere
cadere	partire	stare
correre	restare	uscire
entrare	tornare	venire

Idiomatic Use of Certain Tenses.—In English when we indicate how long something has been going on and is still continuing, we use the present perfect: *I have been* in Italy five years. But this tense in Italian would not mean the same thing. Translated literally: *Sono stato in Italia cinque anni,* it means, "I have been in Italy for five years" BUT I AM NO LONGER THERE, for the present perfect indicates that the action is over in the past, though its results may be felt in the present. To render the meaning of the English tense—"I have been in Italy"—and am STILL THERE, Italian uses the simple present: *Sono in Italia da cinque anni* (= I am in Italy since five years), or *Sono cinque anni che sono in Italia* (= There are five years that I am in Italy).

Similarly when speaking of something which has been going on in the past with respect to a time in the past as: I had been in Italy five years when I met your sister in Florence = *ero in Italia da cinque anni quando incontrai tua sorella a Firenze.* And similarly with the future: On the fifteenth of next month I shall have been in Italy five years = *Il 15 del mese prossimo sarò in Italia da cinque anni,* or *Il 15 del mese prossimo saranno cinque anni che sono in Italia.*

This use of the tenses seems strange to us; just as our use of these perfects bewilders the Italian. The student would do well to learn by heart the literal English equivalent to each of the above sentences, so as to become familiar with the turn of the Italian phrase.

Study the verbs: *parere, piacere, piovere, valere.*

Translation VII

A Pisa riuscii a liberarmi con difficoltà da quella folla di commissionari di alberghi, di ciceroni e di fiaccherai che ingombrano l'uscita della stazione; ma, lasciata la valigia al deposito, una volta fuori con la pianta della città in mano, m'incamminai verso la piazza del duomo. In meno di una mezz'oretta ci arrivai.

Han * chiamato questa piazza il prato dei miracoli; e c'è

* *Hanno* may be thus abbreviated before a past participle which does not begin with s impure.

davvero del meraviglioso nella visione di quei quattro monumenti candidi che s'innalzano maestosi in mezzo a un campo, e
che risaltano con tanta grazia sul verde del prato e sull'azzurro
del cielo. Costruiti in epoche diverse, fra il secolo decimo primo
e il dugento, quando Pisa era una potente repubblica marinara,
i quattro edifizi—battistero, chiesa, cimitero, e torre pendente—
sono tuttavia legati in armonia mirabile. Di stile romanico,
hanno un loro carattere tipico e originale specialmente nelle
decorazioni esterne di arcate cieche e di ordini di loggiati, le
quali danno a queste moli marmoree leggiadria ed eleganza. Nel
battistero ammirai il pulpito di Nicola Pisano e anche mi divertii
a udire la famosa eco. Cantando una sola nota quella cupola
conica ci rimanda l'eco in un accordo musicale perfetto;
cantando poi tutta una canzone, è come se ci fosse lí un organo
che suonasse in pieno. L'interno della cattedrale è impressionante con le enormi colonne monolitiche, e siccome piove
molta luce dai finestroni della navata centrale potevo vedere
molto bene le numerose opere d'arte. Mi mostrarono anche la
lampada di Galileo (il quale era pisano) e la tradizione vuole
che lo scienziato, osservandone le oscillazioni, scoprisse le
leggi del pendolo. Pagai poi centocinquanta lire per entrare
nel Campo Santo a vedere gli affreschi; e si paga anche per
salire la torre pendente (cento lire). Ne vale la pena per il
magnifico panorama e anche per provar la sensazione singolare
che si ha su una torre che strapiomba (ha una deviazione
di piú di quattro metri dalla verticale). Ci vuole un cuore
forte, però e anche due buone gambe: ci sono quasi trecento
scalini!

Sceso dalla torre, mi sedetti un momento sull'erba. C'era
altra gente lí, per lo piú pisani venuti a far merenda all'ombra
dei loro monumenti. Il sole tramontava; l'aria mite e serena
era piena di voli di rondini; quel bianco dei marmi si era mutato
in un color di rosa. Che pace! Che tranquillità! Riprendendo
il cammino per la stazione, pensai che questo era il mio primo
giorno in Italia: e mi pareva impossibile, già mi sembrava di
essere lí da tanto tempo.

Vocabulary

caduta = fall
esperimento = experiment
grave (m.) = weight (adj. =
  heavy)
sommità = top

strano = strange

cominciare = to begin
iniziare = to begin

Exercise 22

1. Just as he was about to open the door, that thief was arrested by the policeman.
2. The cathedral of Pisa was begun in the year 1063.
3. The leaning tower is among the strangest in the world.
4. How long have you been in Italy?
5. I have been in Italy for three years.
6. Is it worth while visiting the tower? Yes, certainly, there is a magnificent view.
7. But let us not go today, it is cold and windy. We ought to wait for a day when it is fine, or we shall not see anything. (Use the subjunctive "it may be fine" to imply uncertainty.) *
8. How long does it take to go from here to the church, sir? (Say: How much time for it is necessary? using *volere*.)
9. Hasn't he come down for his breakfast yet? What shall we do? The train doesn't wait for anyone. We shall have to leave tomorrow.
10. That book was bought by me and I don't want to give it to anyone.
11. I am very sorry but I shall not be able to come; a friend of mine should (trans. *deve*) arrive today.
12. They say that Galileo did his famous experiments on the fall of heavy weights from the top of the leaning tower.

LESSON XXIII

DEMONSTRATIVES (*CONTD.*)—INDEFINITE ADJECTIVES AND PRONOUNS

WE must now add some other demonstrative words to those we already know: *questo, codesto* and *quello*. These words are both adjectives and pronouns, meaning "this" and "that" when used with a noun, and "this one", "that one" when standing alone. As adjectives they have the various shortened forms we have already learnt; as pronouns they always have their full forms, though they change for gender and number:

Questi mi piacciono piú di quelli = I like these better than those.

* See page 135.

Other demonstratives are:

1. *Ciò*, invariable, "this" or "that" referring to a whole sentence or an idea, not a single word:

Ciò non è vero = That's not true.

2. *Quegli* = "that man", *questi* = "this man" (there is no feminine form and no plural, and these words can be used only for persons and not for things and as subject of a verb). They also mean "former" and "latter":

Questi è italiano e quegli è inglese = This man is Italian and that man English.

Note that *quello* and *questo* also mean the "former" and the "latter":

Maria e Luisa sono partite oggi; questa tornerà stasera, quella domani = Mary and Lucy left today; the latter will come back this evening, the former tomorrow.

3. *Costui* = "this man", *costεi* = "this woman", *costoro* = "those people" or "those men", "those women": all these convey a slight idea of contempt:

Chi è costui? = Who is that fellow?
Non vado a sedermi vicino a costoro = I'm not going to sit near to those people.

4. *Colui* = "that man", *colεi* = "that woman", *coloro* = "those people" or "those men", "those women":

Parlo di coloro = I'm speaking of them, of those people.

Indefinite Adjectives and Pronouns.—On pages 32 and 33 we met some indefinite adjectives and pronouns. There are many such words in Italian, and as we add them to our vocabulary we must distinguish which are pronouns, which adjectives, and which may be used as both. Study the following tables:

1. "Each", "every", "each one", "everyone".

> *ogni* (invariable), adj.
> *ognuno, -a* (no plural), pron.
> *ciascuno, -a* (no plural), adj. and pron.
> *tutto, -a, -i, -e*, adj. and pron.

Examples:

Ogni uomo prese uno per sé = Each man took one for himself.

Ciascuno prese uno per sé = Each one took one for himself.
Ciascuna donna prese uno per sé = Each woman took one for herself.

Ognuno, ciascuno lo dice⎫
Tutti lo dicono   ⎬ = Everyone says so.

Ciascuno as a pronoun is used only of persons; as an adjective it may be used for things also, but *ogni* is preferable. *Ciascuno* lays more emphasis on the partitive sense of the word, and *ognuno* and *ogni* on the collective; it is better to use *ciascuno* for "each" and *ogni* and *ognuno* for "every", "everybody".

2. "None", "no one", "nobody", "nothing".

> *nessuno, -a* (no plural), adj. and pron.
> *alcuno, -a* (with *non* has no plural), adj. and pron.
> *nulla* (invariable), pron.
> *nullo, -a, -i, -e*, adj.
> *niɛnte* (invariable), pron.

Examples:

Nessuno ti crede   ⎫
Non ti crede nessuno⎬ = Nobody believes you.

Non họ alcun amico, nessun amico = I have no friend.
Non ho nulla = I have nothing (also means: I've nothing the matter with me).
Le sue speranze sono nulle = His hopes are vain.

3. "Anybody", "anyone", "anything", "any".

> *alcuno, -a, -i, -e*, adj. and pron.
> *qualcuno, -a* (no plural), pron.
> *qualche* (invariable), adj.
> *qualchecɔsa* (invariable), pron.

Examples:

Conosce alcuni di questi uọmini? = Does he know any of these men?
Conoscete alcuno qui? = Do you know anybody here?
Hai qualche libro da darmi = Have you any book to give me?

Note that *qualche* is always followed by its noun in the singular, and *alcuno* when affirmative has a plural.

4. "Somebody", "someone", "something", "some", are the same words as for "any", etc., see previous paragraph.

5. "Whoever", "whatever", "however".

chiunque (invariable), pron., whoever, whosoever.
chicchessia (plural: *chicchesiano*), pron., whoever, whosoever
qualunque (invariable), adj. and pron., however, whichever
per quanto (*-ti*), adj., however much, however many
checché (invariable), pron., whatever
qualsiasi (*qualsiansi*), adj., whatever

Examples (note that these indefinite words are followed by the subjunctive (see also page 138)):

Chiunque tu sia = Whoever you may be.
Datemi qualunque libro = Give me any book whatever.

Note too that *per quanto* may also be an adverb, in which case it is invariable: *Per quanto cari siano* = However dear they may be.

6. "Some . . . others", "the one . . . the other". *Chi . . . chi*; *altri . . . altri*; *alcuni . . . alcuni*; translate "some . . . others"; *l'uno . . . l'altro* (plural: *Gli uni . . . gli altri*) "the one . . . the other". Note that *alcuni* used in this sense is always plural; but the verb with *chi* and *altri* used in this sense is in the singular:

Alcuni camminano, alcuni corrono ⎫
Altri cammina, altri corre ⎪ Some walk, others run
Chi cammina, chi corre ⎬
Gli uni camminano, gli altri corrono ⎭

7. Finally, an indefinite pronoun meaning "of others": *altrui* (pronounce al-tró-ee) which is invariable, and can *never* be subject of a verb; it is really an inflection of *altri*, and does not require any preposition before it:

Bisogna rispettare i diritti altrui = The rights of others must be respected.

Study the verbs: *dire*, *salire* and *uscire*.

Translation VIII

Firenze, per la sua storia, per l'arte, e anche per la bellezza della sua posizione, è fra le città piú celebri. Il mio soggiorno colà fu troppo breve per permettermi piú di uno sguardo rapido ad alcune cose d'importanza artistica e storica, ma bastò per darmi un'idea delle numerose bellezze naturali e artistiche di quella città in riva all'Arno e per farmene sentire il fascino, cosí da decidermi di ritornarvi al piú presto.

Il primo mattino mi svegliai di buon'ora. La mia pensione era all'ultimo piano di un vecchio palazzo, al pianterreno del quale c'erano dei negozi, da una parte un fioraio, e dall'altra un venditore di antichità e di oggetti d'arte. Scesi le scale (non c'era ascensore), passai per il corridoio oscuro, fresco e profumato dai fiori e dalle piante che stavano lí esposti, e, data un'occhiata ai vecchi quadri, mobili e gioielli della vetrina dell'antiquario, uscii sulla via. Con la pianta in mano mi diressi verso la piazza del duomo. Anche a Firenze, come a Pisa e come in tante città d'Italia, il duomo, il battistero e il campanile sono tre edifizi staccati l'uno dall'altro, ma legati in intima unità dallo stile architettonico. Qui a Firenze il marmo è di un altro colore, un colore piú caldo, quasi rosa, con linee di un verde tanto scuro da sembrare nero. Il duomo fu iniziato nell'anno 1296. L'interno è grandioso e solenne, molto chiaro e sobrio, perché quasi privo di elementi decorativi. Ammirai l'altare di puro argento, ma le due famose cantorie, l'una di Donatello e l'altra di Luca della Robbia, le quali erano prima nella cattedrale, bisogna cercarle ora nel museo lí accanto. Il battistero è un edifizio a pianta ottagonale e dentro è ornatissimo di marmi e di mosaici. Quando entrai battezzavano un bambino; e guardando quel piccolo gruppo intorno al fonte mi ricordai che era qui, in questo stesso luogo, che Dante ricevette il battesimo quasi sette secoli fa. Lí vidi anche le belle porte in bronzo * del Ghiberti; quelle che Michelangelo disse degne di esser le porte del Paradiso: rappresentano scene del Vecchio Testamento, incorniciate da un fregio in cui si alternano statuette di profeti e tondi con teste. Il terzo monumento di questo gruppo, il campanile di Giotto è una torre alta, quadrata, di forma semplice e salda, ma elegante; anche qui bisogna ammirare i bassorilievi nella parte inferiore, dovuti ai discepoli di Giotto, su disegni del maestro.

Vocabulary

opinione (f.) = opinion
peccato = pity
   Che peccato! = What a pity!
pianoforte (m.) = piano
violino = violin

ripetere = to repeat
suonare = to sound, to ring
   (bell); to play (piano, etc.).
tutti e due = both (lit.: all
   and two)

* The Baptistery doors are now gilded, having been restored, since World War II, to their original state.

Exercise 23

1. I have seen both of those pictures; I like the latter better than the former.
2. Who is that woman? Does she always shout with that voice?
3. Mary and Lucy both play very well: the latter the violin, the former the piano.
4. Every time I go there that man follows me to the door.
5. It is a great pity to sell that flower shop; everyone says so. (Say: that shop of flowers.)
6. Have you seen anyone on the road? No, I have not seen anyone.
7. However rich she is, it doesn't make any difference to me (to matter = *importare*). I do not want her for my wife.
8. Whoever you may be I cannot let you in here.
9. Some were going to see the pictures; others to be admired by the rest (say: the others) (*farsi ammirare* = to be admired); all were walking along towards the museum.
10. Whatever has happened? (Whatever? interrogative = *che cosa mai?*) Some are running, others walking, but they are all going along towards the church.
11. You should not repeat other people's opinions; you should have some of your own. (Use *bisognare*, say: *non bisogna ripetere . . .*)
12. Are you going out this morning? Yes, I'm going out in a little while (*fra poco*); do you want anything?

LESSON XXIV

USE OF THE ARTICLES

THE definite and indefinite articles are used in Italian on many occasions exactly as in English; but there are some differences between the two languages. One we know already: the use in Italian of the definite article with the possessive: *il mio libro*; and when doing the exercises you have sometimes been told to add the *definite* article and to omit the *indefinite*. We must now learn the following rules:

A. *The Definite Article, il, lo,* etc., is used in Italian when we do *not* use "the" in the following cases:

1. Before a noun used in a general sense, or before an abstract noun:

L'erba è verde = Grass is green.
I libri sono utili = Books are useful.

2. Before the name of a language (though it may be omitted after *parlare*) and the prepositions *in* and *di*:

Studio l'italiano = I am studying Italian.
Si parla inglese = English spoken.

3. Before a surname, used without a Christian name: *

Il Boccaccio nacque a Parigi = Boccaccio was born in Paris.

But:

Dante Alighieri era fiorentino = Dante Alighieri was a Florentine.

4. Before a surname preceded by a title:

Il signor Bianchi è in città = Mr. Bianchi is in town.
Il dottor Viani viene oggi = Dr. Viani is coming today.

(Note that titles ending in *-ore*, such as *signore, professore*, drop their final *-e* when followed by another title, or by a name.)
    When the title is used in direct address, however, the article is not used:

Buon giorno, Signor Bianchi = Good morning, Mr. Bianchi.

5. Before names of countries, continents, provinces and large islands:

    l'America   La Toscana = Tuscany
    l'Inghilterra   La Sardegna = Sardinia

Exception to rule 5: No article is used with feminine names after the prepositions *in* or *di*, if the noun is not modified:

    in Francia = in France   d'Italia = of Italy

But:

negli Stati Uniti = in the United States
del Canadà = of Canada
La storia dell'Italia meridionale = The history of Southern Italy.

* A few famous surnames may have no article: Garibaldi, Colombo.

Note that when the preposition *di* with the name of the country is not equivalent to an adjective of nationality, the article is used:

La Germania è piú grande dell'Italia = Germany is larger than Italy.

6. The definite article is used instead of the possessive when the latter is not absolutely necessary for clearness:

Mise la mano in tasca = He put his hand in his pocket.

B. *The Definite Article is omitted* in Italian where we would use it in English in these cases:

1. Before a noun in apposition to another:

Roma, capitale d'Italia = Rome, the capital of Italy.

2. Before an ordinal used with a proper noun:

Vittorio Emanuele terzo = Victor Emanuel the third.

C. *The Indefinite Article is omitted* in Italian, and used in English, in the following cases:

1. Before a noun in apposition:

Toscana, provincia d'Italia = Tuscany, a province of Italy.

2. Before a noun in the predicate which is unqualified:

Lui è dottore = He is a doctor.
Io sono forestiero = I am a foreigner.

But:

Il dottor Rossi è un buon medico = Dr. Rossi is a good doctor.

3. In exclamations after *che!* and *quale!*

Che peccato! = What a pity!

4. Before *cento* and *mille*:

Centocinquanta = One hundred and fifty.

5. After the preposition *da* used in the idiomatic sense of "like", "in the manner of":

Parla da sciocco = He talks like a fool.

Study the irregular verbs: *cadere, sedere, tacere* and *tenere*.

Translation IX

Dal centro religioso m'incamminai al centro storico della città, cioè alla Piazza della Signoría, è molto pittoresca, con il

maestoso Palazzo Vecchio a un lato, costruito come una fortezza
con mura merlate, e accanto c'è la Loggia dei Lanzi, dove una
volta venivano a parlare i Signori della città, e dove ora la
gente ammira alcune delle statue piú conosciute del mondo.
Dalla piazza si entra nel lungo piazzale degli Uffizi, che si apre
fra il Palazzo e la Loggia. è circondato da tre lati dall'enorme
Palazzo degli Uffizi, cosí chiamato perché destinato a sede di
uffizi amministrativi: oggi è un museo e contiene la piú importante collezione di pitture in Italia. I giorni feriali bisogna
pagare cento lire d'entrata, quindi rimandai la mia visita alla
domenica. Quando vi andai, vi trovai con mia grande sorpresa,
una folla d'Italiani in abiti festivi, che passeggiavano su e giú
per i lunghi corridoi luminosi, o, seduti sulle panche fra l'uno e
l'altro monumento, chiacchieravano e guardavano i visitatori.
Sembravano indifferenti alle bellezze d'arte che li circondavano;
ma se domandi a uno, come feci io, dove si trovi un certo
capolavoro, o a quale scuola appartenga un certo maestro, ti
sanno quasi sempre rispondere lí per lí correttamente. La
passeggiata domenicale negli Uffizi è per loro un'abitudine;
quelle pitture fanno parte della loro vita.

Passando sotto la loggia in fondo al Piazzale, si sale sul
Lungarno, una delle strade che costeggiano il fiume, e voltando
a destra, poco dopo si giunge al Ponte Vecchio. Questo, il ponte
piú antico della città, è molto pittoresco, con le piccole botteghe
degli orefici che si aggrappano ai lati, appoggiate all'esterno del
ponte da mensole in legno. Cosí piccole sono queste botteghe
che si direbbe che non si possano entrare piú di cinque o sei
persone alla volta; invece ci entrano in gran numero specialmente donne e turisti: per chi ama belle collane, orecchini,
fermagli, cammei e anelli, è difficilissimo resistere alla tentazione
di quelle vetrine, o meglio bacheche, che fiancheggiano la via
strettissima del ponte e che sono disposte con tanto gusto al
livello degli occhi dei passanti.

Traversato il fiume, camminai dapprima per straducole scure
e strette, fra palazzi antichi; poi, salendo per viali e vie di
campagna, su per le pendici di un colle, giunsi al Piazzale
Michelangelo. Di là si vede tutta Firenze entro la cerchia delle
sue colline; colline amene e ridenti al sole, coperte di vigne e di
uliveti e sparse qua e là di ville e di case, su cui a tratti si leva
un albero piú alto e piú scuro degli altri—l'albero tipico della
campagna toscana: il cipresso. Ora uno isolato; ora una bella
fila che disegna la linea di un viale o i contorni di un poggio.
Distinsi in lontananza il colle di Fiesole con in cima il monastero
che volevo visitare. era assai lontano ma l'aria limpida e chiara

lo faceva parer vicino. Suonò mezzogiorno. Come batteva il
sole! Tutto quel che si toccava scottava. Mi guardai intorno
sulla piazza. Non c'era anima viva, e nessun rumore fuorché
l'interminabile canto di miriadi di cicale.

Vocabulary

patria = fatherland, country   negare = to deny
pittore (m.) = painter   sacrificare = to sacrifice
scrittrice (f.) = woman writer   Cristoforo = Christopher

Exercise 24

1. Green is a nice colour. (nice = *bello*)
2. He is studying Italian; he can already speak French.
3. Christopher Columbus discovered America.
4. Mrs. Bianchi is at home. Who wants her?
5. He has fallen from the tree and broken his leg. When will
   Dr. Rossi arrive?
6. He is a great painter; he who denies it, talks like a fool.
7. Florence is one of the most beautiful cities in Italy.
8. Grazia Deledda, a famous Italian woman writer, was born
   in Sardinia.
9. He sacrificed his life for his country.
10. My father is a lawyer and my uncle a doctor.
11. Good morning, Doctor. Would you come up, please?
12. Necklaces, earrings, brooches, cameos and rings are all sold
    in those little shops on Ponte Vecchio. (Say: "sell them-
    selves".)

LESSON XXV

SUFFIXES

ITALIANS often add a particular ending to a word to express
size or quality instead of using another word. (We have the
same thing in English: *e.g.*, Johnny, piggy, doggie, streamlet.)
There are many such suffixes in Italian added to nouns,
adjectives, adverbs and, very occasionally, to verbs. A noun
thus modified usually keeps its original gender, but sometimes
a masculine suffix is added to a feminine noun and the word
becomes masculine: *la finestra* = window; *il finestrino* = the
little window; *il finestrone* = the large window. It will be seen
from these examples that when adding a suffix, the final vowel
of the word is dropped; and when the final vowel is preceded by

a *c* or *g*, the original sound of that letter is kept, by the addition of an *h* or an *i*: *barca* = boat, *barchetta* = little boat; *sεmplice* = simple, *semplicione* = very simple, a simpleton.

The commonest suffixes are these:

1. *-issimo* (= very), added to adjectives and adverbs.

buɔno	buonissimo
pɔco	pochissimo
piccolo	piccolissimo

2. *-one*, fem. *-ona* (= large). The feminine form is used only with nouns and adjectives which have a masculine and feminine form; in other cases the feminine noun takes the masculine suffix and becomes masculine:

il libro	il librone
la casa	il casone
il ragazzo	il ragazzone
la ragazza	la ragazzona
la donna	il donnone (= big woman)

3. *-etto, -εllo, -cεllo, icεllo, -arεllo, -erεllo, -uɔlo* and *-ɔlo* all denote smallness, and all have feminine forms in *-a*:

la piazza	la piazzetta
la donna	la donnetta
il fiume = river	il fiumicεllo = stream

4. *-ino, -cina, -icino*, with feminine form in *-a*, mean small (often with the idea of "nice", "dear"):

il gatto	il gattino = little cat, kitten
caro = dear	carino = darling
la casa	la casina = little house
Giovanni = John	Giovannino = dear little John

5. *-uccio, -uzzo, -ucolo*, feminine forms in *-a*, mean small (with the idea of affection if used with the name of a person; with the idea of pity or contempt if used with a common noun):

Maria = Mary	Mariuccia = dear little Mary
la donna	la donnuccia = silly little woman
la strada	la straducola = back street, poor street

6. *-ɔtto*, fem. *-a*, gives the idea of strength, sturdiness, vigour:

| la contadina (peasant woman) | la contadinɔtta = sturdy peasant woman |

il giovane = the youth

il giovanotto = the grown up or strong young man

7. *-accio*, fem. *-a*, means worthless, bad:

Che tempo! = what weather!

Che tempaccio! = what foul weather!

la casa = the house

la casaccia = the awful, dreadful house

povero = poor

poveraccio = poor wretch

These suffixes may not be used just as one likes; that is, not by a foreigner, whose ear would not be sufficient guide for him to choose the right one; some words take one, other words another. The student is advised to use a suffix with any word *only* if he has already met that word and suffix together. There is also another danger in making words by adding a suffix: many words have been employed so often with a certain suffix that they have taken on special meanings, as:

scala = stair; scalino = stair; scaletta = ladder, staircase; casa = house; casina = nice little house; casino = club, casino; casella = pigeon-hole;

cavalla = mare; cavallina = nice little mare; cavaletta = locust.

A word may sometimes have two suffixes added at once: *fiasco* = flask or bottle, *fiaschetto* = little bottle, *fiaschettino* = very small bottle, nice little bottle; *tovaglia* = table-cloth, *tovagliolo* = serviette, *tovagliolino* = very small serviette, or bib.

In very rare cases suffixes are joined to verbs: *-ello*, *-arello* and *-erello* are joined to the stem, and they lose their final *-o* before the infinitive ending: *cantare* = to sing, *canterellare*, *cantarellare* = to hum continually; *saltare* = to jump; *saltellare*, *salterellare* = to keep on giving little jumps.

Study the verbs: *chiedere, chiudere, perdere, prendere, ridere, rispondere.*

Translation X

—Pronto! Parlo con la Pensione Primavera? No? Oh, mi dispiace, ho sbagliato numero. Pronto! Centrale! Mi dia per favore il numero 25,054 (venti-cinque zero cinque quattro). Grazie. Pronto! Parlo con la Pensione Primavera? Bene. C'è il signore inglese, che è arrivato poco tempo fa? Si chiama. . . .—
—Mi dispiace, Signora, non c'è . . . oh, aspetti, torna proprio adesso. Lo vado a chiamare. Un momento.—

—Signore, scusi.— mi disse il portiere al momento che rientravo per mangiare. —La vogliono al telefono.—

—Dio mio, al telefono,— pensai, —Chi può essere? e come farò a farmi capire in italiano?—

Ma mi riuscí facile. Era una vecchia signora inglese, sposata a un italiano, la quale aveva conosciuto mia madre, e m'invitava a visitarla nella sua villa a Fiesole. Molto volentieri ci andai.

Si può salire a Fiesole col tram e coll'autobus; ma io preferivo andarci a piedi. Partii una sera verso le cinque. Faceva ancora caldo ma non troppo; c'era un bel venticello fresco che veniva dalle montagne. Traversata la piazza del Duomo e fatta tutta una strada lunga e stretta entrai in un'altra bella piazza grande e armoniosa, circondata in tre lati da bei portici, e in mezzo alla quale c'erano una statua equestre e due fontane ornatissime. Sopra ciascuna colonna dei portici notai un tondo in terra cotta con quel famoso putto in fasce su fondo celeste, opera di uno dei della Robbia; allora compresi dove mi trovavo; ero nella Piazza della Santissima Annunziata e quell'edifizio era l'Ospedale degli Innocenti. Proseguii per altre vie e piazze finché mi trovai in piena campagna e, sempre salendo ora fra gli alti muri di ville fiorite, ora fra boschi di cipressi e di ulivi—che offrivano qua e là alla vista il panorama della città—giunsi finalmente alla piazza di Fiesole.

Era giorno di mercato e la piazza presentava uno spettacolo molto vivace. All'ombra degli alberi (la piazza ha due belle file di castagni e di tigli) e degli edifizi in pietra grigia, i venditori avevano disposto le loro baracche e i loro banchi sul marciapiede e li avevano coperti di tende, sotto le quali gridavano la loro merce. Vendevano per lo piú oggetti di paglia: cappelli, ceste, cestini, borse di colori e di disegni vivacissimi, per i quali la cittadina è famosa; e anche oggetti in cuoio che si fabbricano a Firenze, anch'essi con bei disegni a colori: e poi, tante altre cose come scarpe, libri, cartoline, calze, gioie di poco valore, panno, rosarii, crocefissi, biscotti, caramelle e frutta. Vidi grosse ceste piene d'uva, di pere e di fichi, posate in terra. Siccome dovevo aspettare la signora inglese e alcuni suoi amici mi sedetti a una delle tavole di fuori, sotto gli alberi, a bere un vermut col ghiaccio mentre guardavo quella folla animata e allegra.

Vocabulary

campanello = bell (of door)	villino = small villa, cottage
parco = park	
tavolino = small table	regalare = to give a present

Exercise 25

1. He eats very little indeed, that boy.
2. They are rich, those foreigners. They have an enormous house in the middle of a park.
3. Have you any kittens? What little ones! Poor little things! (Suffix -*ino* for both nouns.)
4. Dear little Mary, will you go to the door? Didn't you hear the bell? Somebody has rung.
5. Will you help me carry some water from the well? I haven't time; that sturdy peasant girl will help you.
6. But of whom are you speaking? Of that little woman who came yesterday to help Cook?
7. I left all those papers in my trunk, which will now be closed, and I have lost the key. Haven't you asked the porter? He will perhaps have the key.
8. Have you replied to that girl (*signorina*) who gave you that large book? Yes, I replied the day after.
9. What did that silly little woman reply when you told her that she shouldn't hum like that all the time? She didn't say anything, she only laughed. ("Shouldn't"—use *bisognare*.)
10. He went up the stairs and entered the little bedroom. There was nobody there. He put the parcel and the flowers on the little table near to the window.
11. What an awful house! Who lives there? Some poor wretch!
12. They have a small villa on one of those little country roads which go up the hill. ("To go up the hill" = *andare su per il colle*.)

LESSON XXVI

THE INFINITIVE

Infinitive as a Verbal Noun.—When the English present participle in -*ing* is more of a noun than a verb it is rendered in Italian by the infinitive. The infinitive as a *verbal noun* may be subject or object or predicate; in the first two cases it usually takes the article:

Mi piace il ballare = I like dancing
Amo il viaggiare = I like travelling

but not as predicate (*i.e.*, after the verb "to be"):

è facile şbagliarsi = It is easy to make mistakes.

It is also used after prepositions (except "by", "on", "in" and "through"; refer back to page 65). It usually takes the definite article in this case too, except after *di, dopo di, invece di, prima di, senza* and *oltre*:

Parlò senza esitare = She spoke without hesitating.
Votò contro il dare tanto a uno solo = He voted against giving so much to only one.

Conjunctive Pronouns with Certain Verbs and the Infinitive.
Dovere, potere and *volere* have a kind of auxiliary function when followed by an infinitive; and a pronoun object, which is really the object of the infinitive, may either precede both verbs or follow and be joined on to the infinitive (see Part II, page 173). Two other verbs have a similar construction: *osare* (= to dare) and *sapere*:

Non mi osa dire ciò, *or* Non osa dirmi ciò = He daren't tell me that.
Lo sa parlare bene, *or* Sa parlarlo bene = He can speak it well.

Five verbs, however, when followed by the simple infinitive, take *all* the object pronouns, even when these belong to the infinitive: *fare, lasciare, sentire, udire* and *vedere*:

Glielo fanno spedire ora = They are having it sent to him now.
L'ho sentito dire mille volte = I've heard it said a thousand times.
Glielo vedo dare = I see it given him.

Note that in these constructions the Italian *infinitive* translates an English *past participle*.
In the above examples, of the two pronoun objects one was direct and the other indirect; but each verb may govern a direct object in English. In this case, in Italian, the direct object of the main verb becomes indirect and the object of the infinitive remains direct:

Gliela feci scrivere = I made him write it (letter, understood) (lit.: to him it I made to write).

When the object of either verb is a noun, it follows both verbs in Italian; but again when there are two direct objects, the one belonging to the main verb becomes indirect:

Feci scrivere la lettera = I had the letter written.

Feci scrivere la lettera a quella ragazza = I made that girl write the letter (lit.: I made to write the letter to that girl).

Infinitive Governed by a Preposition.—One or two other verbs take the infinitive after them without any intervening preposition, as: *desiderare* = to desire, *preferire* = to prefer, *solere* = to be accustomed, in addition to the impersonal verbs already mentioned (pp. 107–108); but certain verbs require a preposition after them before a following infinitive: some *a*; others *di*; *essere* and *avere* may be followed by *da* to express duty or necessity; and when the English "to" means "in order to" it is rendered by *per*:

È abituato *ad* alzarsi presto = He is used to getting up early.

Ha cercato *di* farlo = He has tried to do it.

Non ho niente *da* fare = I have nothing to do.

È tornato *per* vederla = He has come back to see her.

The following verbs require *a* after them before an infinitive: verbs meaning accustoming, beginning or continuing, compelling, helping, hastening, inviting, learning, preparing, teaching and verbs of motion or rest in a place. The most common are:

abituarsi, aiutare, cominciare, continuare, destinare (= to destine), *costringere* (= to compel), *imparare* (= to learn), *insegnare* (= to teach), *invitare, riuscire*.

Andrò a vederla domani = I will go and see her tomorrow.

È riuscito a vincere il concorso = He has succeeded in winning the competition.

Most other verbs take *di*. We may note the following:

cercare (= to try), *credere* (= to believe), *dire, finire, maravigliarsi, permettere* (= to permit), *pregare* (= to beg), *proibire* (= to prohibit), *promettere* (= to promise), *rifiutare* (= to refuse), *sperare* (= to hope).

Ha finito di scrivere quel capitolo = He has finished writing that chapter.

Prometto di venire subito = I promise to come at once.

The infinitive preceded by *di* is often used after some of these verbs where we in English would use a noun clause, when the subject of the principal sentence and the dependent clause is the same:

Credo di dover andare fra poco = I think I shall have to go in a little while.

Disse di averlo finito tutto = He said he had finished it all.

With verbs denoting command, permission or prohibition, this same construction may be used in Italian when the subject of the main clause is different from that of the dependent clause (when no doubt or uncertainty is implied—see lesson on the subjunctive, page 136):

Ti proibisco di parlare = I forbid you to speak.

Mi prega di andare a vederlo = He begs me to go and see him.

Gli ho detto di venire alle sei = I have told him to come at six.

Study these verbs: *aprire*, *offrire* and *udire*. When translating the following passage, note verbs which are followed by an infinitive, whether they take any preposition, and if so, which.

Translation XI

Eravamo seduti sulla terrazza del villino della signora inglese dopo un'ottima cena, a godere la veduta della città di notte— tutto uno scintillio di luci laggiú nella valle—quando i miei ospiti decisero di condurmi a Signa a vedere il Palio.* —Noi si va ogni anno,— mi dissero, —è uno spettacolo bellissimo e divertente. Vedrà che le piacerà.—Avevano ragione; mi divertii proprio immensamente.

Si prese la littorina.† Fra parentesi, non raccomanderei questo trenino automobile a persone nervose, ma è il mezzo piú

* Name given to a horse-race run in the city square: a competition between the different wards, the winner receiving as a prize a special banner, beautifully embroidered, called the "Palio". This race dates from mediaeval times.

† A train which came into service just before World War II. It runs along the ordinary track, but instead of an engine, it has a motor driven on petrol. Small, light and very stream-lined, it develops a high speed, but is meant for short journeys only; it holds less than 100 passengers and heavy luggage is not allowed. The main Italian railway system is electrified; the *littorina* is to take the place of the old steam trains which served (and in some few cases still serve) the less important local lines.

rapido. Va tanto veloce che sembra volare sul binario senza toccarlo; ma quando lo tocca, dà una tale scossa che i viaggiatori balzano sui cuscini; e i pacchetti che stanno ballando nella rete cascano in testa alla gente. Così s'arrivò alla graziosa e pulita stazioncina di Signa; modernissima e da far convertire allo stile novecento, tanto belle e armoniose ne sono la forma e le proporzioni.

E poi, dopo una scarrozzata per una strada ripida, mi trovai entro le mura della città medioevale, la quale, dai suoi tre monti, domina tutto il paesaggio circostante. I maestosi palazzi gotici, di pietra grigia, alcuni con merli, e i vicoli scuri e stretti (qualchevolta non ci passa nemmeno la carrozza), mi parvero dapprima austeri e freddi. Ma vennero i giorni del Palio. Che trasformazione! Tutto appariva inondato di gioia: abitanti, strade, palazzi. Da quegli edifizi solenni pendevano bandiere, arazzi, panni—ogni finestra dava il suo contributo; le strade erano uno sventolio di bandiere; e i senesi, a qualunque ora del giorno o della notte, passeggiavano su e giú a braccetto, cantando e ridendo, tutti allegri. Questa corsa di cavalli, che celebra un'antica festa religiosa, è la piú strana del mondo. Ha luogo in mezzo alla città, cioè nella Piazza del Campo, e tutti i partecipanti sono vestiti in costumi medioevali di colori vivaci bene armonizzati. Non sapendo io niente del significato religioso e non avendo fatto nessuna scommessa, non potevo partecipare a quell'entusiasmo frenetico per la corsa; nondimeno quello fu per me come uno spettacolo teatrale interessantissimo, di cui mi colpirono di piú le scene seguenti:

Atto primo.—Una chiesetta di una delle contrade. Personaggi—un cavallo, un prete, un fantino (tutti vicino all'altare); una folla che ride e chiacchiera tutt'il tempo. Il prete, ripetendo una certa preghiera asperge il naso del cavallo. Grida e risa della folla. —Bravo! bravo! Viva la lupa *!— Escono tutti ridendo. Sipario.

Atto secondo.—Una piazza grande, che ha la forma di una conchiglia o di un ventaglio. È affollatissima. A tutte le finestre, gente; su tutti i tetti, gente. Un pigia pigia nella piazza stessa, fuorché nello spazio riservato per la corsa tutt'intorno. Un urlo tremendo della folla; la corsa pazza di dieci cavalli; mentre per un minuto e mezzo l'aria è in tempesta per il gridare e il fischiare

* Each district or ward has its own flag and emblem, and is represented in the race by horse and jockey wearing its colours. Each has, too, its own small church in which the ceremony of blessing the horse takes place. The *contrada* in question was that of the *lupa* or "She-wolf".

di diecine di migliaia di persone, per il rullio di tamburi, lo squillo di trombe, i colpi di mortaretto, e il suonare delle campane di più di venti chiese. Sipario.

Atto terzo.—La strada principale della contrada vincitrice, a notte inoltrata. Ad una lunga tavola cenano all'aperto parecchie centinaia di persone; la scena è illuminata dagli antichi torchietti che pendono dalla facciata dei vetusti palazzi. E in capo alla tavola sta l'attore principale, il cavallo vincitore, con la sua propria mangiatoia dentro la quale ci sono—fra altre cose—maccheroni. Esso sta mangiando. Fine. Sipario.

Exercise 26

1. He gave me that book before leaving for Rome.
2. Why has he said that? He speaks without thinking.
3. I hear that said a thousand times a day.
4. Have they had that door opened?
5. Yes, Cook opened it, and now we cannot close it.
6. Instead of reading a novel he ought to study that lesson.
7. Yes, *I* would make him study it, and at once.
8. The motor-train leaves at eleven, I think. Could you reserve me a seat?
9. I told him to buy the tickets yesterday.
10. Yes, he tried to (. . . to do it), but he couldn't—everything was closed.
11. He had promised to go immediately, but he can't—there isn't a train before tomorrow.
12. I forbid you to go to that house.

LESSON XXVII

PREPOSITIONS

THESE short invariable words, which connect a noun, pronoun or infinitive to a word preceding them, sometimes present difficulties, for corresponding prepositions in English and Italian are often used on different occasions and with very different meanings. Also some verbs which take a direct object in Italian require a preposition in English, and vice versa.

Only a few Italian verbs require a preposition which in English take a direct object. The most common are: *entrare IN, credere A* (when the object is a person), *ricordarsi DI*, and *fidarsi DI* (= to trust):

Entrò nella camera = He entered the room.

Non credere a quell'uomo, è bugiardo = Don't believe that man, he's a liar.

Ti ricordi di quel giorno? = Do you remember that day?

There are more Italian verbs which govern a direct object which in English require a preposition: for example, *fischiare* (= to hiss AT), *guardare* (= to look AT), *aspettare* (= to wait FOR), *pagare* (= to pay FOR), *cercare* (= to look FOR).

Lui me la pagherà = He'll pay me *for* it.

Sta cercando quel libro = He's looking *for* that book.

The following verbs require a preposition in both languages, but a different one:

adornare di = to adorn with
approfittare di = to profit by, to take advantage of
caricare di = to load with
maravigliarsi di = to wonder at
occuparsi di = to busy oneself with, look after, see to, attend to
ridere di = to laugh at
vivere di = to live on
dipendere da = to depend on

Lei si occupa anche del giardino? = Do you look after the garden too?

Ride sempre di me = He always laughs at me.

Note the constructions with the following verbs:

chiedere = to ask (Italian: to ask something to someone).
   Chiedo il conto al cameriere = I ask the waiter for the bill.
pensare (followed by *a* = to think of).
   Hai pensato a me? = Have you thought of me?
pensare (followed by *di* = to have an opinion about).
   Che cosa pensa di quel romanzo? = What do you think about that novel?
perdonare (Italian: to pardon a thing to a person).
   Non vuoi perdonare quello a tua sorella? = Aren't you going to pardon your sister for that?

We must not get the impression that the use of the prepositions in Italian is never the same as in English; many verbs take the same in both languages; on the other hand, it must not be thought that the above list of words is by any means exhaustive. Only by continuous reading and careful observation can the student hope to master the use of the prepositions thoroughly.

We have often met the preposition *di* after an adjective or past participle doing the service of our "with". Note the following, which are always followed by *di*:

> abbondante di = abundant in
> carico di = laden with
> contɛnto di = contented with
> fornito di = provided with
> povero di = poor in'
> pratico di = experienced in
> ricco di = rich in
> soddisfatto di = satisfied with
> sorpreso di = surprised at
> vestito di = dressed in

and three which take *a*, where we use "for: *adatto a* = fit for," *buono a* = good for, *dirɛtto a* = bound for.

The prepositions *a*, *di*, *da* are *simple* prepositions. Others (some of which also exist as adverbs) are: *in, con, su, per, tra* or *fra, sɛnza, vɛrso, sopra, sotto, dentro, dopo, diɛtro, contro*; others again are phrases made up of another word and a true preposition, as *fuori di* = outside of. The following when governing a personal pronoun take *di* after them, and thus become prepositional phrases: *contro, diɛtro, dopo, sɛnza, sopra, sotto* and —sometimes—*fra* and *vɛrso*.

> sɛnza di te = without you
> vɛrso di loro = towards them

We must now gather together idiomatic uses we have already met and add a few others to them. We will begin with *da*, which has the most varied meanings:

DA, besides meaning "by" and "from", also means:

1. "at", "at the house of", "with", "in the district":

Non può venire da me oggi? No, mi dispiace, dɛvo andare dal mɛdico = Can't you come to me today? No, I'm sorry I have to go to the doctor's.

2. "like", "in the manner of":

Ho una fame da lupi = I am ravenous (lit.: I have hunger like wolves).

3. "of such a kind as to":

Non è uomo da fare ciò = He's not the man to do that.

4. It describes a personal or characteristic quality:

Quell'uomo dal naso lungo = That man with the long nose.

5. It indicates the purpose for which something is intended:

la sala da pranzo = the dining-room
la stanza da bagno = the bathroom
una bottiglia da vino = a wine-bottle
una tazza da tè = a tea-cup

(Note that a bottle *of* wine is *una bottiglia di vino*, a cup *of* tea = *una tazza di tè*.)

6. Before the word "parte" it means "on":

da questa parte = on this side

DI = "of", and the partitive "some", is also used before adverbs to mean "from":

è lontano di qua = It is far from here,

and it also indicates certain times of the day or year, rendered in English by "in" or "by":

di mattina, di sera, di notte, di giorno = in the morning, in the evening, by night, by day
di primavera, d'inverno = in spring, in winter.

A = "to", and "at", is also:

1. "in" before the name of a town:

Mia moglie è a Roma = My wife is in Rome.

2. It indicates the way a thing is done in certain idiomatic phrases:

chiudere a chiave = to shut with a key (= to lock)
andare a piedi = to go on foot
andare a cavallo = to ride
alla romana = in the Roman fashion (*maniera* understood)

Note: *pagare alla romana* means "to pay one's own share".

3. It also forms compound nouns:

> una barca a vela = a sailing boat
> una macchina a vapore = a steam engine

IN translates "to" before the name of a country:

> è andato in Francia = He has gone to France

FRA = "among", translates "in" when expressing future time:

> Sarà pronto fra un'ora = He'll be ready in an hour.

Study the irregular verbs: *cogliere, scegliere* and *sciogliere.*

Translation XII

Oltre a essere una delle città piú romantiche e pittoresche, Venezia è anche fra le piú originali del mondo. Chi non l'abbia veduta non può figurarsi questa città di marmo e di acqua. Vi manca la vegetazione, o quasi; non ci sono né erbe, né piante, né alberi, eccetto che in pochi giardini. Mancano strade larghe; le vie di Venezia sono canali e rii; quindi né automobili, ne autobus, né carrozze. Il taxi di Venezia è la gondola o il vaporetto. In questo luogo singolare l'occhio deve abituarsi a un panorama del tutto diverso da quello di ogni giorno: un panorama di palazzi, acqua e cielo: palazzi candidi, palazzi gialli, palazzi color di rosa, tutti scintillanti nella luce purissima e forte, e tutti lambiti a pianterreno dal mare. L'orecchio nota l'assenza dei soliti rumori; la prima impressione è di un gran silenzio, rotto ogni tanto dal grido melanconico del gondoliere che s'avvicina all'angolo di una strada o dal lontano fischio del vaporino che fa servizio alle isole vicine.

Questi e altri pensieri mi passavano per la mente, una sera, seduto a un tavolino in piazza San Marco. C'erano con me parecchi amici (conoscenze fatte al Lido, dove andavo a bagnarmi tutti i giorni) venuti a sentire la serenata sul Canal Grande.

—E pensa, Carlo,— mi diceva uno di loro, —che questa città fantastica è costruita in mezzo a una laguna, sopra un arcipelago di quasi centoventi isole, e ha centosessanta canali e quattrocento ponti.—

—La sua storia dev'essere molto interessante,— dissi io.

—Avanti, Luigi, lo storico— gridarono tutti.

—Bene, bene,— rispose Luigi. —Era fondata nel quinto secolo— mi pare —dai profughi dalle invasioni barbariche, e andò sempre acquistando maggior importanza e potere con le sue relazioni commerciali coll'oriente. I veneziani, sapete, erano un popolo pratico e intraprendente: seppero approfittare di ogni occasione per arricchirsi e per estendere la loro potenza. Nel medioevo si erano acquistato il monopolio del commercio del sale, un prodotto allora molto scarso e caro; ai tempi delle crociate con le loro navi trasportarono in oriente le truppe cristiane e naturalmente da quei furbi mercanti che erano fecero pagar cari quei viaggi. Nel dugento Venezia era già una potenza importante nel Mediterraneo, con colonie nell'Egeo e nell'Asia Minore, e nel trecento cominciò a farsi paladina del cristianesimo contro i Turchi, e fu allora, se mi ricordo bene, che le sue navi raggiunsero i porti della lontana Inghilterra. Avendo conquistato molta parte dell'Italia settentrionale, questa repubblica marittima divenne poi uno dei cinque grandi stati italiani. La decadenza data dal cinquecento coll'aprirsi di nuove vie marittime alle Indie e col principio di lunghe guerre contro la Turchia. Oggi può sembrare una città morta; ma è un ricchissimo museo e un paradiso per i turisti . . . e per studenti in vacanza.— soggiunse, con un sorriso.

—Bravo Luigi!— —Trenta con lode!—

—Grazie, Luigi,— dissi io, e mi guardai intorno sulla piazza.

Ci stava di fronte nella lontananza la facciata della basilica, e ai due lati i bei portici con i negozi di cristallerie e di pizzi, dove andava su e giú a passi lenti la folla (era l'ora della passeggiata serale). L'orchestra suonava una musica sentimentale, e tutt'intorno volavano quegli abitanti sfrontati della piazza—i piccioni—i quali venivano ogni tanto sul marciapiede o a posarsi sulle tavole per cercarvi delle briciole. —Venga pur qui a Venezia chi ha bisogno di riposarsi— pensai. —Cullandosi al ritmo lento della gondola, un senso di calma e di pace gl'invaderà l'anima come in nessun altro luogo. Qui si è pigri, qui nessuno ha fretta, c'è tempo per tutto, perchè il tempo stesso pare che si sia arrestato.—

Vocabulary

adriatico = Adriatic

fedele = faithful (adj. and noun)

marinaro = seafaring

nord (m.) = north

orientale = eastern

patriottico = patriotic

sentimento = feeling

abbellire (1st group) = to beautify

animare = to animate

attestare a = to bear witness *to*

fare guerra a = to make war on

Exercise 27

1. He is a cheeky boy: he was looking at me all the time.
2. Haven't you paid for that ticket yet?
3. He will not allow me to see those books; he has locked the door of his room.
4. What do you think of that man? He is a liar; I do not believe what he says.
5. The bottle of wine is on the table in the dining-room; that new maid with the red hair has left it there.
6. Venice was one of the largest and most important cities of the Middle Ages. Built on an archipelago of 120 islands in a lagoon at the north of the Adriatic, it was destined to become a maritime power. The Venetians were a practical and enterprising people. They acquired the monopoly of the salt trade and charged a high price for that commodity. In the times of the Crusades they knew how to take advantage of the opportunity of enriching themselves and of extending their power in the Eastern Mediterranean, and their ships carried thousands of the faithful who were making war on the Turks. On the return journeys to their own country, those same ships came laden with rich marble and mosaics, which that seafaring people used to beautify their city. The beautiful Venetian monuments and buildings which we admire today bear witness to the strong patriotic feeling which animated the sons of this famous maritime republic of the Middle Ages.

(Note: In the times ... translate *at* the times; *on* the return ... *in* the journeys of return; their own country ... is *their own* necessary if you use *patria*?)

LESSON XXVIII

THE SUBJUNCTIVE

THE Subjunctive Mood has almost disappeared from English, and except for an occasional "Long live!" and an "If I were you", we no longer use it. Italian, however, observes the mood strictly, and we must learn to use it correctly.

The *indicative* makes a plain statement about something which is an actual fact; the *subjunctive* expresses something which is possible but uncertain, some action which is dependent upon another action, sometimes resulting from emotion or thought expressed in that other action. It is chiefly found in subordinate clauses, though it appears, too, in principal sentences, to express a wish:

> Voglia il cielo che torni in tempo = Heaven grant he returns in time!

and we have met it as supplying the third persons of the imperative:

> Mi dia quel libro per favore = Give me that book, please.

In this lesson we will confine ourselves to the *Present Subjunctive*. The three model verbs are conjugated on page 76. Note that the three persons singular are identical for all verbs; that the first person plural is the same as that of the present indicative; and that the third conjugation verbs which have the *-isc* in the present indicative also have it in the present subjunctive. We might also study at this point the irregular present subjunctive of the following verbs: *andare, dare, dire, fare, potere, sapere, stare, venire* and *volere*. These will be found in the appendix, where it will be seen that the three persons singular are identical and that the endings are the same for all these verbs (i.e., *-a, -iamo, -iate* and *-ano*). The same remarks apply to the auxiliary verbs, which are conjugated as follows: *essere*: sia, sia, sia, siamo, siate, siano; and *avere*: abbia, abbia, abbia, abbiamo, abbiate, abbiano.

Uses of the Subjunctive

The subjunctive is used in clauses depending on verbs which express:

1. desire, will, preference:

   > *Voglio* che *veniate* voi tutti = I want you all to come.

2. request, command, prohibition, hindering or preventing:

   > Il capitano *comanda* che tu *venga* subito = The captain orders you to come at once.

3. doubt, uncertainty, ignorance:

   > *Dubito* che quella *sia* vero = I doubt that that is true.

4. belief, opinion, supposition:

   > *Credo* che *sia* già partito = I think he's already gone.

(Where there is no doubt, but simply a future idea with *credere*, the indicative is used: *Credo* che *partirà* alle nove.)

5. a negative idea:

> *Non so* se *sia* già partito = I don't know whether he's already left.
>
> *Non* c'è *nessuno* che essa *conosca* = there is no one she knows.

6. emotion (joy, sorrow, fear, wonder, shame, expectancy):

> *Sono* tanto *contɛnto* che *sappiano* ogni cɔsa = I'm so glad that they know everything.
>
> Mi *dispiace* che tu *abbia* lɛtto quello = I'm sorry that you have read that.

7. It is also used after an impersonal expression, except when that expression denotes something clear and evident, an actual fact:

> *Bisogna* che ci *vada* = I must go there.

But:

> ɛ *vero* che ci *sono* stato = It's true that I've been there.

All the dependent clauses quoted above are noun clauses; they stand as subject, object or predicate of a verb. Note that the subject of the main clause and of the dependent clause is always different; if the subject is the same in both clauses, the subordinate clause would not require the subjunctive, but the infinitive (see page 127).

Another type of subordinate clause is the adjectival clause, modifying a noun or pronoun, and introduced by a relative pronoun = who, which, that. They have their verbs in the subjunctive:

1. After a relative superlative and the words *primo, ultimo, solo* and *unico*, in the main clause:

> ɛ *la più grande* chiɛsa che *abbia* mai vista = It's the largest church I've ever seen.

2. After a negative or an interrogative:

> *Non ha* chi lo *pɔssa* aiutare = He has nobody who can help him.
>
> Non c'è nessuno che lo possa aiutare? = Isn't there anyone who can help him?

3. When the subordinate clause expresses purpose:

Scelgono dieci volontari che *prendano* d'assalto la fortezza = They are choosing ten volunteers to take the fort by assault.

4. When the relative pronoun has an indefinite antecedent:

Cerco *una giacca* che *vada* bene con questa gonna = I'm looking for a coat (jacket) to match this skirt (uncertain as to whether there will be one).

BUT:

Cerco *la giacca* che *va* con questa gonna = I'm looking for the short coat that goes with this skirt (a definite coat).

5. After the indefinite words: *chiunque, qualunque, checché, dovunque, per quanto*:

Chiunque tu *sia*, non puoi entrare = Whoever you are, you cannot go in.

Study the irregular verbs: *leggere, muovere, scrivere*.

Translation XIII

A Venezia la vita della città si svolge intorno alla Piazza San Marco, e piú precisamente intorno a quei tavolini di caffè; a Milano il centro vitale è la Piazza del Duomo con la contigua galleria Vittorio Emmanuele, anch'essa coi suoi tavolini occupati a tutte le ore del giorno. La galleria, tradizionale luogo di ritrovo dei milanesi, è enorme. Dalla Piazza del Duomo ci si entra per una maestosa arcata, e, attraversata tutta la galleria, si esce nella Piazza della Scala dove c'è il famoso teatro di quel nome. Per tutta la sua lunghezza la galleria è fiancheggiata da eleganti negozi e da molti caffè, e io certo ho passato ore molto gradevoli seduto con amici a un tavolino a guardare e a criticare la folla che passava e a mangiar gelati, che sono davvero squisiti!

Un giorno, dopo una visita al convento di Santa Maria delle Grazie in compagnia di due turisti americani per vedere la celebre Ultima Cena di Leonardo da Vinci, tornai alla galleria per riposarmi. Sedutomi alla mia solita tavola, chiesi un vermut al cameriere e mi misi a guardare i passanti. Mi rimanevano soltanto pochi giorni di vacanze, e pensavo che sarei dovuto andare al teatro almeno una volta. Chiamato il cameriere, che mi era già amico—tante volte mi aveva aiutato e consigliato, gli chiesi un giornale, per leggervi la rubrica dei teatri.

—Molto volentiᴇri, Signore,— rispose, —a momenti passerà il giornalaio col Corriᴇre della Sera, e glielo comprᴇrò io, Signore. Ma in quanto ai teatri, temo che ci sia bᴇn poco ora perché si è fuori di stagione. La maggior parte dei teatri son chiusi e gli artisti sono via in vacanza. Ma ci sono moltissimi cinema; non vorrᴇbbe vedere qualche buona pellicola?— Ma sapevo già che ai cinema non c'ᴇra gran che.

Mentre aspettavo il giornalaio comprai carta da scrivere e francobolli dal camerieᴇre, e lí, al mio tavolino scrissi ai miei in Inghiltᴇrra per annunciare la data del mio ritorno a casa. Stavo mettᴇndo i francobolli da settanta lire alla mia lᴇttera quando tornò il camerieᴇre col giornale. Egli lo aveva già consultato e me lo porse dicᴇndo:

—C'è una cosa che fose le andrà a gᴇnio, Signore. Le place la musica?— Alla mia risposta affirmativa continuò:

—Allora, c'è una rᴇcita straordinaria di beneficᴇnza, la bellissima opera di Puccini, Madame Butterfly—Lᴇi la conosce certamente, Signore—con un tenore bravissimo e una cantante giapponese con una voce divina. Vale la pena di sentirla. Ma la danno in un teatro piccolo, un po' fuori del cᴇntro, vicino a casa mia.—

—Benissimo, Beppino— risposi (cosí si chiamava quel brav'uomo); —se è vicino a casa sua, vᴇnga con me stasera a sentire Madame Butterfly, eh?—

Vocabulary

affari (m.pl.) = business	bancario (adj.), of banks, banking
movimento = movement, bustle	
penisola = peninsula	industriale = industrial
speranza = hope	
trᴇgua = respite	discutere (irreg.) = discuss

Exercise 28

1. Give me some of that writing-paper, please; I want to write to my people at home (omit "some").
2. He wants you all to go away immediately; he cannot see anybody.
3. I doubt whether they will come now; it is so late.
4. He is glad you know it now; but he did not dare tell you himself.
5. Do you know whether they have gone or not?
6. He is the naughtiest boy I know.
7. Isn't there anyone here who can play the piano?

8. Milan is one of the largest towns in Italy, with more than a
million inhabitants. It is the most important city of
northern Italy, and the largest industrial, commercial and
banking centre in the whole of the peninsula. When I am
in Milan I go to the Victor Emanuel Arcade every day.
It is the traditional meeting-place for the Milanese, and
there are some smart shops and very many cafés there.
I sit down at one of the little tables and ask the waiter for
a vermouth or a coffee, and while I am there drinking
I watch the crowd go by. Some come here to walk up and
down, some to chat, some to meet their friends, and others
to discuss business; but they all come in the hope of
having a moment's peace and respite from the noise and
bustle of the large modern industrial town. (Say: of the
large town industrial modern. "whole" = tutto.)

LESSON XXIX

THE SUBJUNCTIVE (*CONTD.*)

On page 76 the *Imperfect Subjunctive* of regular verbs is given.
Note that the double *ss* appears in all persons except the second
person plural; that the second person plural is the same as that
of the past definite; and that, except for the characteristic
vowel, the endings are the same for all three conjugations.
Study also the irregular imperfect subjunctives (in the Appendix) of: *dare, fare, stare* and *dire*; and of the auxiliary *essere*;—
fossi, fossi, fosse, fossimo, foste, fossero. (*avessi* from *avere* is
regular.)

Use of the Tenses of the Subjunctive

In our last lesson we translated the Italian present subjunctive into English by the present indicative, by the infinitive
or by "may" and "might". Where Italian requires the subjunctive, if the English verb is in the *present* indicative, in
Italian it will often be in the *present* subjunctive; and if the
English verb is a *past* tense, Italian will on most occasions
employ the *imperfect* subjunctive. But we cannot take the
English equivalents as a basis to decide which tense of the
subjunctive to use in every case in Italian; our "may" and
"might" are sometimes interchangeable, and the infinitive in
English is sometimes rendered by the Italian present and sometimes by the imperfect subjunctive:

Vuole che tu *venga* subito = He wants you to come at once.
Voleva che tu *venissi* subito = He wanted you to come at once.

The tense of the subjunctive in the subordinate clause is determined by what tense of the indicative is to be found in the main clause. The two sentences just quoted show that a present subjunctive follows a present indicative, and an imperfect subjunctive follows an imperfect indicative. We may formulate the rules as follows:

1. When the verb in the main clause is in the present indicative or the future or the imperative, the verb in the subordinate clause is in the present subjunctive or in the present perfect subjunctive:

Temo che non *venga* oggi = I'm afraid he won't come today.
Crederà che tu *sia uscito* = He'll think you've gone out.

2. When the verb in the main clause is in any other tense of the indicative (except the present perfect), the verb in the dependent clause is in the imperfect subjunctive, or in the past perfect subjunctive:

Credeva che tu *scherzassi* = He thought you were joking.
Credeva che tu *fossi uscito* = He thought you had gone out.

3. When the verb in the main clause is in the present perfect, the verb in the subordinate clause may be either present or imperfect subjunctive, according as to whether it expresses a present or a past action:

Ha scritto che tu *debba* tornare subito = He has written that you should return at once.
Ha voluto che tu *rimanessi* a casa = He wanted you to stay at home.

The imperfect or past perfect subjunctive is also used in clauses expressing a condition,* and in independent sentences to express a wish that cannot be fulfilled:

Avesse dato retta a me! = Had he only listened to me! (Dare retta a = to pay attention to.)

and occasionally it is used instead of the present in such sentences as:

Volesse il cielo! = Would to heaven!

* See page 146.

Further Uses of the Subjunctive
The third type of subordinate clause, the adverbial clause, modifying a verb and introduced by a conjunction (as *sebbɛne*, or *benché*), has its verb in the subjunctive after certain of these conjunctions. These may best be listed under the different types of clause they introduce:

1. Purpose: perché } = so that, in order that
               affinché }
               di mɔdo = in such a way that
2. Time: prima che } = before
               avanti che }
               finché, finché . . . non = until, as long as
               (only followed by subjunctive when it contains the idea of doubt, uncertainty or possibility).
3. Condition: purché = provided that
               a meno che . . . non = unless
               nel caṣo che = in case
               dato che = given that
               se mai, se pure, se anche = even if
4. Concession: benché, sebbɛne = although
               non ostante che = in spite of the fact that
               per quanto = however much
5. Manner: come se, quasi = as if
6. Negation: sɛnza che, sɛnza che . . . non = without
7. Than-clause, introducing a comparison when implying uncertainty: di quel che, che non = than.

Examples:

1. *Purpose.*

   Studia molto *affinché pɔssa* vincere un prɛmio = He's studying a great deal so as to win a prize.

2. *Time.*

   Vɔglion partire *prima che* lɛi vɛnga = They want to go before she comes.
   Aspettate *finché* io tɔrni = Wait till I come back.

But:

   Finché l'autobus non si fɛrma, non si puɔ̀ scɛndere = Until the bus stops, you cannot get off.

3. *Condition.*

Glielo venderò *purché* mi *paghi* bene = I'll sell it to him so long as he pays me well.

4. *Concession.*

Benché abbia ricevuto tante lettere, non è contento = Although he's received so many letters, he's not satisfied.

5. *Manner.*

Trasalí *come se avesse visto* uno spettro = He started as if he had seen a ghost.

6. *Negation.*

Aprite la porta *senza che* lui se ne *accorga* = Open the door without his noticing. (Accorgersi *di* = to notice.)

7. *Than-clause.*

Quel ragazzo lavora meglio *che* tu *non pensi*, or: meglio *di quel che pensi* = That boy works better than you think.

Two further uses of the subjunctive remain to be considered: the indirect question and the indirect statement. The verb of an indirect question is in the subjunctive if it depends on a verb in the past tense or in the conditional, when there is uncertainty in the indirect statement:

Ci *chiese* se *potesse* venire = He asked us if he might come.
Avrebbe voluto sapere dove tu *fossi stato?* = Would he have wanted to know where you had been?

The verb of an indirect statement—that is, the verb in a clause depending on a verb of saying—is also in the subjunctive if the main verb is (1) negative, (2) interrogative or (3) in a past tense or the conditional, unless, in the case of (3), the speaker wishes to indicate that the indirect statement is true:

Non dico che non *sia* intelligente = I don't say that he's not clever.
Ha chiesto che *andasse* anche lo zio? = Has he asked for uncle to go too?
Dissero che il re *fosse morto* = They said that the king was dead.

In this last sentence the person who is repeating the statement is not absolutely certain that it is true: in the one that follows he is:

Dissero che il re morí ieri sera alle undici = They said the king died at eleven o'clock last night.

Study the verbs: *correre, giungere, piangere* and *rompere*.

Translation XIV

—Grazie, Signore, Lei è troppo gentile,— continuò Beppino. —Oggi per l'appunto sono libero, e se le fa veramente piacere. . . .—

Cosí finí per venire al teatro con me non solamente Beppino, ma anche tutta la sua numerosa e simpatica famiglia—la moglie, la sorella, il fratello, il nonno e quattro bambini. Ma che buona gente! Non vollero in nessun modo che io pagassi i biglietti, neppure il mio, malgrado tutte le mie proteste. E che ressa! Poche volte in vita mia ho visto tanto entusiasmo. Non era possibile prenotare i posti, tanta era la gente; anzi si dovette fare la coda. Ma all'aprirsi delle porte ci fu un pigia pigia e fra risa e grida ognuno si precipitò per entrare per primo, e io mi sentii trasportare su per le scale e a un buon posto nella galleria. Beppino perdette di vista alcuni membri della sua famiglia, ma non pareva preoccuparsene molto; era un po' piú ansiosa però, la moglie, che aveva perso una scarpa, ma fortunatamente la trovò piú tardi.

Non dimenticherò mai quel pubblico italiano: critico, persin severo; fischiò senza complimenti un cantante che non gli piaceva e non gli permise di continuare. Tutti conoscevano l'opera nota per nota, e le arie molto famose le cantava anche il pubblico, il che mi infastidí. Se il cantante era veramente buono, però, e l'esecuzione musicale eccellente, c'era nel pubblico un tal rapimento e silenzio che pareva tutti trattenessero il respiro, fino all'ultima nota, poi scoppiò una tempesta di applausi e di "bis" che non finivano piú. Per una certa aria di quel tenore cosí bravo gridarono "bis" sette volte! E per accontentarli il pover'uomo tornò a cantarlo sette volte!

Come si può imaginare era molto tardi quando uscimmo da teatro; due bimbi già si erano addormentati e noi tutti eravamo stanchi ma tanto soddisfatti. Io dovetti affrettarmi all'albergo per fare la valigia, perché partivo il giorno dopo. Tutti m'accompagnarono al tram, e dopo tante strette di mano e "addio" e "torni presto", lasciai finalmente quella brava gente.

Vocabulary

ciao = good-bye! so long!   accompagnare = to accompany
fischio = whistle   lagnarsi = to complain
saluto = greeting   raccontare = to relate, to tell

insieme = together

Exercise 29

1. I was glad that they had gone.
2. I thought that you were all in Italy.
3. If only he had never seen her!
4. Although she had not been the one to break the Venetian mirror, she kept on crying. (Say: Although it had not been she who had . . .; to keep on = to continue.)
5. Did your wife ask where you had been last night?
6. No, I got in without her seeing me.
7. Dear John,

> Do you know where I have come to spend my holidays? My father has always wanted me to see Italy, and now here I am at last! I have visited various famous cities: Pisa, Florence, Siena, Venice, and now I am in Milan, where I have met some of my Italian friends. Yesterday they took me to the theatre (accompanied me to . . .) to hear the opera. They all sang very well; but what interested me most was the Italian audience. What enthusiasm! If only you had seen it. (Omit "it" in translating.) What encores! (How many times encore!) A very good tenor had to come back and sing one of the songs they liked seven times. Seven times! On the other hand (d'altra parte), what whistling and shouts when there was one that couldn't sing! What a pity that you weren't here too with me! We would have had a good laugh together! (We would have laughed so much!)
> Don't reply to this; I may have to leave for England in a short time. And excuse this short letter; I'll have heaps of things to tell you (. . . a thousand things . . .); at least you can't complain that I haven't written. My greetings to your people. So long! Yours, Charles.

(Note: Use *tu* throughout this letter, which is obviously to an intimate friend.)

LESSON XXX

THE CONDITIONAL—NOTE ON *DOVERE* AND AUXILIARY VERBS

THE conditional is used to express future time in relation to a verb of saying, thinking and believing in the past; for example:

Direct statement: *Scriverò* la lεttera = I will write the letter.
Indirect statement present: Dice che *scriverà* la lεttera = He says he will write the letter.
Indirect statement past: Disse che *scriverεbbe* la lεttera = He said he would write the letter.

If the indirect statement in the conditional tense has not yet come true, the *conditional perfect* is used in Italian. The last example therefore implies that he has already written the letter, as he said he would; had he not done so the sentence would be:

Disse che *avrεbbe scritto* la lεttera.

It is often clear from the sentence that the action in the dependent clause has not yet been performed:

Risposi che avrεi fatto tutto il possibile per aiutarlo = I replied that I would do everything possible to help him.

In such cases, therefore, when translating from English, it must be remembered that Italian requires the conditional perfect where we would use the simple conditional.

The most common use of the conditional is in conditional sentences; sentences stating that *if* such a thing happened, something else depending on it *would* come about. The use of the tenses in such sentences is as follows:

1. When a condition is contrary-to-fact in the present, or doubtful in the future, the if-clause (stating the condition) is in the imperfect subjunctive, and the would-clause (drawing the conclusion) in the conditional:

Se avessi abbastanza denaro, comprεrεi un automọbile = If I had enough money, I should buy a car

(implying that I have not enough money—a condition contrary-to-fact in the present);

Se venisse in tɛmpo, potremmo partire insiɛme = If he came
in time, we could leave together

(a condition doubtful in the future).

2. When the if-clause refers to past time, the past perfect
subjunctive is used, and the would-clause is in the conditional
perfect:

Se avessi avuto abbastanza denaro, avrɛi comprato quell'automɔbile = If I had had enough money, I should have
bought that car.

3. Any other condition is expressed by the indicative:

Se Lɛi va in città, mi cɔmpri dell'inchiɔstro, per favore = If
you're going to town, buy me some ink, please.

Note that sometimes in Italian, and particularly in the
spoken language, the *imperfect indicative* is used in both clauses
of a contrary-to-fact condition in the past, instead of the past
perfect subjunctive and the conditional perfect:

Se avevo abbastanza denaro, compravo quell'automɔbile =
If I had had enough money, I should have bought that
car.

The conditional is also used idiomatically to express doubt or
uncertainty: *Chi è quello lì? Non saprɛi* = Who is that man
there? I don't know.

There remain two more points to consider before we finish
the last lesson of this little book. First the translation of
"should have" when it means "ought to have". The literal
translation of: "I should have read that book" = *Avrɛi lɛtto
quel libro* gives no idea of obligation, so we go to *dovere* and use
the conditional perfect followed by the infinitive:

Avrɛi dovuto lɛggere quel libro = I ought to have read that
book. It would be useful to list the meanings of the various
tenses of this semi-auxiliary verb:

Dɛvo lɛggere quel libro = I must, have to, am to read that
book.
Dovevo lɛggere quel libro = I had to, was to read that book.
Dovɛtti lɛggere quel libro = I had to read that book.
Dovrɔ lɛggere quel libro = I shall have to read that book.
Dovrɛi lɛggere quel libro = I should, ought to read that
book.
Ho dovuto lɛggere quel libro = I have had to read that book.
Avrɛi dovuto lɛggere quel libro = I ought to have read that
book.

ITALIAN

The second point is the use of the auxiliary with *dovere* when followed by an infinitive, for it is the *infinitive* which determines which auxiliary should be used. Study these examples:

Avrei dovuto *scrivere* quella lettera = I ought to have written that letter.
Sarebbe dovuto *andare* prima di me = He ought to have gone before me.

Four other verbs, besides *dovere*, when followed by an infinitive may take either auxiliary, according to which the infinitive usually takes: *potere, volere, cominciare* and *finire*:

Non è potuto venire? = Hasn't he been able to come?
Non ha potuto vederla = He hasn't been able to see her.
Ha cominciato a scrivere il libro = He has begun to write the book.
È cominciato a invecchiare = He has begun to get old.

(Verbs conjugated with *essere* are indicated in the Appendix and in the Vocabulary.)

Study these verbs: *condurre, distinguere, proteggere* and *trarre*.

Translation XV

La mattina dopo partii per Como in compagnia di alcuni americani che proseguivano per Parigi. Como è soltanto un'ora da Milano col direttissimo, e ci arrivai prima delle dieci. Dopo aver fatto un giro per la città mi decisi a salire colla funicolare a Brunate, piccolo borgo sopra una collina a est, da dove c'è una bella veduta del lago. Seduto su una panca a contemplare il panorama, tirai fuori la carta topografica a cercai di orientarmi. In basso si stendeva la città di Como colla sua baia, e con le sue colline oltre le quali si apre la pianura lombarda; in faccia e a destra, il lago, coi suoi monti alti e ripidi, e lontano lontano * all'orizzonte le maestose cime bianche delle Alpi, che brillavano al sole. —Sono ora nel paese di Don Abbondio e di Lucia,— pensai, ricordandomi del famoso romanzo, —e al di là di quelle montagne all'est ci dev'essere Lecco sull'altro ramo del lago—. Consultai di nuovo la carta, pensando, —Invece di rimanere a Como, preferirei un posto più solitario sul lago, un po' fuori di mano. Vediamo un po'.—Seguii col dito l'itinerario del piroscafo: —Como, Cernobbio, Cadenabbia, Bellagio. . . .

* Adverbs and adjectives may be repeated to give emphasis.

Ecco un luogo ridente, su un promontorio, all'incontro dei tre rami del lago; sí, questo va bene. Ci sono cinque o sei alberghi non molto grandi. Tanto meglio.— Scesi di nuovo a Como, e, ritirata la valigia dal deposito m'imbarcai sul piroscafo per Bellagio.

—Buona sera,— dissi al proprietario che stava oziando sulla soglia del suo albergo, —Ha una camera libera?—

—Si accomodi, Signore,— e data la valigia a un portiere che si fece avanti, mi precedette nel vestibolo.

L'albergo era piccolo, ma bianco e pulito; sul davanti aveva un bel giardinetto con balcone e pergola che si stendeva fino alla riva del lago.

—Si fermerà molto?— mi chiese il proprietario.

—No, soltanto tre o quattro giorni.—

—Allora Le posso offrire una bella camera con terrazza e veduta sul lago, lire 2,000 al giorno, tutto compreso; in piú la tassa di soggiorno e per il servizio il dieci per cento. Ce ne sarebbe un'altra piú piccola e senza terrazza con veduta sulle montagne per 1,800. Tutte e due sono belle e ariose, con acqua corrente. Le vuol vedere, Signore?—

—Sí, grazie,— E benché fosse un po' piú caro di quel che avrei voluto pagare, finii per lasciarmi tentare dalla bella vista e scelsi quella con la terrazza.

Ma ogni cosa ha la sua fine. Venne il mio ultimo giorno di vacanza; mi bagnai per l'ultima volta in quelle acque fresche e feci l'ultima gita in barca col vecchio barcaiuolo Antonio. La mattina della partenza mi alzai prestissimo, e, fatta la valigia mi feci portare il caffè sul terrazzino. Mentre mangiavo guardavo passar le barche da pesca con le vele rossicce. Poi a un tratto vidi il mio vecchio amico Antonio, il quale, lasciati i remi, si alzò in piedi, e agitando in aria il beretto, mi gridò:—

—Arrivederci, Signore, buon viaggio; si ricordi di Antonio e torni presto.—

—Certamente—, pensai salendo a bordo del piroscafo per Como, la mia prima tappa del viaggio di ritorno, —certamente, mio caro Antonio, mi ricorderò di te; e, in quanto al tornare presto; sí, anche questo te lo posso promettere: tornerò nel tuo bel paese il piú presto possibile.—

Vocabulary

barca a remi = rowing-boat	prezzo = price
conoscenza = acquaintance	rabbia = anger, rage
molo = jetty	Che rabbia! = How annoying!
motoscafo = motor-boat	importare = to matter

Exercise 30

1. They said they would come at three, but it is half-past and they have not arrived yet.

2. If you go to the theatre, don't come back as late as you did the other time.

3. If I had that book, I should study.

4. If I had had that book I should have studied.

5. If I have that book I shall study.

6. If he had asked *me* where the church was, I should have told him straight away. (Translate in two ways.)

7. He ought to have come earlier if he had wanted to see me.

8. If I had not arrived at Como too late to take the steamer for Bellagio I should not have got to know Antonio (Should not have known . . .). That old boatman with his blue eyes and white beard and with that queer red cap was lounging about on the jetty when I arrived at a run (running), my suitcase in my hand, just in time to see the steamer leave. . . . "How annoying! Who knows how long I'll have to wait!" I thought. "I'm sorry you've missed the steamer. Would you like a boat, sir?" asked the old man, coming up to me. "Thank you," I replied, "it's a bit far to go in a rowing-boat." "Oh, but I have a motor-boat, sir." "No, thank you; I'm afraid that would cost too much." "But, sir, you want to go to Bellagio, and I want to go there too; my home is there (say: *there* is my house . . .), and my wife and children are expecting (waiting for) me for supper. Let's go together; if you wish to pay me, pay me the price of the steamer ticket; if you don't want to pay me, it doesn't make any difference; I shall be going all the same." And so I ended by going with Antonio and in getting to know one of the nicest men I have ever met.

CONCLUSION

Lesson XXX brings us to the end of this little book, and the student who has worked through it conscientiously should now be able to go forward on his own account. His first aim should be to read as much Italian as possible. A beginning could be made with the readers, short stories and plays in Harrap's modern language series, which are provided with notes and vocabularies. The easiest to start with would be: *Andiamo in Italia. Venti scenette italiane*, by Christabel Fowler and Teresa Della Torre; or: E. Goggio, *A New Italian Reader for Beginners*, which contains anecdotes, short stories and a few poems; and three small books of Italian conversation, based on topics of everyday interest, by C. E. Kany and C. Speroni: *Elementary, Intermediate* and *Advanced Italian Conversation*. Two books in the bilingual series might then be tried: *Introduction to Italian*, by Ena Makin; and L. Pirandello, *Quattro novelle*, translated by V. M. Jeffrey; but keep the English side covered up as long as possible! Other editions in the annotated series are, in ascending order of difficulty: (1) C. Collodi, *Avventure di Pinocchio* (the Italian child's classic), ed. E. Goggio, (2) *Modern Italian Short Stories*, ed. T. G. Bergin, a collection of contemporary authors, mostly of the generation that came to fame between the two world wars, as C. Alvaro, M. Bontempelli, G. A. Borgese, G. Lipparini, G. Papini; (3) Massimo T. D'Azeglio, *I miei ricordi*, edited with notes by V. Cioffari and J. van Horne; and (4) A. Manzoni, *I promessi sposi* (the first eight chapters of this famous novel which contain a story in themselves), ed. Geddes and Wilkins.

For those who are interested in plays the Harrap series includes: *Six Easy Italian Plays* (very farcical and of no literary merit, but useful for learning colloquial idiom), ed. E. Goggio; *Modern Italian One-Act Plays* (three in number: G. Verga, *Cavalleria rusticana*, G. Giacosa, *Diritti dell'anima*, and R. Bracco, *Pietro Caruso*), ed. C. A. Swanson; and a play by Pirandello: *Così è, (se vi pare)*. In addition to notes and vocabularies, many of these books have an introduction telling briefly about the author and his work and an appendix containing exercises and drill in idiomatic phrases.

By this time, however, the enthusiastic student will be looking for a dictionary of his own. There is not a large choice; but

it is varied, ranging from the very small pocket ones, such as
the Collins Gem edition and the similar one in the E.F.G. series,
Eyre & Spottiswoode, to the large ones, *e.g.*, G. Orlandi,
Dizionario italiano–inglese, inglese–italiano, Signorelli, Milan,
1950; or N. Spinelli, *Dizionario scolastico italiano–inglese,
inglese–italiano*, S.E.I., Turin, 1951; while those who require a
dictionary including commercial and technical terms have a
choice of the following: *Modern Italian–English, English–
Italian Dictionary*, with commercial supplement, by Lysle-
Severino, Allen & Unwin; N. Spinelli, *Dizionario commerciale
italiano–inglese, inglese–italiano*, S.E.I., Turin, 1951; and G.
Marolli, *Dizionario tecnico inglese–italiano, italiano–inglese*, Le
Monnier, Florence, 1950. Between the very small and these
larger dictionaries come three medium-sized ones; N. Spinelli,
Dizionario tascabile italiano–inglese, inglese–italiano, S.E.I.,
Turin, revised ed. 1952, 2 vols.; J. Purves, *Dictionary of
Modern Italian*, Routledge, 1953 and *Cassell's Italian–English,
English–Italian Dictionary*, 1958. If an all-Italian dictionary is
required a really sound investment would be: G. Cappuccini
and B. Migliorini, *Vocabolario della lingua italiana*, Paravia,
Turin, revised ed. 1958.

With the knowledge he now has and with the help of a dictionary the student will be surprised at the rapid progress he
will make in reading contemporary novels and short stories.
One of the main characteristics of the neo-realist writers of
post-war Italy (*i.e.*, of post world war II) is the natural spon-
taneity and unselfconscious freshness of their stories, which are
told in a correspondingly simple and straightforward style.
Most of the following, therefore, will be found fairly easy to
read: L. Bartolini, *Ladri di biciclette* (which made a famous
film); E. Vittorini, *Conversazione in Sicilia*, and *Il garofano
rosso*; G. Berto, *Il cielo è rosso*, and *Il brigante*; C. Pavese, *La
luna e i falò*, and *Prima che il gallo canti*; and, with an interesting present-day Florentine background: V. Pratolini, *Il
quartiere, Un eroe del nostro tempo*, and *Cronache di poveri
amanti*; while G. Marotta's *L'oro di Napoli* and *San Gennaro
non dice mai no* have contemporary Naples for their scene. Two
more might be mentioned, rather more difficult than those just
listed, and in such complete contrast to one another as to seem
to come from two different worlds, yet both giving, in their
different ways, a true-to-life picture of Italy today: the tragic
and impressive: *Cristo si è fermato a Eboli* by C. Levi; and the
delightfully satirical and witty: *Don Camillo, Piccolo Mondo*,
by G. Guareschi, while many of the outstanding Italian novels

which have appeared recently, Carlo Cassola's *La ragazza di Bube*, Einaudi, Turin, 1958 may be recommended, with Giuseppe Tomasi di Lampedusa's *Il Gattopardo*, Feltrinelli, Milan, 1959, as two of the finest, the latter became internationally famous almost as soon as published.

While reading Italian, grammatical studies should not be neglected if the student wishes to learn to write Italian correctly. He would be well advised to attend some class, or arrange for a teacher or an educated Italian to correct his efforts. The following will be useful, with or without a teacher: V. Cioffari, *Italian Review Grammar*, Harrap, intended for those who have studied Italian for at least a year, and offering many exercises in conversation and drill in colloquial and idiomatic Italian; W. Shewring, *Italian Prose Usage*, a supplement to Italian grammars, Cambridge University Press; and if he would like to study the grammar and read about the language in Italian, the student will find the following of interest and not too difficult: B. Migliorini and F. Chiapelli, *Lingua e stile*, 1952, Le Monnier, Florence; B. Migliorini, *La lingua nazionale*, 1947, the same publisher; G. Devoto and D. Massaro, *Grammatica italiana*, La Nuova Italia, Florence, 1953. Also the following: E. Bianchi, *La lingua italiana*, Salani, Florence, 1943, illustrated, an elementary book on the history of the Italian language, on its structure and position in the Romance family, containing long passages from the classics, both prose and verse in a section devoted to the art of writing; and B. Migliorini, *Conversazioni sulla lingua*, a series of short talks given on the wireless on various aspects of language study, such as: meanings, metaphors, the disappearance of words, the influence of biblical language on Italian, Spanish words in Italian, etc., Le Monnier, Florence, 1949; while a more difficult, but entertaining and at the same time very useful and well-informed book about foreign words which have passed into Italian as a result of the last war and which gives, to the observant reader, an interesting glimpse of contemporary Italy, is: A. Menarini, *Profili di vita italiana nelle parole nuove*, Le Monnier, Florence, 1951.

To the student of the history of Italian literature the following manuals may be recommended: V. Rossi, *Storia della letteratura italiana*, new edition brought up to date by U. Bosco, 1943, 3 vols., Vallardi, Milan, and rather more detailed: N. Sapegno, *Compendio di storia della letteratura italiana*, 1948, 3 vols., La Nuova Italia, Florence; and shorter than either of these: A. Momigliano, *Storia della letteratura italiana*, in one volume, G. Principato, Milan, new ed. 1947, all of which contain full and up-to-date bibliographies. There are many anthologies of Italian literature, a useful one would be *Antologia di letteratura italiana per stranieri*, ed. O. Prosciutti and U. Pittola, Perugia University, 1952; and two inexpensive ones of contemporary works are: *Poeti del novecento*, compiled by G. Spagnoletti, Edizioni scolastiche Mondadori, Milan, 1958; and *Narratori del novecento*, by L. Fiorentino, and the same publisher, 1960; while the *Oxford Book of Italian Verse*, revised and augmented by C. Dionisotti, 1952, is a treasure coveted by many English students of Italian.

For the student who aspires to read Dante in the original there is J. D. Sinclair's edition of the *Divina Commedia* in 3 vols., John Lane, the Bodley Head, revised ed. 1948. This contains brief but adequate notes, an admirable commentary and a very readable English version in prose printed opposite the Italian text. An introduction to Dante studies should include Dean Church's *Essay on Dante* (in *Dante and St. Anselm*, Routledge); E. G. Gardner, *Dante*, Dent; P. H. Wicksteed, *From Vita Nuova to Paradiso* (Manchester University Press); D. G. Rossetti's version of the *Vita nuova* (or in the original in the Temple Classics); and in Italian: M. Barbi, *Dante, Vita, opere e fortuna*, Sansoni, Florence, 1933, and U. Cosmo, *Guida a Dante* (this last has an English translation: *A Handbook to Dante Studies*, trans. by D. Moore, Oxford, Blackwell, 1949). Useful Dante bibliography will, of course, also be found after the relative chapters in each of the manuals of History of Literature mentioned above.

And so, in the hope that this short bibliography will prove useful and will also be an urge to further endeavour, we take our leave of the patient reader, and while advising him to "read, read more, read much more", we would wish him, most cordially, "Buono studio e . . . buon divertimento!"

PART II

KEY TO EXERCISES AND TRANSLATIONS

Preliminary Exercise

1. Virtú, portò, perché, mercoledí, credé, onestà, caffè, città, sincerità.
2. arena (ah-ráy-nah), cupola (kóo-poh-lah), incognito (een-cón-yee-toh), pianoforte (peeah-noh-fáwr-tay), vermicelli (vair-mee-chéll-ee), terra cotta (tay-rrah-cáw-tah), ultimatum (ool-tee-máh-toom), Galli-Curci (Gah-lee Cóor-chee), Marco Polo (Mahr-coh Páw-loh), Medici (Máy-dee-chee).

Exercise 1 (a)

1. Maria è una donna e Piero è un uomo.
2. Maria e Piero hanno una casa.
3. Piero e Maria hanno un figlio e una figlia.
4. Chi ha un fratello? Maria ha un fratello e anche una sorella.
5. Ha Piero uno zio? Sí, Piero ha uno zio e anche una zia.
6. Dov'è una porta e dov'è una finestra?
7. Chi ha un libro? Piero ha un libro? Che cosa ha Maria? Maria ha uno specchio.
8. Dov'è uno sbaglio? Ecco uno sbaglio in un libro.

Exercise 1 (b)

1. Mary is a woman and Peter is a man.
2. Mary and Peter have a house.
3. Peter and Mary have a son and daughter. (Note that in Italian the article must be repeated before each noun.)
4. Who has a brother? Mary has a brother and also a sister.
5. Has Peter an uncle? Yes, Peter has an uncle and also an aunt.
6. Where is a door and where is a window?
7. Who has a book? Has Peter a book? What has Mary? Mary has a mirror.
8. Where is a mistake? Here is a mistake in a book.

Exercise 1 (c)

1. Maria ha una casa e Piero ha una casa.
2. Piero ha un figlio e una figlia.
3. Ha Maria una zia? Sí, Maria ha una zia e anche uno zio.
4. Dov'è uno sbaglio? Ecco uno sbaglio.
5. Chi ha un libro? Maria ha un libro. Maria dà un libro a Piero.
6. Maria ha un fratello e una sorella.
7. Che cosa ha Piero in una mano? Piero ha un libro in una mano.
8. Maria ha uno specchio? Sí, Maria ha uno specchio.

Exercise 2 (a)

1. Vendo una vacca e compro un gatto.

vendi	compri
vende	compra
vendiamo	compriamo
vendete	comprate
vendono	comprano

2. Mentre scrivo, uso una penna, inchiostro e un foglio.

   scrivi, usi
   scrive, usa
   scriviamo, usiamo
   scrivete, usate
   scrivono, usano

3. Quando leggo, guardo un libro.

   leggi, guardi
   legge, guarda
   leggiamo, guardiamo
   leggete, guardate
   leggono, guardano

(Note that the g of *leggere* has the hard sound before the -*o* in the first person singular and third person plural; otherwise it is soft as the *j* in *July* in the other persons, as in the infinitive.)

Exercise 2 (b)

1. Io parlo con Piero.
   tu parli
   egli, ella, lui, lei, esso, essa parla
   noi parliamo
   voi parlate
   loro, essi, esse parlano

Exercise 2 (c)

1. Who finds a book? I find a book.
2. Are Mary and Peter speaking? Yes, they are speaking.
3. Is Mary writing a letter to Peter?
4. Yes, and while she is writing I am looking at a book.
5. What is Peter buying today?
6. Today Peter is buying a book.

Exercise 2 (d)

1. Dov'è una tavola?
2. Vende una vacca e compra un gatto.
3. Scrivono una lettera a Maria.
4. Mentre lei legge io scrivo.
5. Che cosa vedi? Io vedo una donna e un uomo, un ragazzo e una ragazza.
6. Lei compra uno specchio e io compro un libro.
7. Parlano italiano Maria e Piero? Sí parlano italiano.
8. Lui guarda Maria mentre lei scrive una lettera.

Exercise 3 (a)

1. Dov'è la donna? La donna è a casa.
2. I fratelli e le sorelle di Maria sono in città. Comprano i cappelli e le cravatte.
3. Lo zio di Piero è alto, ma la zia è molto piccola.
4. Ecco la casa nuova. Dov'è l'entrata?
5. Il tetto è rosso e i muri sono gialli.
6. Questo muro è alto ma l'altro è basso.
7. Il giardino è bellino, l'erba è bella e ci sono molti alberi.
8. Piero guarda lo zio: perché ha un cappello giallo, una cravatta azzurra e i calzini sono rossi.
9. Maria non è in casa, è in città e compra gli specchi.

Exercise 3 (b)

1. Where is the woman? The woman is at home.
2. Mary's brothers and sisters are in town; they are buying the hats and ties.
3. Peter's uncle is tall, but his aunt is very small. (The article is often used instead of the possessive "his", "her", etc., when the context makes it quite plain whose "aunt", etc., is meant.)
4. Here is the new house. Where is the door?
5. The roof is red, but the walls are yellow.
6. This wall is high, but the other is low.

7. The garden is pretty; the grass is lovely and there are many trees.
8. Peter is looking at uncle, because he has a yellow hat, a blue tie and his (the) socks are red.
9. Mary is not at home; she is in town, and she is buying the mirrors.

Exercise 3 (c)

1. Gli alberi sono molto alti.
2. La casa nuova ha un tetto rosso e muri gialli. È in un giardino molto bellino.
3. Le finestre sono molto alte, ma la porta è bassa.
4. Lo zio è a casa ma la zia è in città. Lei compra un cappello.
5. Lui è molto alto ma la zia è piccola.
6. Questo ragazzo compra una penna, ma l'altro ragazzo compra calzini e una cravatta.
7. La casa ha cinque porte e diciassette finestre.
8. Loro non scrivono le lettere; guardano il cappello giallo e i calzini rossi di Piero.

Exercise 4 (a)

1. The mother opens the window while the child is sleeping.
2. I do not understand why the lady is going today and not tomorrow.
3. We understand this word, but not the other.
4. This house has twelve rooms.
5. The dining-room has a terrace, and the two large rooms have balconies.
6. The dining-room and the terrace are lovely, but the kitchen is too small.
7. We open the window and we see the garden.
8. We have a very fine garden.
9. Where is Peter's sister? She is in the kitchen.
10. They open the door and they see the terrace.
11. The drawing-room is not small and the chairs are comfortable.
12. The drawing-room is on the ground floor, but the study is on the upper floor.
13. Where do you sleep, Mary and Lucy? We sleep in a room on the upper floor.
14. Do you find Italian easy, madam? (or miss?).
15. Yes, I find Italian easy. Spanish is easy too; but I prefer Italian.

Exercise 4 (b)

1. Questa sedia è molto comoda, ma preferisco l'altra.
2. Non capisco questa parola.
3. Capisce Lei questo libro?
4. Dove sono le signorine? Partono oggi?
5. Sí, partono oggi. Sono in cucina con Piero.
6. Piero dorme al pianterreno.
7. La camera di Maria è al piano superiore.
8. È in casa Piero? No, è in città.
9. Sono in città Maria e Piero? Sí, comprano mele.
10. Perché partono oggi? Non capisco perché.
11. La cucina è piccola, ma la sala da pranzo è grande.
12. Comprano una casa nuova (or: una nuova casa) con un giardino.
13. Preferiamo una casa in città.
14. Ecco lo studio. Piero apre la porta e vediamo lo zio. Lo zio dorme:
15. Mentre lo zio dorme, la zia è in città. È in città con Maria. Comprano cravatte, calzini, cappelli e un soprabito per lo zio.

Exercise 5 (a)

1. Mary is in the garden and Aunt is in the dining-room.
2. John gives some apples to the guests and then leaves for the town in Uncle's car.
3. Uncle is with the children in the drawing-room.
4. What have you got in your pocket, Peter? I have two handkerchiefs and a tie of Uncle's.
5. Where is Peter? He is in the study with the girl.
6. The dining-room chairs are on the balcony.
7. They are looking in the mirror. What do they see?
8. They see Aunt's hat and gloves. They are on the table.
9. Where is Uncle's yellow hat? Uncle's yellow hat is in the river.
10. Poor Uncle! John and Peter buy a new hat for Uncle.
11. Haven't we any bread? Yes, it is on the table in the kitchen.
12. What is there in the river? I do not see anything.
13. Have you any yellow ties, please?
14. No, sir, but I have some white and blue ties.
15. John is very lazy! He never writes to anybody.

Exercise 5 (b)

1. Maria è nello studio con lo zio. Scrivono lettere.
2. Piero compra calzini, fazzoletti e cravatte da un ragazzo nella strada.
3. Giovanni compra un cappello e guanti dallo stesso ragazzo.
4. È un ragazzo molto povero; non ha scarpe.
5. Che cosa ha nella tasca? Ho tre fazzoletti e una cravatta.
6. Che cosa vedi tu nel fiume, Giovanni? Non vedo niente.
7. Guardo nello specchio: vedo i tre bambini col gatto.
8. Maria cerca il gatto nel giardino.
9. Dov'è il pane? Non abbiamo pane.
10. L'uomo nel salotto è il fratello di Giovanni.
11. Dov'è la cravatta di Giovanni? È sulla tavola nella sala da pranzo con i guanti della zia.
12. Non vedo né la cravatta né i guanti.
13. Non ha dell'inchiostro? Sí, è sulla tavola nello studio.
14. Questa sedia è per l'ospite. Ma non è molto comoda.
15. Il libro che Lei cerca è nello studio.

Exercise 6 (a)

1. He sold the two fine horses last week.
2. Three weeks ago I lost a lovely ring in the garden.
3. Two days ago I received a registered letter and a parcel, and I signed a receipt.
4. The cook offered the postman some tea.
5. Last week the postman brought the cook a lovely red rose.
6. The postman has a good salary? but he is of a poor family.
7. Where did Cook go yesterday? She went to the post office and met the postman. She is a good friend of the postman.
8. I went to the post office too, and at the entrance I met the doctor.
9. The doctor is a good friend of the lawyer.
10. Then we met the lawyer too in the writing-room.
11. I bought twelve postcards and twenty stamps; I finished a letter and then we went to a café.
12. Yesterday the postman brought two postcards from the aunt in America.
13. He is a handsome man, the postman, and the cook is not ugly.

Exercise 6 (b)

1. Vendei un bell'anello ieri e comprai questi libri.
2. Perdé un bell'anello tre settimane fa.
3. Dove perdette l'anello? Nel giardino.
4. La zia ricevé un pacco raccomandato ieri e firmò una ricevuta.
5. Maria fu alla posta con la cuoca. Comprarono francobolli e cartoline.
6. Il fratello di Maria è un uomo molto bello.
7. Ricevei una lunga lettera dallo zio ieri e anche due cartoline e un gran pacco.
8. Non ricevé niente ieri Lei, Signor Pazzi?
9. No, ieri non ricevei niente.
10. I teatri in questa città sono molto belli.
11. Sí, fummo al teatro la settimana scorsa.
12. L'avvocato ricevette una cartolina dal dottore ieri.
13. L'anno scorso comprò una macchina, due cavalli, una vacca e una casa con un gran giardino: ora è molto povero.

Exercise 7 (a)

1. When he was in Florence he went to the library every day.
2. Where did you go? We used to go to a café in Tornabuoni Street.
3. Tornabuoni street was one of the smart streets in that town.
4. I met the lawyer in town yesterday. He was in Tornabuoni Street, looking at the new books in the bookshop.
5. He was looking for that book on the history of Italy which we saw in Rome last week.
6. Do you see that old woman without shoes? Once she was very rich; now she is very poor.
7. This morning I was looking for Cook. Where was she? Wasn't she in the kitchen?
8. No, she was in town. She was buying meat and vegetables at the market.
9. Yesterday I met Mary's brother and the postman in town; they were talking to that girl from the bookshop.
10. What a lovely study Mr. Pazzi used to have! It was a large room with a balcony and two windows.
11. The desk was in front of the balcony, and on the round table near the door there was a lovely lamp.
12. It had a beautiful green carpet too, and a large bookcase with many books.

Exercise 7 (b)

1. Andava in chiesa tutti i giorni quando era a Firenze?
2. Sí, andava colla zia tutte le mattine.
3. Scriveva a Giovanni tutte le settimane.
4. Cercavo il fratello di Maria. Dove era? (or Dov'era?)
5. Era nella libreria e parlava coll'avvocato.
6. Il dottore entrò mentre loro parlavano.
7. L'avvocato finiva una lettera quando loro entrarono nello studio.
8. Guardava l'avvocato che era vicino alla scrivania.
9. Cercavano quel giornale che quelle donne leggevano.
10. La cuoca era al mercato stamattina, Signora Pazzi?
11. Sí, comprava carne e legumi, pane e vino.
12. Hanno vini buoni al mercato? No, non sono molto buoni.

Exercise 8 (a)

1. Who is that gentleman? He is one of my friends (or a friend of mine).
2. I am writing to a girl friend of mine in Rome?
3. For whom is that registered parcel? It is for my father.
4. How much bread is there in the kitchen, Mary?
5. There isn't any bread; that boy ate all our bread yesterday.
6. Why do you not buy a bookcase for your books?
7. What good wine! Do you drink wine every day?
8. That cook of theirs is very good.
9. What a good fire that is! Yes, Cook always has a good fire.
10. How much wine does that man drink every day? He usually drinks five or six bottles every day.
11. That wardrobe (cupboard) is for my clothes, and this is for yours.
12. Which trunk is yours, miss? This is mine, that is my mother's and that one over there is that gentleman's with the beard.

Exercise 8 (b)

1. Chi è quel signore dalla barba? È un amico di mio padre.
2. Mio padre e mia madre furono in città ieri. Incontrarono quel tuo amico nella libreria (or: quel suo amico).
3. Di chi è questo baule? È di mia madre.
4. Quanti libri ci sono in quello scaffale?
5. Abbiamo diversi (molti) vini buoni, Signore; quale preferisce, rosso o bianco?

6. Un mio amico comprò quella macchina ieri. Quale? Quella macchina lí nell'autorimessa.
7. Che cosa vende quella vecchia? Vende fazzoletti e calzini.
8. Dove compra Lei i Suoi cappelli? Quel Suo cappello nuovo (or: quel Suo nuovo cappello) è molto elegante.
9. Quale vestito preferisce? Preferisco quello azzurro.
10. Quel suo cappello verde è molto vecchio. Non comprò uno * nuovo la settimana scorsa?
11. Molti miei libri sono nel mio baule.
12. Quanti bauli ha Lei, Signore? Ho due bauli. Questo è il mio e quello là è anche il mio.

Exercise 9 (a)

1. When I sell the house I shall buy a car.
2. What time will the train arrive?
3. It will arrive at half-past five. We shall have time to take tea before going to the station.
4. We usually have tea at five.
5. What time will your son arrive, madam? He will arrive by the twenty-to-eight train.
6. When will they leave? John leaves tonight at midnight, but his brothers will leave tomorrow morning for Florence.
7. We generally have dinner at one (eat at one), but tomorrow we shall dine at half-past twelve and take the two-o'clock train.
8. It is eleven o'clock and Cook is still at the market.
9. What will she be buying at the market? She will be buying lots of things at the market, and she will be talking to her friends.
10. According to my father, Cook is a clever woman, but she doesn't look it.
11. I am sure that my son would not sign this letter.
12. Journeys by train are not always comfortable.

Exercise 9 (b)

1. Che ore sono? Sono le tre e mezzo.
2. A che ora arriva il treno? Alle otto meno un quarto.
3. Quanti cappelli ha quella donna? Ne avrà nove, credo.
4. Quando venderemo i cavalli, compreremo una macchina.
5. Sono sicuro che mia madre non comprerebbe quel cappello.

* *uno*, pronoun, does not have the shortened forms like the definite article.

6. Prendiamo il tè alle quattro e mezzo generalmente, ma domani prenderemo il tè alle quattro prima di andare alla stazione.
7. L'avvocato manderà la lettera al giudice domani.
8. Quando arriverà a casa? Non prima di mezzanotte.
9. Stasera i suoi quattro figli saranno a casa.
10. Comprò ieri un cappello grigio e domani comprerà una sciarpa e dei guanti grigi.
11. Sono le quattro meno un quarto e la cuoca è ancora al mercato.
12. Secondo la signora Pazzi la nostra cuoca sarebbe pigra.

Exercise 10 (a)

1. Today we have guests to dinner.
2. Cook has gone to the market to buy meat and vegetables, and the maid has washed the plates, the cups and glasses.
3. Mary will help the maid to lay the table and clean the forks, spoons and knives.
4. When she has helped the maid she will go to the station to meet the guests.
5. The woman had washed all the plates, but she had not cleaned the knives.
6. When you see the doctor he will already have sold his car.
7. As soon as she had broken a cup she let a bottle fall too.
8. Has she broken all the things on the tray? Yes, all.
9. They had been at the doctor's house when they met the lawyer.
10. Will they already have arrived when Charles returns home? Yes, they will already be in the house.
11. She may be intelligent, that maid, but she doesn't look it. She has already broken twelve plates and two glasses. She also let three bottles fall, and we have lost some good wine.
12. What time did Cook return from the market today? She arrived home very late, I think. She must have met the postman on the way.

Exercise 10 (b)

1. Abbiamo invitato il signore e la signora Pazzi (i signori Pazzi) a pranzo oggi.
2. La cameriera (la donna) ha già apparecchiato per dodici.
3. Aveva già pulito i coltelli e le forchette quando la cuoca tornò dal mercato.

4. La cuoca era stata al mercato molto tempo perché aveva perduto la borsa.
5. Appena ebbe perduto la borsa, parlò col poliziotto.
6. Incontrò anche il postino stamane.
7. C'erano molte cose sul vassoio; piatti, bicchieri, tazze e piattini.
8. Ha rotto molte cose? Sí, due tazze, tre piattini e cinque piatti
9. Appena ebbe apparecchiato, gli ospiti arrivarono.
10. Avrà veduto Maria, crede?
11. Ha perduto la borsa nel treno stamane.
12. Tutti i miei libri erano in quel baule che ho mandato a Napoli.

Exercise 11 (a)

1. I've lost my trunk. Have you seen it?
2. No, I've lost my suitcase; I've looked for it everywhere, but I haven't found it yet.
3. Hasn't the porter taken it to the train?
4. No; he may have left it at the hotel.
5. Isn't it already in the carriage? No, I've looked in the carriage; perhaps I've left it in the waiting-room.
6. Have you bought the tickets, madam? No, I have not bought them yet.
7. Has Cook brought the bread and butter and fruit? Yes, she has brought them; she has brought some sausage and a bit of ham too.
8. Where is that porter? Haven't you found him, John? But the train is going and we shall be going without trunks.
9. Here comes the porter. Here he is! Let's go and meet him. But he's got some red roses in his hand!
10. Good Lord! Red roses! But the trunks! Where are they? Where are the trunks? Oh, here they are; here they are at last!
11. Now we are ready. But where is Mary? Run, run, Mary; the train is going. We're off at last. Good-bye, good-bye.
12. But who were those red roses for? They were for Cook.
13. Poor Cook! We've lost her lovely red roses. Mary has let them fall out of the carriage window.

Exercise 11 (b)

1. Abbiamo perduto le nostre valigie, le ha vedute, facchino?
2. No, Signora, non le ho vedute.
3. Le ho cercate dappertutto nella carrozza.

4. Compra i biglietti, per favore, Giovanni.
5. Giovanni e Maria, andate a comprare i biglietti.
6. Ha della frutta? No, non ne ho.
7. Vado io a comprare della frutta? Sí, vada a comprare
   frutta e un po' di prosciutto (or: va' a . . .).
8. Vende anche salame? Sí, lo vende.
9. Compriamo della frutta, pane e burro e un po' di prosciutto.
10. Ha portato anche le salsicce? Si, eccole.
11. Perché non ha portato il baule? Lo ha lasciato nel ristorante
    (or: L'ha lasciato . . .).
12. Andremo noi a cercarlo?
13. No, bambini, rimanete qui, perderete il treno.

Exercise 12 (a)

1. On going out of the post office I met the dentist.
2. Where is the chemist's, please, madam? There is one at the
   corner, miss; there it is.
3. While he was crossing the square a policeman stopped him
   and asked him for his passport.
4. What lovely red roses! Give me one, please!
5. They are not mine, they are Cook's; but I will give you one
   with pleasure.
6. While speaking of it to him (or to her) he missed the bus
   and went home on foot.
7. There is no bus; let us take a carriage. Look, there is one
   in the square, waiting.
8. While she was opening the box, all were looking at her.
9. Have you been to Florence? Yes, sir, we are coming from
   there now.
10. Have you been to Milan, madam? Yes, I've been there.
11. Wait for me, wait for me. We're not waiting for anyone.
    The train is going. Have you given the tip to the porter?
    Yes, I have given it him.
12. Have they given us the tickets? Yes, they have (given
    them to us). And has the porter got his tip? Yes, he has.

Exercise 12 (b)

1. Uscendo dalla chiesa incontrarono il dentista e il dottore.
2. C'era una grande scatola in quel cassetto. L'ha trovata lei?
3. Sí, gliel'ha data.
4. Perché non me lo dà? L'ha già dato a loro.
5. Camminando per via Tornabuoni la cuoca incontrò il
   postino.

6. Ha perduto il suo passaporto. L'ha veduto Lei?
7. No, ma il facchino l'ha trovato. Glielo darà.
8. Gliene dia (or: *dagliene, dategliene*); ma non ne ho piú.
9. Dov'è quella chiesa famosa? Alla cantonata, non la vede?
10. Il dentista le ha dato una ricevuta? Sí, me l'ha data.
11. Hai comprato i biglietti? Sí, li ho comprati e li ho dati a Maria.
12. Ve li ha dati? (or: *Glieli,* or *te li*). Io glieli ho dati. Perché non li avete dati loro? Perché non ce ne aveva dato lui. E perché non ve ne aveva dato? Perché non ne aveva.

Exercise 13 (a)

1. Do not give it to him; give it to her.
2. I met her in town today, but not him.
3. Have you seen the lake? Yes, we went there today. The water was very calm and there were many boats.
4. These sheets are very old; they are not for the guest; let us look for some new ones.
5. This telegram is for you, not for me.
6. The boats arrived at the port laden with fish. (Note carico *di* = laden *with*.)
7. Are the chemists not open today? Yes, madam, they are open.
8. Has the little girl learnt to write already? Yes, she has written a letter by herself.
9. The duke has a long white beard and his hair is white. He is old, but his wife is older than he.
10. The old woman was sleeping; she still had that book in her hand, and the cat was on her knees, sleeping too.
11. The members of the Turin Alpine Club have arrived today.
12. What a girl she is! Yesterday she lost two pairs of gloves in the train, and today in the kitchen she has dropped six eggs (drop = let to fall).
13. Give me a clean towel, please.

Exercise 13 (b)

1. Lo dia a me, non a lui (or: dallo a . . ., datelo a . . .).
2. Quei due uomini con i buoi arriveranno domani.
3. Incontrai loro in città stamane, ma non ho veduto lei.
4. Quel libro era scritto da lui.
5. Questa lettera è per me non è per lui.
6. Mi porti quelle lenzuola, per favore (or: portami . . . portatemi). Eccole.

7. Quelle barche erano cariche di pesce quando arrivarone al porto.
8. Quante uova ha comprate?
9. Quel vecchio è molto elegante. Ha una camicia pulita tutti i giorni.
10. Quella vecchia ha venti paia di scarpe.
11. Fortunata lei! Aveva lasciato il suo portamonete nel treno, e il facchino lo trovò.
12. Ho perduto due paia di calzini nuovi. Li avevo con me la settimana scorsa quando portavo dalla città tutte quelle uova. Li avrò lasciati nell'autobus.
13. Andava a vederla quando io lo incontrai.

Exercise 14 (a)

1. At dinner we shall eat the fish we caught this morning.
2. The young lady with whom I was speaking yesterday is my sister.—She is a nice-looking girl. What is her name?
3. The study in which I work is very comfortable. It is a large room with three windows, from which I have a lovely view of the lake and the mountains.
4. The man to whom you sold the car has left. What, left! and he hasn't paid me for it yet.
5. What is the name of this square? The square through which we are now passing is the Victor Emanuel Square.
6. The gentleman, whose daughter we saw in town this morning, is a professor at the university.
7. The doctor's daughter, to whom you wrote today, is a friend of mine.
8. What time do you get up in the morning, madam? I get up early, generally at six; but my sister is lazy, and she gets up very late.
9. What a glorious sun! How lovely it is here in the heat!
10. Yes, here on the beach one is always happy.
11. Excuse me, madam, the young lady whose ring was lost on the beach is at the door.
12. Do you remember that lovely day on the beach last year? I should think I do! (lit.: and how!). I remember it very well.

Exercise 14 (b)

1. Quella donna a cui lei parlava è la sorella della cuoca.
2. Quel libro di cui lei parlava non è nella biblioteca.

3. La ragazza, da cui ho ricevuto questa lettera, arriverà la settimana prossima.

4. Quell'uomo che ha comprato la Sua macchina è già partito per l'Italia.

5. Il cuoco, i cui piatti erano cosí famosi, ha lasciato quel ristorante.

6. A che ora si alza tuo padre? Si alza generalmente alle otto, ma ieri si alzò alle sette e partí col treno delle otto per Roma.

7. Si metteva il soprabito, quando arrivò sua sorella.

8. Quella ragazza non si è lavata. Che mani! e che faccia!

9. Scusi, Signore, come si chiama questa piazza?

10. La strada che cerco è vicino a questa piazza.

11. Si è ricordato di quel libro? Sí, fui a quella libreria dove si parla inglese.

12. Parte già lo zio? Sí, si sta mettendo il cappello. Dove sono quei nuovi guanti che gli ho comprati? Eccoli. Lui non se ne ricorda mai.

Exercise 15 (a)

1. The man of whom we are speaking has been here this morning. Didn't you see him, Uncle?

2. Of course Uncle did not see him, for he was in bed.

3. But what time does your uncle get up? Never before ten.

4. And you, what time did you get up this morning? But I have never even been to bed. I travelled in the train all night and slept very badly.

5. What are you looking for, sir? My spectacles; they've just fallen from my nose this moment. Poor me! I can't see anything.

6. Leave it to me, sir; I'll look for them.

7. Here they are, here they are, I've found them. They were under that chair. Thank you, miss.

8. I bought this suit when I was in Milan last week. Do you like it?

9. Yes, I like it very much; that colour suits you very well.

10. The house had a little garden in front, which separated it from the road, and there every evening that old man with the white beard used to work.

11. Has the lawyer arrived? No, he will arrive by the half-past seven train. We will go and meet him at the station.

12. Immediately he had finished the letter, he called up John on the telephone, but the number was engaged.

Exercise 15 (b)

1. Non mi piace il nuovo vestito di Maria, dove l'ha comprato?
2. Quel colore non le sta bene; preferisco il vestito che aveva l'anno scorso.
3. La zia perde sempre i suoi occhiali. Non si ricorda mai dove li ha lasciati.
4. Lunedí scorso li stava cercando per delle ore, e le stavano sul naso tutt'il tempo.
5. Per favore, siamo vicino a Firenze? Sí, ci saremo in cinque minuti.
6. La signora di cui parla è partita ora. Sí, la incontrai quando entravo.
7. Questo non è un letto molto comodo. Com'è il suo? (or: il tuo, . . . il vostro?).
8. Ha dormito bene Signore? No, ho dormito molto male.
9. Parto per Firenze stasera.
10. Viaggerò in treno tutta la notte e ci arriverò alle sei della mattina.
11. Di chi è quel soprabito? È il tuo o il suo? (È il vostro o il suo . . . or: È di Lei, o di lui?)
12. Appena che il professore ebbe finito la lettera, l'avvocato telefonò (or: chiamò per telefono) la polizia.

Translation I

Literal Version

"Good day, sir. In what thing can I serve you ". to me asked the clerk when I entered in the office of the tourism Italian at London.

I did not reply immediately, because although I had studied the Italian, not it I had never spoken, and the words not to me were coming quickly to the lips. But, happy of the opportunity of to practise the language before the my journey in Italy, to him I said in Italian, a little timidly:

"Good day. I should have need of some information. I should like to go in Italy for the holidays this summer, but I have little time and money at my disposal."

"Is it the first time that you go in Italy, sir?"

"Yes, not there am I never been."

"I have understood. But, first of all, to me tell, have you the passport in order?"

"Yes, it is in order. I come just now from the office passports, and the consul Italian to me has said that not is necessary a visa special."

"Very good. Then which cities would you like to visit? You yourself interest of art? Then you will want to see Florence, perhaps also Pisa and Siena or Venice? Or have you the intention of to go to Rome and to visit the antiquities? Or of to make a tour through the lakes? Or perhaps you prefer to stop yourself in some station bathing? Or in some place of resort in mountain? To the English please much the beauties natural, it I know; and in Italy there are so many beautiful places . . . Which are your plans, sir?"

"You me should advise. Of art not myself of it I understand much, I must confess it, and very little of antiquities Roman. I was wanting above all to visit Florence, where was born my mother, and perhaps other cities of Tuscany, and to me it would please very much to see Venice if there is time and if the journey not costs too much. Rome is a little too far; it will be for another time."

Free Version

"Good morning, sir. What can I do for you?" the clerk asked as I entered the Italian tourist office in London.

I did not reply at once because although I had studied Italian I had never spoken it and the words did not come very readily. But pleased to have the opportunity of practising the language before my journey to Italy, I said to him rather timidly:

"Good morning. I'm needing some information. I want to go to Italy for my holidays this summer, but I've only a little time and not much money at my disposal."

"Is it the first time you're going to Italy, sir?"

"Yes, I've not been before."

"I see. Then first of all, is your passport in order?"

"Yes, quite. I've just come from the passport office and the Italian consul told me that a special visa isn't required."

"Very good. Now which towns do you want to visit? Are you interested in art? If so, you'll want to see Florence, perhaps Pisa too, or Siena or Venice? Or are you thinking of going to Rome to see the antiquities? Or perhaps of making a tour through the lakes? Or would you rather stay at some seaside resort? Or at some resort up in the mountains? I know the English are very fond of the beauties of nature, and in Italy there are so many lovely places. . . . What are your plans, sir?"

"You must advise me, please. I'm not well up in art, I must confess, and I know precious little about Roman antiquities.

I wanted particularly to go to Florence, where my mother was born, and perhaps to other places in Tuscany; and I'd very much like to see Venice, if there's time and if it doesn't cost too much. Rome is a bit far off; that will have to wait for another time."

Notes

Buon giorno.—Similarly: *buona sera* = good afternoon, good evening; *buona notte* = good night. *mattina* = morning and *pomeriggio* = afternoon, are not used in salutations.

a Londra.—Before names of towns "in" is translated by *a* in Italian, though *in* may be used if the meaning is "within".

sebbene = "although" and *benché* (same meaning) are followed by the subjunctive, see page 143. Conjunctions ending in *-ché* have the acute accent on the final *-é*.

mi venivano . . . alle labbra.—Note the use of the conjunctive pronoun *mi* instead of the possessive adjective, with a part of the body.

contento di.—Some adjectives which in English are followed by "with" or "to" in Italian take *di*: *carico di* = laden with; *soddisfatto di* = satisfied with.

Avrei bisogno.—*Aver bisogno* = to have need. The conditional here rather than the present infers uncertainty in the speaker's mind: *if* I could go to Italy, I should need . . . Note other phrases formed with the verb *avere* and a *noun* as object, which we render in English by the verb "to be" and an *adjective*:

aver fame,	lit.: to have hunger	= to be hungry
aver sete	to have thirst	to be thirsty
aver sonno	to have sleep	to be sleepy
aver ragione	to have reason	to be right
aver torto	to have wrong	to be wrong

in Italia.—"to" before the name of a country is usually *in*; before the name of a town *a*.

a mia disposizione.—The definite article is omitted after certain prepositions (*con, senza, per, di, a* and *da*) when the preposition and the following noun form an adverbial expression, as: *con piacere* = with pleasure; *senza denaro* = without money; *di giorno* = by day.

ufficio passaporti.—Similarly *ufficio viaggi* = tourist office, without any intervening preposition.

benissimo.—From *bene* = well. The ending *-issimo* stands for "very", see page 121.

s'interessa di arte.—*Interessarsi* = to interest oneself in, here followed by the preposition *di*, may also be followed by *a*, as: *s'interessa alla condizione dei profughi* = he interests himself in the state of the refugees.

l'intenzione di andare.—The infinitive is used after a preposition where in English we have the present participle in "-ing"; see page 125.

stazione balneare.—Bathing resort. *Stazione* here has the original meaning of "station"—that is, stopping-place, place to stay.

villeggiatura.—Comes from the word *villa*, which originally was a large country house, equivalent to country seat. From *villa* we have *villeggiare* = to go and stay in a villa, and the noun, *villeggiatura* = the act of going to stay in the country, also the place where one stays. "Resort" is the best translation in this instance.

Agl'Inglesi piacciono . . ., and in the last paragraph, *mi piacerebbe.* Note the use of the impersonal verb *piacere* = "to please", to translate our verb "to like".

mi dovrebbe consigliare . . . debbo confessarlo.—When the infinitive following *dovere, potere* and *volere* has a pronoun object or objects, these conjunctive pronouns may come either before both verbs, as in the first case here quoted, or they may come after both verbs, as in the second case. They must NEVER come *between* the verbs. Ex.: I can send it to him = *Posso mandarglielo* or *Glielo posso mandare.*

non me ne intendo molto = I don't understand much about it, I am not well up in it. *Intendersi di una cosa* has the meaning of "to be expert in", "to be a good judge of"; *intendersi* also means "to agree", and *intendere* (not reflexive) has three meanings: "to understand", "to intend" and "to hear".

un po' (short for *un poco*) = a little. *troppo* = too, too much; but "too", meaning "also", is *anche.*

Exercise 16

1. Dove va lui per le vacanze quest'estate?
2. Andrà in Italia, se il viaggio non costerà troppo (or: va . . . costa).
3. Parla italiano? Sí, lo parla molto bene (or: benissimo), era nato a Roma.
4. Vuol andare a teatro oggi o domani?
5. Domani, per favore. Non posso andare oggi perché lo zio arriverà stasera e dovrò andare a incontrarlo.
6. Buon giorno, Signora, in che cosa posso servirla?

7. Vorrei vedere delle sciarpe, per favore.
8. Con piacere (or: molto volentieri), Signora. Che colore le
   piacerebbe? (or: che colore vorrebbe?).
9. Lui va molto spesso al concerto, ma non s'intende di
   musica.
10. Quando avrà finito con quel libro? Ne avrò bisogno per la
    settimana prossima.
11. Noi andiamo al mare quest'anno per le vacanze: e non ci
    andate voi?
12. No, quest'anno andremo in villeggiatura in montagna.
13. Ho bisogno di una gruccia. Me ne può dare uno?
14. Ho molta sete. Mi dia un bicchiere d'acqua, per favore.

Translation II

Literal Version

"Well, sir, you decide then for Florence," continued the
clerk, while he was opening a drawer and was taking out
various papers and books and an enormous map.

"And would it be possible to go to Florence," I asked,
"passing through Genoa and Pisa, and then to return by
another road?"

"Very possible."

"What would you say if I went from Florence to Venice,
then from Venice to Milan, and in the journey of return I made
a tour through the lakes? I know that the ticket of going and
return is more cheap; but with that tour, should I have to
spend much of more?"

"No, no. Here, here is the thing that does for you; a ticket
circular tourist, valid for 45 days; and to you it is convenient,
because to you it gives a reduction of the fifty per cent, provided you stop yourself in Italy for a period of at least twelve
days."

"It goes just well for me, for myself I shall stop at least two
weeks, perhaps even three."

"Let us see a little the map for to fix more exactly the your
route. Therefore, leaving from London the morning early, you
arrive at Paris the evening towards the six. There you will
have the time of to eat before of to leave again with the express
Paris–Rome; just your route: Modane–Turin–Genoa–Pisa. It
is a very best train. It arrives at the frontier Italian at dawn,
and at Pisa in the afternoon. And with the ticket circular you
can stop yourself when and where you wish, and you can travel
with any train: therefore leave Pisa when you wish and stop

yourself at Florence how much to you it seems, naturally always in the limit of the 45 days."

"I understand."

"After Florence the your route is this: Bologna, Venice, Milan, and then Como and Lugano, where you will take the express for Paris. Thus you enter in Italy through the Pass of the Mont Cenis and you exit through the St. Gotthard. Goes it well thus?"

"Thanks, it goes very well indeed. Would you prepare me the ticket? I shall leave Friday next, and I shall travel in second."

"Here, done. This is the ticket; and here there is also a book which perhaps to you will be useful: 'Annual Hotels of Italy', and a magazine tourist with other indications interesting."

"Very kind, thousand thanks."

"Nothing, sir, I pray. Good journey and good enjoyment."

Free Version

"Very good, sir; you decide on Florence then," said the clerk, opening a drawer and taking out various papers and books and a large map.

"And would it be possible to go to Florence," I asked, "via Genoa and Pisa and then come back by another route?"

"Why, yes, of course."

"Supposing I went from Florence to Venice, then from Venice to Milan, and on the return journey go for a tour through the lakes? I know the return ticket is cheaper; but if I go round like that, would I have to pay very much more?"

"Not at all. Here's just what you want; a circular tourist ticket valid for 45 days; and it pays you to get it, for there's a reduction of 50 per cent, provided you stay in Italy for a period of at least twelve days."

"That'll just do for me, for I'll be there at least two weeks, perhaps three."

"Let's look at the map a moment and fix your route. Now, if you leave London early in the morning you arrive at Paris in the evening towards six o'clock. There you'll have time to dine before leaving again by the Paris–Rome express, which goes just the way you want: Modane–Turin–Genoa–Pisa. It's a very good train. It arrives at the Italian frontier at dawn and at Pisa in the afternoon. And with the circular ticket you can stop when and where you want and travel by any train you like; so you can leave Pisa when you wish and stay in Florence as long as it suits you—always of course within the period of the 45 days."

"Of course."

"After Florence here's your route: Bologna, Venice, Milan and then Como and Lugano, where you'll take the express for Paris. So you enter Italy by the Mont Cenis Pass and leave by the St. Gotthard. Will that do?"

"Thank you, that'll do excellently. Will you get me my ticket? I want to go next Friday, and I shall travel second class."

"Here you are. This is your ticket, and here is a book which might be useful: 'Annual Italian Hotel Guide', and a tourist review with other information of interest."

"You are very kind indeed. Thank you very much."

"Don't mention it, sir. A good journey, and I hope you enjoy yourself."

Notes

A buon mercato.—*mercato* "market", also "bargain"; therefore "at a good bargain", that is "cheap".

Le conviene.—*convenire* "to agree", "to suit", used impersonally may mean: "to be necessary", or "to be of advantage to": *non ci conviene farlo* = it isn't to our advantage to do it.

purché is followed by the subjunctive. See page 142.

proprio as an adverb means: "just", "exactly"; as an adjective: "own", "proper", "appropriate": *la mia propria casa* = my very own house.

Partendo . . . la mattina presto . . . arriva la sera.—No preposition *in* is required in the adverbial phrases "in the morning", "in the evening"; but with the word *pomeriggio* "in" is used: *nel pomeriggio*. Note the following expressions: *di giorno* = by day; *di notte* = by night; *Vi andrò lunedì* = I shall go there on Monday (no "on" in Italian); *Ci vado il martedì e il venerdì* = I go there *every* Tuesday and Friday; *Il piroscafo fa servizio solamente la domenica* = The steamer goes only on Sundays.

Direttissimo = express train. The names of the trains in Italian, in descending order of speed (!), are: *rapido* = express; *direttissimo* = express through train, stopping more frequently; *diretto* = through train; *accelerato* = stopping train; *treno omnibus* = slow stopper; *treno merci* = goods train.

Prego (from *pregare* = to beg, pray) is commonly used where we might say: "please don't mention it". "excuse me".

Buon viaggio e buon divertimento.—*Buono* is often used in expressions containing a greeting or wish. Just before a meal you say to the others who are going to partake of it: *Buon appetito!* When going to a theatre or concert you may hear: *Buon divertimento*, or *buon concerto*, and if you're going to work, someone might even wish you: *Buon lavoro* or *buono studio*—according to the kind of work.

Exercise 17

1. Parlando (or: mentre parlava) aprí un cassetto e tirò fuori un'enorme carta geografica.
2. Non potrebbe venire con noi al cinema? Dicono che c'è un film molto buono (or: si dice che c'è . . .).
3. Un biglietto di andata e ritorno per Londra, per favore, seconda classe. Devo comprare un biglietto anche per il cane? Sí, Signora, il cane deve avere un biglietto.
4. Non voleva venire a parlarLe ieri; oggi è contento di farlo.
5. Hai messo (or: posto) i colletti dello zio in questo cassetto? (or: mettesti, or if you use porre, ponesti). No, lui stesso ce li ha messi (posti), (or: ce li mise, pose). (Or, to make the pronouns more emphatic: Did *you* . . . no, *he himself*: Hai messo *tu* i colletti . . . No, ce li mise *lui stesso.*)
6. È mai stata a Londra, Signora? Sí, ci sono stata molte volte (*diverse volte, parecchie volte*).
7. Non è arrivato ancora? No, Maria andò a incontrarlo, ma è tornata sola (or: *tornò sola*).
8. Forse è andato per un'altra strada? Sí, è possibile.
9. Ieri si alzò alle sette, ma rimase nella sua camera a leggere il giornale, e scese soltanto alle dieci per prendere il caffè.
10. Mi dia la carta geografica un momento, per favore; voglio cercare Siena.
11. Buon giorno. Ho bisogno di (or: *voglio*) una cravatta per portare con questo vestito.—Ho proprio la cosa che fa per Lei, Signore. Questo blu marino con strisce gialle andrà molto bene con il verde scuro del Suo abito.
12. Dovrebbe comprare un biglietto circolare. È il piú a buon mercato; e può fermarsi dove e quando vuole e quanto le pare. (Using the other modes of address: *Dovresti . . . puoi fermarti . . . quando vuoi e quanto ti pare*; *Dovreste . . . potete fermarvi . . . quando volete e quanto vi pare.*)

Translation III

Literal Version

Of usual I do not sleep well in train: but perhaps this time
I was tired, or I had eaten too well at the restaurant of the
station of Paris (there one eats divinely, but one pays too, very
generously), or perhaps because I was all alone in the compartment and myself I was able to stretch out on the cushions as in
a bed; fact stands that, taken off the shoes, the tie and the
jacket, as soon as I placed the head on the pillow—hired for
100 francs at the station—myself I fell asleep profoundly, and
I continued to sleep like a dormouse all the night.

Myself I awakened that it was already day; the train was
going slowing down and at last itself it stopped. Looking out
of the little window I saw on the platform of a station wayside
a small group of employees of the railway, porters and soldiers,
with two policemen and various other guards, who were laughing and joking among of themselves, with the air of not to take
no notice of us and of our train. But a whistle sharp sent out
by the express Paris–Rome loosened that group. One of them,
the station-master (him one recognized by the cap red), went
to speak with the engine-driver, while all the others, always
talking and laughing, ascended on to the train. The clock of the
station marked the five. Only the five of the morning, and
already it was making hot and there was a lovely sun, a sky
blue and clear, and the air was so mild and fragrant (sweet). I
drew out the watch to regulate it, but in that moment, someone
opened brusquely the door of my compartment, and shouted
with a voice hoarse but strong: "Gentlemen, the customs
Italian, prepare the luggage." Three men in uniform to me
were standing in front on the doorway.

Free Version

I do not usually sleep well in a train; but perhaps this time
I was tired, or I had eaten too much at the station restaurant
in Paris (the food there is marvellous . . . but so are the bills!)
or perhaps it was because I was all alone in the compartment
and was able to stretch out on the seat as if I were in bed;
the fact is, having taken off my shoes, my tie and jacket, no
sooner had I put my head on the pillow (hired for 100 francs
at the station) than I fell fast asleep, and I went on sleeping
like a log the whole night.

It was already light when I awoke; the train was gradually
slowing down, and at last it stopped altogether. On looking out
of the carriage window I saw, on the platform of a wayside

station, a small group of railway officials, porters and soldiers, with two policemen, and various other guards, laughing and joking together, as if they weren't going to take any notice of us and our train. But a shrill whistle from the Paris–Rome express broke up the group. One of them, the station-master—you could see that from his red cap—went to talk to the engine-driver, while all the rest, still laughing and talking, got into the train. It was five o'clock by the station clock. Only five in the morning, and it was already warm, and there was a lovely sun, a clear blue sky, and the air was so mild and fragrant! I took out my watch to put it right, but at that moment somebody suddenly opened the door of my compartment and a loud hoarse voice bawled: "Italian Customs! Get luggage ready, please," and three men in uniform stood before me in the door-way.

Notes

fatto sta che (or: *il fatto è che*) . . .—The verb *stare* is used in many expressions in place of *essere*. In speaking of the condition of health of a person in greetings, such as: Good morning, how are you? = *Buon giorno, come sta?* Very well, thank you, and how are you? = *Molto bene, grazie, e Lei?* He is ill = *Sta male*. It should be noted, however, that *stare* implies a temporary condition, and *essere* a permanent state: He is lame = *Lui è zoppo*.

tolte le scarpe.—A past participle is often used alone in Italian where we would use a perfect past participle or a dependent clause. When the verb is transitive, the participle agrees with its object; when intransitive, with its subject: *Finita la lettera, uscì* = Having finished the letter (or: When he had finished) he went out; *La ragazza, rimasta sola, cominciò a piangere* = The girl, having remained alone (or: When the girl was left alone), she began to cry.

posi il capo.—We are quite sure whose head it is, so no possessive adjective is necessary.

continuai a dormire.—Some verbs require a preposition after them before a following infinitive. *Continuare* and *cominciare* (see previous note) both take *a*. See also page 126.

andava rallentando.—The use of *andare* to form a progressive tense is not very common; it implies particular attention focussed on the action of the present participle, an action which is progressively increasing. In this sentence it gives the idea that the train is slowing down "more and more" ("more and more", by the way, is in Italian—*sempre più*).

due carabinieri.—There are different kinds of police in Italy (one organization looking after the roads, another after the railways, another after public safety, etc.), but the ones the foreigner notices most are the *carabinieri* (public safety), for they wear a picturesque uniform of the last century, a coat with tails (navy blue), trousers with red stripes, Napoleonic-shaped hat, gold buttons and white gloves, and they always go about in twos.

salirono.—To get into a tram, train, bus, etc., use *salire*; and to get out of such vehicles: *scendere*. *Dove scende lei?* = Where are you getting out?

faceva caldo.—Lit.: it was making hot. Similar idioms with *fare* are: *fare freddo* = to be cold, *fare bel tempo* = to be fine, *fare vento* = to be windy. See, too, page 108.

Exercise 18

1. Buon giorno, Signore, e come sta Lei oggi? Grazie, oggi non sto molto bene. Sono molto stanco.
2. Ha dormito bene nel treno ieri? Sí, grazie, ho dormito benissimo, ho viaggiato in una carrozza-letti.
3. Si mangia bene a quel ristorante dove è stato Lei ieri? Sí, si mangia molto bene, ma è un po' caro.
4. Andate già alla stazione? Ma il treno arriva soltanto alle dieci.
5. Abbiamo fatto un buonissimo viaggio. Non c'era nessuno nel nostro scompartimento, e abbiamo dormito molto bene.
6. Che bel tempo fa! Andiamo a fare una passeggiata sulla spiaggia? (or: faremo una passeggiata).
7. Chiuse la porta e le finestre dello scompartimento, si tolse la cravatta, la giacchetta e le scarpe, pose il denaro, il passaporto e l'orologio da tasca sotto il guanciale, e, sdraiatosi sui cuscini, in un momento s'addormentò.
8. Dove scende Lei, Signora? Io scendo a Firenze, sono salita a Parigi.
9. Lei è piú alto di me; ma Giovanni è piú alto di Lei.
10. Chi è il piú intelligente di quella famiglia? La cuoca; è piú intelligente di quel che Lei pensi (or: ... *che Lei non pensi*).
11. Quello è l'uomo piú ricco della città. È un suo amico? Mi vuol presentare a lui?
12. Non ho tanto denaro quanto lui; ma ne ho piú di Lei.
13. Non voglio fare una passeggiata; mi fa male il piede.

Translation IV

Literal Version

"You," to me asked the most near of the three, "have you forwarded the luggage?"

"No, it I have all here," I replied quickly, drawing down from the rack the my only suitcase. As I was come in Italy for little time, not I had need of trunks.

"He has only luggage at hand, this gentleman," then two of the Customs officers themselves of it they went, without doubt to look for other victims, while the third, remained alone with me, went on:

"Have you anything to declare, sir?"

"No, nothing."

"Absolutely nothing? No tobacco, cigarettes, cigars, chocolate . . ." a pause . . . "articles of silk? . . . perfumes?"

I outlined a smile.

"But good heavens; what thing myself of it should do I, of perfumes?"

"Oh, sir, one never knows, one never knows! A little present for some girl friend Italian, perhaps?" he suggested; then, with a large piece of chalk white, he drew some his line mysterious on the my case.

"No, sir, leave to stand," he said, when I made for to open it. "It doesn't matter."

"Thousand thanks," replied I, happy of not to have to open the case and put all in disorder.

"You come to pass the holidays in Italy, not is it true? Well. Excellent! Yourself enjoy! Good day." And himself of it he went finally also he.

But, hardly outside in the corridor, he made a step backwards, and, all smiling, himself he faced once again at the door, saying:

"And good luck . . . to that perfume."

Listening to that joker of a Customs officer not myself was I aware that the train was again in motion, and with surprise, looking out of the little window, I saw that already one was passing quickly between high mountains. Myself I accommodated in the my place of corner to contemplate the scenery. The railway, flanked on one side and on the other by precipices rocky was following the course of a torrent, one of those many courses of water which, rising from the Alps, themselves turn upside down in little cascades down for the steep slopes of the long valleys narrow for to empty in those more large, tributaries of the Po. This was a torrent impetuous; every so often one was hearing the swish of its waters above of the noise of the train; and to us it was flowing at the side, as if it wished to say: "There I shall arrive before you."

Free Version

"Have you forwarded your luggage, sir?" the nearest of the three asked.

"No, all I have is here," I quickly replied, and I got down my one and only suitcase from the rack. As I had come to Italy for so short a time I had not needed any trunks.

"This gentleman only has hand luggage," at which two of the Customs officers went off, doubtless to look for other victims, while the third stayed with me and went on:

"Have you anything to declare?"

"No, nothing."

"Absolutely nothing? No tobacco, cigarettes, cigars, chocolate" . . . a pause . . . "silk goods . . . scent?"

I began to smile.

"Good heavens! Whatever should I be doing with scent?"

"Oh, one never knows, sir, one never knows! A little present for an Italian girl, perhaps?" he suggested; then with a large piece of white chalk he drew some mysterious lines on my case.

"No, sir, leave it as it is," he said, when I made as if to open it. "It doesn't matter."

"Oh, thank you," I replied, very pleased at not having to open the case and turn everything upside down.

"You're coming to Italy for your holidays, aren't you? Very good. Excellent. Have a good time. Good morning." And at last he went off too.

But no sooner was he in the corridor than he took a step backwards, and once again his face, wreathed in smiles, peeped round my door as he said:

"Good luck to that scent of yours, sir!"

While listening to that joking Customs officer I hadn't realized that the train was moving again, and it was with surprise therefore, when looking out of the carriage window, that I saw we were travelling rapidly between high mountains. I settled myself down in my corner seat to watch the scenery. The railway, flanked on either side by rocky precipices, followed the course of a mountain stream—one of the many streams which rise in the Alps and hurl themselves in little waterfalls down the steep slopes of long narrow valleys to empty into those larger rivers, the tributaries of the Po. This was a raging torrent; every now and then you could hear the roar of its waters above the rumble of the train; and it flowed there alongside us as if to say: "I'll get there before you."

Notes

spedito.—From *spedire* = to forward, to send. Luggage registered through to Italy from London normally awaits its owner at the Customs house at the frontier station, or it contrives to be in the luggage van of his train. To register luggage is: *fare registrare il bagaglio* (lit.: to make to register). Note this special construction with *fare*. Followed by the infinitive, *fare* expresses the idea of making someone else do something: *Fatelo venire qua* (lit.: make him to come here), *i.e.*, "Have him come here". *Fece chiamare il dottore* = He had the doctor called. Similarly: Please have my luggage brought up = *Per favore faccia salire il mio bagaglio*; Have it taken down, please = *Lo faccia scendere per piacere*.

se ne andarono.—*andarsene* = to go away; a reflexive verb with *ne* added. Here *ne*, "of it", is used in the sense of "thence" *i.e.*, "away". In all the tenses and with the various parts of the verb, *ne* must have its correct position with regard to the reflexive pronoun: *Io me ne vado* = I go away; *Te ne vai?* = Are you going?; *andandosene* = going away; *andatevene* = go away (*voi*); *vattene* = go away (*tu*); *se ne vada* = go away (*Lei*).

Ha qualchecosa da dichiarare.—The preposition *da* implies obligation or necessity. *Avere da* has the same meaning as *dovere*; I must write a letter: *Ho da scrivere una lettera*, or *Devo scrivere* . . . Turn also to page 126.

lasci stare.—Lit.: "let be", "let stand". *Lasciami stare* (*tu*) or *Mi lasci stare* (*Lei*) = Leave me alone, don't bother me.

importa.—*importare* = to matter. *Fare* is also used to mean the same thing: *Ciò non fa niente* = That doesn't matter, that makes no difference; *Ciò fa molto* = That matters a great deal.

tutto sorridente.—*sorridente* is an adjective from the verb *sorridere* to smile. A similar kind of adjective is formed from any verb. Those of the first conjugation form this verbal adjective by adding *-ante* to the stem, and the other two conjugations add *-ente*: *parlare*, *parlante*; *seguire* (to follow), *seguente*; *la lezione seguente* = the following lesson; *gli animali parlanti* = the talking animals. A relative clause is, however, often preferable to this verbal adjective: a singing bird = *un uccello che canta*. Like other adjectives, this verbal adjective is inflected (changing its final *-e* to *-i* for the plural), and it may be used as a noun. Certain of them have been so continuously

used as nouns, that they are now regarded as such: *il* (or *la*)
cantante = the singer; *l'amante* = the lover; *l'insegnante* = the
teacher. Refresh your memory on the present participle
(page 64).

mi ero accorto.—*accorgersi* "to notice", when not followed by
a dependent clause and *che*, is followed by the preposition *di*:
I did not notice that girl = *Non mi accorsi di quella ragazza.*
I always notice it = *Me ne accorgo sempre.*

finestrino.— *-ino* is a suffix meaning "small". See page 121.

mi accomodai.—*accomodarsi* = to make oneself comfortable,
to seat oneself (*comodo* = comfortable). Pray be seated,
madam = *Si accomodi, Signora. Accomodatevi* = sit down.

ogni tanto = every now and then, every so often.

ci scorreva allato.—The same construction as *mi stavano
davanti*: instead of a preposition governing the pronoun in the
predicate—"it flowed alongside us"—the verb governs the pronoun, and the preposition becomes an adverb of place—"us it
flowed alongside".

Exercise 19

1. Ha spedito tre bauli o quattro per quel signore dalla barba?
2. Tre solamente; dovrò spedire l'altro domani (or: *avrò
   da . . .*).
3. C'era una volta una contadina che aveva cento pecore,
   ventotto vacche, cinquantacinque porci, diciannove
   capre, un cane e un gatto ed era molto contenta.
4. Qual'è la data di oggi? È il 4 luglio 1940 (*mille novecento
   quaranta*).
5. In che anno scoprí Colombo l'America? Nel 1492 (*mille
   quattrocento novantadue*) non è vero?
6. Quanti anni hai, bambino? Compirò sei anni lunedí
   prossimo, Signorina.
7. Quando è il tuo compleanno? Il nove maggio.
8. Faccia salire il mio bagaglio in camera subito, per favore.
9. Sei milioni di tonnellate di carbone passano per questo
   porto ogni settimana (or: *tutte le settimane*).
10. La chiesa piú grande del mondo è la chiesa di San Pietro a
    Roma: ha una superficie di 15,160 (*quindicimila cento-
    sessanta*) metri quadrati e la cupola è alta piú di 130
    (*centotrenta*) metri.

Translation V

(From this point onwards only one English version of the
extracts will be given. Where the translation differs a great

deal from the original Italian, a literal version will be added in brackets.)

The valley was now getting broader; bare rocky mountains were giving place to hills covered with pines and firs; then these to the plain with its vineyards, farms (houses of farms) and fields yellow with corn and ripening maize. What surprised me most was the small amount of land kept for pasture; almost all of it was cultivated: a succession of yellow fields, dotted here and there with the dark patches (shadows) of the olives and small maples, with their festoons of vines. I was very interested in the cultivation of the vine. The stalks climbed up the trunks and branches of low trees, such as the maple and elm, and hung in graceful festoons from one tree to another; and beneath them some green plant was growing. I could not see very well what it was. "This land must be very fertile," I thought. "And the people want to make the most of it. But how different this landscape is from ours!" At first the colours and the light seemed too strong; I missed the lovely green of the English meadows. "And where are the cows?" I wondered. "Oh, there they are!" In the distance there were two white ones, and I stood up to see better. But I was very surprised to see that, instead of sitting peacefully chewing their cud, these two animals were working! "But those aren't cows!" They were two enormous oxen yoked to a cart laden with hay. "Then they use the ox as a beast of burden here," I thought: "Oh, and the mule too," for as we passed along by a main road I saw several carts drawn by mules; and very soon cars, buses, tall houses and factories all began to appear (did not delay to appear . . .). We were getting near to some large town (there one was getting near).

"Papers, magazines, *Sunday Post*." I opened the carriage window and calling the newspaper boy I bought a paper for 35 lire and a review for 150. It was still early, but there were plenty of people on the station. "Perhaps they're already going to work," I thought, remembering that in Italy they go to work earlier than we do, for with the great heat in the summer months they need to rest during the day. So, many shops and offices are open from eight to midday, and then they close, and only open again at three or four, and they stay open in the evening until eight, and in some cases even later. The meal times are therefore somewhat different from ours. One might say that the Italians have two meals a day: dinner at one, and supper at eight. Most of them don't eat anything early in the morning; their breakfast consists of coffee and milk and nothing else; but they have a good meal at dinner, and again at supper. That doesn't stop them going to the cafés very often, both in the morning and the afternoon, as I was to find out later (as I came to know . . .).

Notes

coperti di.—Note that an Italian says "covered *of*".

loppio = a low maple, and *olmo* = elm, are both cultivated specially for the trailing of the vine over them. They are both rather short, stunted trees.

lavorassero.—Subjunctive after the verb *maravigliarsi* = to wonder. See page 137.

carico di fieno.—Note the preposition: "laden *of*".

tardarono ad apparire.—*tardare* = to delay, is followed by *a* before a following infinitive.

da noi.—Note the idiomatic use of the preposition *da* to mean: "at our house", "with us", "in our land", etc. *Vado dal dentista* = I'm going to the dentist's. See also page 131.

i più.—Note the adverb used as a noun to mean "majority".

Prima colazione.—Lit. = first lunch—that is, breakfast. Some Italians talk about their midday meal as *colazione* (= lunch), and their evening meal as *pranzo* (= dinner); but this is not so usual as *pranzo* and *cena*; in any case, the two meals are in quantity about the same, whatever they are called.

Ciò non toglie . . . Lit. = that does not prevent that they may go very often. This idiomatic expression is followed by the subjunctive. See page 136, section 2.

spesso, spessissimo.—The *-issimo* superlative ending is not often added to adverbs of manner; the student is advised to use only those he has met in reading, and not to form them for himself.

tanto di mattino che di sera = both in the morning and the evening. Note this use of *tanto . . . che*, meaning literally: "so much . . . as"; note too *di mattino*, "in the morning"; and *di sera* = "in the evening".

Exercise 20

1. Quel signore ha ricevuto tre bauli, ma non il quarto.
2. Il fiume Po è il fiume più lungo d'Italia; è lungo più di seicento chilometri.
3. Sorge dalle Alpi piemontesi, attraversa una pianura molto fertile, e scorrendo dall'ovest all'est, sbocca nel mare adriatico.

4. Il Petrarca nacque nel 1304 (*mille trecento quattro*) e morí nel 1374 (*mille trecento settantaquattro*); egli aveva soltanto 17 anni nel 1321 (*mille trecento ventuno*) quando morí Dante, il quale era nato nel 1265 (*mille duecento sessantacinque*).

5. Sa Lei chi è quella Signora? No, Signore; Lei è la terza persona che mi ha fatto quella domanda.

6. Mi ha comprato due dozzine di uova? No. Non potevo comprarne due dozzine, ne trovai soltanto una ventina.

7. Quanto va avanti il vostro orologio al giorno? Non va avanti, rimane indietro dieci minuti al giorno.

8. Qual'era la data di ieri? Ieri era il 10 giugno 1941 (*il dieci giugno mille novecento quarantuno*).

9. L'anno comincia il primo gennaio, e finisce il 31 (*trentuno*) dicembre.

10. Il re Enrico VIII (*ottavo*) ebbe sei mogli, ma non tutte allo stesso tempo.

11. Che bel vigneto! Sí, produce migliaia e migliaia di bottiglie di vino all'anno.

12. Suonavano le dodici un anno fa stasera, e io stavo per andare a letto quando improvvisamente la porta della mia camera s'aprí, e quell'uomo alto e magro mi stette davanti.

Translation VI

"Take your seats, please; seats, please!" (lit.: "In carriage!") and once more we were off. This time I was no longer alone. Two men, one young, the other about fifty, came and sat down in my compartment. The older man, of a very swarthy complexion, had very dark hair and black eyes; the young man, on the other hand, with his fair hair and blue eyes, could easily have been taken for an Englishman. They were commercial travellers, by the look of them (to how much it was seeming), and they were talking loudly and animatedly, but all the time in Piedmontese, a dialect which is so different from Italian that I could not understand them. I read the paper a bit; there was nothing special in it, and in a little more than two hours we were at Genoa.

"Ices, biscuits, sweets, fresh grapes, luncheon baskets!" I looked out of the window. What a noise! What a crowd! Some people getting in; others getting out; some coming to the station to meet new arrivals and others to say goodbye to those who were going; and in the midst of the throng, porters, with bags on their shoulders, trying to push their way through (making themselves forward by dint of pushes), and the news-vendors, ice-cream sellers and the men selling sweets and drinks were doing the same (*non meno di* = not less than). At last I managed to attract the attention of one of these, and I bought a luncheon-basket. It was really very cheap, for I paid only 500 lire for it (it I paid only 500 . . .), and it had a plate of hot macaroni, two slices of roast veal, ham, cheese, fruit, biscuits, two rolls and even a small flask of red wine. I was ravenous, but it was still a little early to have lunch.

"Hope you enjoy your meal, sir!" said the man sitting opposite, with a smile. By now the train was full and there were no empty seats in my compartment. "Thank you, the same to you," I replied, seeing that he was going to eat as well. My other travelling companions were doing the same, and some of them, guessing that I was a foreigner, pointed out objects of interest for me. "This is the gulf of Spezia where the poet Shelley was drowned," they told me. In the distance we could see the white gleam of the mountains of Carrara with the famous marble quarries. Later, while we were passing through a lovely pine forest, they asked me whether I liked music, and told me that there was the house and the tomb of the composer, Giacomo Puccini.

Notes

un uomo sulla cinquantina = a man nearing fifty.

commesso = clerk or employee; *commesso viaggiatore* = an employee who travels for his firm to buy or sell goods.

niente di speciale.—Note this use of *di* before an adjective after a word like "something", "nothing", "anything": *Ho qualchecosa di buono per te* = I've something (of) good for you.

chi arrivava . . . chi partiva = some . . . others. See page 114.

farsi avanti = to come forward, make one's way.

riuscii a richiamare.—*riuscire* takes *a* before a following infinitive.

maccheroni caldi.—Luncheon baskets, or rather heavy paper bags, supplied on the Italian trains often include a small dish of cooked macaroni (with a cover on to keep it hot), and with it there is a small tin fork!

fettone.—*una fetta* = a slice, *fettona* = large slice. See page 121.

fiaschettino.—*fiasca* = flask. See again page 122.

aver una fame da lupi = to have a hunger like wolves, *i.e.*, to be ravenous. For this use of *da*, see page 131.

fare colazione = to have lunch.

colui che = he who, or simply *chi* = he who, the one who . . .
altrettanto = the same to you; lit. = as many, as much as,
again; the same amount again.

mi chiesero se amassi.—The verb of an indirect question has
its verb in the subjunctive if it depends on a main verb in the
past tense. See page 143.

Exercise 21

1. Non faccia nessun caso di ciò che dice; lei ha sempre parlato
   così.
2. Ieri stava un po' meglio; ma oggi sta peggio. Hanno fatto
   chiamare il medico?
3. Qual'è la via più corta (or: *breve*) per andare alla stazione,
   per favore?
4. Vada sempre diritto Signore, fino alla chiesa, e lì volti a
   destra e troverà la stazione di faccia.
5. Parla piano, non vedi che ci stanno ascoltando (or: *parli . . .
   vede*).
6. A che ora fa prima colazione Lei? Alle otto di solito, ma non
   prendo molto, soltanto caffè latte.
7. A che ora si fa colazione qui? Generalmente all'una,
   Signore. Bene. Mancano soltano dieci minuti; ho una
   fame da lupi.
8. Hai (or: *Ha*) mangiato bene sul treno? Sì, molto bene. Ho
   comprato un cestino e dentro c'erano tante buone cose:
   pollo, prosciutto, biscotti, formaggio e frutta.
9. C'era tanta gente e non un posto libero. Ma un signore lì
   vicino alla porta si alzò dicendo molto cortesemente:—Si
   accomodi, Signorina, si accomodi, per favore.—
10. Un altro viaggiatore venne a sedersi nel mio scomparti-
    mento. Era un uomo sulla sessantina, piccolo e grasso,
    calvo e con la barba bianca.
11. Non sono venuti i ragazzi con Lei al teatro? No, sono
    rimasti a casa; volevano sentire la radio; trasmettevano
    un bel concerto dalla Scala.
12. Che cosa fece Lei ieri? Niente di speciale. Son rimasto in
    casa.

Translation VII

At Pisa it was with difficulty that I got free of that crowd of
hotel porters, guides and cabbies who throng around the station
entrance; but having left my case in the cloakroom, once outside, I set off, plan in hand, towards the cathedral square, and
I was there in less than half an hour.

This square has been called the "meadow of miracles"; and there is something marvellous in the sight of those four gleaming white monuments towering up majestically in the middle of a field and standing out so gracefully against the green of the meadow and the blue of the sky. Built at different times—between the eleventh and thirteenth centuries, when Pisa was a powerful maritime republic—the four buildings, baptistry, church, cemetery and leaning tower, are nevertheless all bound together in wonderful harmony. They are romanesque in style, but have their own peculiar and original character, particularly in their external ornamentation of applied arcading with rows of covered galleries above, which gives the marble masses a delicate grace and elegance. In the baptistry I admired the pulpit by Nicola Pisano and I also enjoyed hearing the famous echo. If you sing a single note, the conical dome sends back the echo in a perfect musical chord; if you sing a whole song, it's just as if there were an organ there going full blast. The interior of the cathedral is impressive, with its enormous monolithic columns, and as the light streams down from the huge windows of the central nave, I was able to examine the many works of art there. They also showed me Galileo's lamp (he was a Pisan), and tradition has it that the scientist discovered the laws of the pendulum while watching it swinging. Afterwards I paid 150 lire to go into the Campo Santo (lit.: field holy = cemetery) to see the frescoes; and you have to pay to go up the leaning tower—100 lire. But it is worth it for the magnificent view and also to have the queer sensation of being on a tower that leans so—it is more than four metres from the vertical. You need a stout heart, however, and a strong pair of legs: there are nearly three hundred stairs!

When I came down the tower, I sat down on the grass for a moment. There were other people there, mostly Pisans who had come to picnic their supper in the shade of their monuments. The sun was setting; the soft, clear air was full of the flight of swallows; the white of the marble was changing to a rosy colour. What peace! what calm! As I wended my way back to the station I remembered that this was my first day in Italy: it seemed impossible; I already felt as if I'd been there for some time.

Notes

oretta.—etto, meaning "small", indicates less than an hour; *mezz'oretta* = a little less than half an hour.

maestosi.—Note the use of an adjective for an adverb in -*mente*.

arcate cieche.—Lit.: blind arcades—that is, arcades of which the central space is filled in. A glance at a photograph (if available) of these buildings will show these arcades on the ground floor, while the upper storeys are rows of pillared galleries, the *ordini di loggiati.*

se ci fosse . . . suonasse.—For the use of the subjunctive after *come se,* see page 142.

scoprisse.—Subjunctive after the verb *volere* in the main clause, the statement being a supposition, not an actual fact. See page 136.

ci vuole.—Note the verb *volere* used impersonally with *ci* meaning "to be required" (see page 107). Note the following: *Ci voleva tutta la mia forza* = It required all my strength; *Ci voleva un uomo come lui* = He was the man for it; *È la parola che ci voleva* = That's the word that was wanted; *Quanto tempo ci vuole per andare alla stazione?* = How long does it take to get to the station?

Exercise 22

1. Proprio quando stava per aprire la porta, quel ladro venne arrestato dal poliziotto.
2. La cattedrale di Pisa fu cominciata nell'anno 1063.
3. La torre pendente è fra le piú strane del mondo.
4. Da quanto tempo è in Italia Lei? (or: *Da quando è in Italia Lei?*).
5. Sono in Italia da tre anni.
6. Vale la pena di visitare la torre? Sí, certamente, c'è un panorama magnifico.
7. Ma non andiamo oggi che fa freddo e tira vento. Bisogna aspettare un giorno che faccia bel tempo, o non si vedrà niente.
8. Quanto tempo ci vuole per andare di qua alla chiesa Signore?
9. Non è sceso ancora per la prima colazione? Che cosa faremo? Il treno non aspetta nessuno. Bisognerà partire domani (or: *dovremo partire . . .*).
10. Quel libro era comprato da me, e non lo voglio dare a nessuno (or: *non voglio darlo . . .*).
11. Mi dispiace molto, ma non potrò venire; deve arrivare oggi un mio amico.
12. Si dice che Galileo fece i suoi famosi esperimenti sulla caduta dei gravi dalla sommità della torre pendente.

Translation VIII

Florence is among the most famous of cities by reason of its history and art, and also because of its lovely situation. My stay there was too short to permit me more than a rapid glance at some of the things of historic and artistic importance, but it was enough to give me an idea of the very many lovely things, both of nature and of art, that are to be found in that city on the banks of the Arno, and to make me feel its fascination so strongly that I decided I would return there as soon as ever I could.

The first morning I wakened up early. My boarding-house was on the top floor of an old palace, and on the ground floor there were shops: on one side a florist's, and on the other a seller of antiques and art treasures. I went down the stairs—there was no lift—through the dark passage, cool and sweet smelling from the flowers and plants on view there, and after a look at the old pictures, furniture and jewellery in the antique dealer's window, I went out into the street. With the plan of the town in my hand, I made my way to the Cathedral Square. At Florence, as at Pisa and in many other Italian towns, the cathedral, baptistry and belfry are three buildings separate from one another, but bound together in close unity by the architectural style. Here at Florence the marble is another tint, a shade warmer, almost a pale pink colour, with lines of green, so dark as to look like black. The cathedral was begun in 1296. The interior is dignified and solemn, clear and sober, for it is almost free from ornamentation. I admired the altar of pure silver, but the two famous choir stalls, one by Donatello and the other by Luca della Robbia, which used to be in the cathedral, are now to be found in the museum at the side. The baptistry is octagonal in plan, and the interior is very ornate with marble and mosaic. When I went in they were christening a child; and as I looked at that little group gathered round the font, I remembered that it was here, in this very same place, that Dante was baptized, almost seven centuries ago. There too I saw the beautiful doors in bronze by Ghiberti; those which Michelangelo said were fit to be the gates of Heaven. They represent scenes from the Old Testament, framed in an alternating design * of little statues of the prophets and of round plaques with sculptured heads. The third monument of this group, Giotto's belfry, is a high, square tower, simple and solid in shape, and yet graceful; here too the low reliefs in the bottom

* Lit.: framed by a frieze in which alternate little statues, etc. . . .

part should be seen, done by followers of Giotto, from designs by the master.

Notes

colà = there, in that place; more emphatic than *là*.

da decidermi = as to make me decide. See page 132, for the use of *da*.

stavano lì esposti.—Many of the shops on the ground floor of the old buildings and palaces have no windows in which to exhibit their goods; these are therefore arranged round the wide stone doorway, on the pavement on either side of the door, and even hanging on the outside walls of the building (whenever this is possible).

esposti.—Note that an adjective (*esposti*, past participle, has here the force of an adjective) agreeing with more than one noun is in the *masculine plural* if the nouns are of different genders; when both nouns are masculine, it is of course masculine, and feminine when both nouns are feminine.

vetrina = shop window. *Finestra* is never used in this sense.

tondo, as an adjective = round, circular; as a noun: circle, dish. *parlare chiaro e tondo* is an idiom meaning: "to speak out flatly".

bassorilievo = low relief—that is, shallow carving or sculpture on a background, from which the figures are shaped to stand out to give the appearance of perspective.

Exercise 23

1. Ho veduto tutti e due quei quadri; questo mi piace piú di quello.
2. Chi è costei? Grida sempre con quella voce?
3. Maria e Lucia suonano bene tutte e due; questa il violino, quella il pianoforte.
4. Ogni volta che ci vado, quell'uomo mi segue fino alla porta.
5. È un gran peccato vendere quel negozio di fiori; ognuno lo dice.
6. Hai visto qualcuno per la strada? No, non ho visto nessuno.
7. Per quanto sia ricca, ciò non m'importa (or: *mi fa niente*), non la voglio per moglie.
8. Chiunque siate, non vi posso lasciar entrare qui (or: *chiunque sia . . . non la posso . . .*; or: *non ti posso . . .*).
9. Chi andava per vedere i quadri; chi andava per farsi ammirare dagli altri; tutti camminavano verso il museo.
10. Che cosa mai è successo? Altri corre, altri cammina, ma tutti vanno verso la chiesa.

11. Non bisogna ripetere le opinioni altrui; bisogna avere alcune opinioni proprie.

12. Esce Lei stamane? Sí, esco fra poco; ha bisogno di qualche-cosa?

Translation IX

From the religious centre I set out for the historical centre of the town: the Square of the Signoria. It is very picturesque, with the majestic Palazzo Vecchio (Old Palace) at one side, built like a fortress with battlemented walls, and near by, the Loggia dei Lanzi (Lancers' Loggia), where once the lords of the town: came to make speeches, and where now people come to admire some of the world's most celebrated statues. From the piazza you enter into the long avenue (*piazzale* = open space, large square) of the Uffizi (Offices), which opens out between the Palazzo Vecchio and the Loggia. It is surrounded on three sides by the enormous Uffizi palace, so named because it was destined to be the seat of government offices: today it is a museum and contains the most important collection of paintings in Italy. On ordinary days you have to pay L.100 admission, so I postponed my visit until Sunday. When I went I was surprised to find a crowd of Italians all dressed in their Sunday best, walking up and down the long, light corridors, or sitting on the benches between the monuments, chatting and watching the visitors. They seemed indifferent to all the beauty of art around them; but if you were to ask one of them, as I did, where a certain masterpiece is kept or to which school of painting a certain master belongs, they can almost always give you a correct answer right away. With them the Sunday walk in the Uffizi is a habit; those pictures have become part of their lives.

If you go under the loggia at the end of the avenue you come out on the Lungarno, one of the streets which run along the river; and if you turn to the right, a little afterwards you come to Ponte Vecchio (Old Bridge). This bridge, the oldest in the town, is very picturesque, with little goldsmiths' shops clinging on to its sides, which are supported on the outside of the bridge by wooden brackets. So small are these shops that you would think that not more than five or six people could get in at once; but they do, and in large numbers, particularly ladies and tourists: for, for those who like beautiful necklaces, ear-rings, brooches, cameos and rings, it is very difficult indeed to resist the temptation of those windows, or rather show-cases, which line the very narrow road over the bridge, and which are arranged so tastefully, just at the eye-level of the passer-by.

Having crossed the river, I walked first through dark, narrow back streets between ancient palaces; then, climbing up through avenues and country roads, up over the slopes of a hill I reached the Piazzale Michelangelo. From there you can see the whole of Florence encircled by its hills; hills gently sloping and bathed in sunlight (lit.: laughing in the sun), covered with vineyards and olive groves, dotted here and there with villas and houses, among which every now and then rears up a taller and darker tree, the tree so characteristic of the Tuscan land-scape: the cypress. Sometimes one all by itself; at other times there is a lovely row marking the line of some avenue or the contour of some low hill. I could see in the distance the hill of Fiesole with the monastery at the top that I wanted to visit. It was some distance away, but the clear, pure air made it seem quite near. The clock struck twelve noon. How the sun was beating down! Everything you touched was burning hot. I looked around me at the square. Not a soul to be seen, and no noise except the ceaseless chirping of myriads of crickets.

Notes

Signoria = lordship; also: "power", "authority". Name given to the council of chief magistrates, chosen from the merchant class, who ruled Florence at the end of the 13th and during the 14th centuries.

Lanzi.—From *Lanzichenecchi* (landsknecht = German mercenary soldiers who were placed on guard in this loggia).

abiti festivi = holiday clothes, best clothes.

dove si trovi . . . a quale scuola appartenga.—The subjunctive is used here in the indirect question, although the main verb is in the present and not the past tense (see pages 136 and 143) because that verb expresses a supposition: the idea is "were you to ask", "should you ask", "suppose you asked".

li per lì (idiomatic) = straight away.

si direbbe che non si possano.—The subjunctive in an indirect statement. See page 143.

sparse . . . di.—*spargere* = to scatter, sprinkle, is followed by *di*.

parer vicino.—Remember that the final *-e* of the infinitive may be dropped before any word except one beginning with *s impure*.

Exercise 24

1. Il verde è un bel colore.
2. Sta studiando l'italiano, già sa parlare francese.
3. Cristoforo Colombo scoprì l'America.
4. La signora Bianchi è in casa; chi la vuole?
5. È caduto dall'albero e si è rotto una gamba. Quando arriverà il dottor Rossi?
6. È un gran pittore; chi lo nega parla da sciocco.
7. Firenze è una delle più belle città d'Italia.
8. Grazia Deledda, famosa scrittrice italiana, nacque in Sardegna.
9. Sacrificò la vita alla patria.
10. Mio padre è avvocato e mio zio è medico.
11. Buon giorno, Dottore, vorrebbe salire, per piacere.
12. Collane, orecchini, fermagli, cammei e anelli, tutti si vendono in quelle piccole botteghe sul Ponte Vecchio.

Translation X

"Hello! Am I speaking to the Primavera boarding-house? No? Oh, I'm sorry, I've got the wrong number. Hello, Exchange! Please give me number 25,054. Thank you. Hello! Am I speaking to the Primavera boarding-house? Good! Is the English gentleman there, who arrived a short while ago? His name is . . ." "I'm sorry, madam, he's not in. . . . Oh, wait, he's just coming in now. I'll call him; one moment."

"Excuse me, sir," the porter called just as I was coming in for lunch. "You're wanted on the telephone."

"Good lord! the telephone!" I thought. "Who can it be? However shall I make myself understood in Italian?"

But it turned out to be quite easy. It was an old English lady, married to an Italian, who had known my mother, and who wanted to invite me to go and see her in her villa at Fiesole. And very willingly I accepted.

You can go up to Fiesole by tram and by bus; but I preferred to walk. I started out in the afternoon about five. It was still hot, but not too much so; there was a lovely cool breeze coming down from the mountains. I crossed the Cathedral square and followed a long, narrow street until I came into another large square, harmonious in its effect, and surrounded on three sides by fine porticos, and in the middle of it there was a statue of a man on horseback and two very ornate fountains. Over each column of the porticos I noticed a terra-cotta plaque with that famous child in swaddling clothes on a pale blue ground, the work of one of the Della Robbia; then I knew where I was; this was the Santissima Annunziata Piazza (Holy Annunciation Square), and that building was the Foundling Hospital. I continued through other squares and along more roads until I found myself right in the country. Then, always climbing up, sometimes between high walls of villas with their gardens in bloom, other times through woods of cypresses and olives—which cleared every now and then to give a glimpse of the town below—until at last I arrived in the square at Fiesole.

It was market day, and that square presented a very lively spectacle. In the shade of the trees—there are two very fine rows of chestnuts and limes—and of the grey stone buildings, the sellers had arranged their stalls and benches on the pavement, and having covered them with tents, they stood beneath these, crying out their wares. They were selling mostly things made of straw: hats, baskets, carriers, bags, all very gay in colour and design, things for which the little place is famous; there were also leather goods in gay designs and bright colours, which are manufactured in Florence; then, too, other articles, such as shoes, books, post-cards, stockings, cheap jewellery, cloth, rosaries, crucifixes; and biscuits, sweets, and fruit. I saw large baskets full of grapes, pears and figs standing on the ground. As I had to wait for the English lady and some of her friends, I sat down at one of the tables outside under the trees, to drink an iced vermouth and to watch that cheery and animated crowd.

Notes

Pronto (lit. = ready) is used on the telephone, as we say "Hello".

mi riuscì (lit. "it succeeded to me", "it turned out to be to me"). This verb is often used impersonally to mean "to turn out to be" and "to seem". *Ciò mi riesce molto strano* = That strikes me as very strange.

portico, with the stress on the first syllable, follows the rule for words so stressed, and does not retain the hard sound in the plural.

Della Robbia.—Luca della Robbia (1400–1482) and his nephew Andrea (1437–1528 c.) revived the use of terra cotta for sculpture, and introduced the fashion of glazing their plaques in brilliant colours, particularly a lovely china blue. These blue plaques, with the charming little babe on each, give the square a particularly gay and cheerful appearance.

per lo piú = "for the most part".

vermut = vermouth. Italians usually find it difficult to pronounce a word ending in a consonant, and have a tendency to add a final vowel to foreign words which Italian has adopted, such as: *vermutte, autobusse, tramme*; and "beefsteak" has become *bistecca* in Italian. (The first three examples are not spelt with the final vowel; but the fourth, *bistecca*, is so written as well as pronounced.)

Exercise 25

1. Mangia pochissimo quel ragazzo.
2. Sono ricchi, quei forestieri. Hanno un casone in mezzo a un parco.
3. O avete dei gattini? Che piccini (or: *piccolini*), poverini!
4. Vuoi andare alla porta, Mariuccia? Non hai sentito il campanello? Qualcuno ha suonato.
5. Vuoi aiutarmi a portare dell'acqua dal pozzo? Non ho tempo io; quella contadinotta t'aiuterà (or: *vuole aiutarmi . . . l'aiuterà*).
6. Ma di chi parli? (or: *parla?*). Di quella donnetta che è venuta ieri per aiutare la cuoca?
7. Lasciai tutti quei fogli nel mio baule, che ora sarà chiuso; e ho perso la chiave. Non ha chiesto al facchino? Lui avrà la chiave, forse.
8. Ha risposto a quella signorina che Le regalò quel librone? Sí, risposi il giorno dopo.
9. Che cosa rispose quella donnuccia quando le disse che non bisogna canterellare cosí tutto il tempo? Non disse niente, rise soltanto.
10. Salí le scale (or: *gli scalini*) ed entrò nella cameretta. Non c'era nessuno. Pose il pacchetto e i fiori sul tavolino vicino alla finestra.
11. Che casaccia! Chi ci vive? Qualche poveraccio!
12. Hanno un villino in una di quelle stradette di campagna che vanno su per il colle.

Translation XI

We were sitting on the terrace of the English lady's villa after an excellent supper and enjoying the view of the city by night—all a twinkling of lights down there in the valley—when my hosts decided to take me to Siena to see the Palio. "We go every year," they said. "It is a fine sight and most amusing. You'll like it, you'll see." And they were right; I thoroughly enjoyed myself.

We took the *littorina*. By the way, I would not recommend this motor-train for nervous people, but it is the quickest way. It goes so fast that it seems to fly over the rails without touching them; but when it does touch them, it gives such a bump that the travellers bounce up and down on their seats, and the parcels dancing about on the luggage-rack jump out and land on the heads of the people below (lit.: fall on). And so we arrived at the charming, clean and neat little station at Siena. It is very modern, and would make anyone like the modern style of architecture (lit.: very modern and of such as to make to convert to the 20th-century style), so lovely is it in shape and proportion.

Then, after a carriage drive up a steep road, I found myself within the walls of the mediaeval town, which looks down upon the surrounding country from the height of its three hills. The imposing Gothic palaces of grey stone, some battlemented, and the dark, narrow little streets—down some even a carriage cannot pass—all seemed to me rather cold and forbidding at first. But then came the days of the Palio. What a change! Everything and everybody seemed transported with joy: the inhabitants, even the streets and the palaces. Hanging from those sombre buildings were flags, tapestries and pieces of cloth; every window had something; the streets were all a-flutter with banners; and the Sienese, at all hours of the day and night, went walking up and down, arm in arm, singing and laughing, all very merry. This horse race, run in commemoration of some ancient religious festival, is the strangest in the world. It takes place in the middle of the town, in the Piazza del Campo (lit.: Square of the Field), and those taking part dress up in mediaeval costumes in the brightest of colours, but well harmonized together. As I did not know anything about the religious significance, and as I had not backed a horse, I could not share in the wild enthusiasm for the race; all the same, for me it was the most interesting theatrical show, and the scenes which most impressed me were these:

Act I.—A little church in one of the wards. Characters—a priest, a horse, a jockey (all near to the altar); a crowd of people laughing and chatting all the time. The priest recites a prayer, sprinkling meanwhile the horse's nose with holy water. Shouts and laughter of the crowd: "Well done! hurrah! long live the she-wolf!" They all go out laughing. Curtain.

Act II.—A large square the shape of a shell or a fan, crowded with people. There are people at all the windows and people on all the roofs; the square itself is a jostling crowd except in the space all around reserved for the racecourse. A deafening roar from the crowd; a mad rush of ten horses; and for just one minute and a half the air is rent with the shouting and whistling of tens of thousands of people, with the beating of drums, the blowing of trumpets, the firing of guns, and the ringing of the bells of more than twenty churches. Curtain.

Act III.—The main street in the winning ward, at a late hour of the night. At a long table several hundred people are having supper in the open air. The scene is lit up by old-fashioned flares hanging from the ancient palaces. At the head of the table is the principal actor: the winning horse, with his own manger, and in it there is—as well as other things—macaroni! He is eating! The end. Curtain.

Notes

Eravamo seduti . . . a godere.—Note the preposition *a* after a verb of rest (*sedere*), before a following infinitive.

condurmi.—The few verbs of the second conjugation whose infinitive ends in *-rre* drop the final *-re* before adding the conjunctive pronouns.

Noi si va.—The indefinite *si* construction is often used in conversation together with the subject pronoun *noi* instead of the ordinary first person plural. This very idiomatic use should be remembered for conversation, but it should not appear in written Italian, except when reporting conversation.

Va tanto veloce.—Note the adjective instead of an adverb in *-mente.*

in testa alla gente.—Where we should say "on to the heads of", Italian has "in head to", for *in testa a* has become a prepositional phrase formed by a noun preceded and followed by a preposition, in the same way as: *in mezzo a* = in the middle of. See also the last paragraph of this extract: *in capo a* = at the head of.

scarrozzare = to drive in a carriage.

scarrozzata = drive, driving in a carriage.

abitanti.—From what verb is this noun formed?

partecipare a.—Note the preposition after this verb.

grida e risa.—Irregular plurals of *grido, riso.* See page 70.

l'aria è in tempesta.—Lit.: "the air is in a storm".

Exercise 26

1. Mi diede quel libro prima di partire per Roma.
2. Perché ha detto ciò? Parla senza pensare.
3. Odo dire ciò mille volte al giorno.

4. Hanno fatto aprire quella porta?
5. Sì, la cuoca l'aperse, ma ora non possiamo chiuderla.
6. Invece di leggere un romanzo, dovrebbe studiare quella lezione.
7. Sì, io gliela farei studiare, e subito.
8. La littorina parte alle undici, credo, mi potrebbe prenotare un posto?
9. Gli dissi di comprare i biglietti ieri.
10. Sì, ha cercato di farlo, ma non poteva, tutto era chiuso.
11. Aveva promesso di andare subito, ma non può, non c'è un treno prima di domani.
12. Ti proibisco di andare in quella casa.

Translation XII

Besides being one of the most romantic and picturesque of cities, Venice is also one of the strangest in the world. It is difficult for anyone who has not seen it to imagine what this city of marble and water looks like. There is no vegetation, or very little; no grass, no plants nor trees, except in a few gardens. There are no wide streets, the roads of Venice are canals and waterways; so there are no cars, no buses, no carriages. The Venetian taxi is the gondola or the motor-boat. In this strange place the eye has to get accustomed to a view quite different from that which it sees every day; it is a view of palaces, water and sky; white palaces, yellow palaces, pink palaces, all glittering in the very strong, clear light, and all have the sea lapping their walls at ground-floor level. The ear notes the absence of the usual sounds; the first impression is of a great silence, broken only by the melancholy call of the gondolier as he comes near a street corner, or by the far-off whistle of the steamer which plies regularly to the neighbouring islands.

These and other thoughts were passing through my mind one evening, as I sat at one of the little tables in St. Mark's Square. Several friends were with me—acquaintances I had made at the Lido, where I used to bathe every day—and they had come to hear the evening concert on the Grand Canal.

"And just think, Charles," one of them was saying to me, "this extraordinary city is built in the middle of a lagoon, on an archipelago of nearly a hundred and twenty islands, and it has one hundred and sixty canals and four hundred bridges!"

"It must have a very interesting history," I said.

"Come on, Lewis, the historian," they all shouted.

"Very well," said Lewis. "It was founded in the 5th century —I think—by refugees fleeing before the invasions of the barbarians, and it went on gaining in power and importance by reason of its trade connections with the east. The Venetians, as you know, were a practical and an enterprising people: they managed to seize every opportunity of enriching themselves and of extending their power. In the Middle Ages they acquired the monopoly of the salt trade, a product which was then very scarce and very dear; during the crusades they carried the Christian troops to the east in their boats, and of course, like the crafty merchants they were, they charged a good bit for those voyages. In the 13th century Venice was already an important power in the Mediterranean, with colonies in the Aegean and in Asia Minor; and in the 14th she came forward as the champion of Christianity against the Turks. It was at this period, if I remember rightly, that her ships reached the ports of far-off England. Later, when she had conquered a large part of northern Italy, this maritime republic became one of the five great Italian states. Her decline dates from the 16th century with the opening of new sea routes to the Indies and with the beginning of long wars with Turkey. Today Venice might seem to be a dead city; but it is a very rich museum and a paradise for tourists . . . and for students on holidays," he added, with a smile.

"Good for you, Lewis! Full marks!"

"Thank you, Lewis," I said as I looked around at the square.

In the distance the cathedral façade was facing us; and at either side were the fine porticos with their shops selling glass-ware and lace, and where a large crowd was now sauntering leisurely to and fro, for it was the hour for the evening walk. The band was playing a slow, sentimental tune, and flying all around were those impudent inhabitants of the piazza—the pigeons. Every now and then they came down on to the pavement or perched upon the tables looking for crumbs. "Let him who needs a real rest come here to Venice," I thought; "for, lulled by the slow rhythm of the gondola, a sense of calm and content enters one's soul here, as in no other place. Here one can be lazy; here no one hurries, there is time for everything, for time itself seems to be standing still."

Notes

Oltre a essere.—Note the infinitive after the preposition where we in English use a present participle. See page 125.

abbia.—Present subjunctive of *avere*. The subjunctive is required here as *chi* has the force of "whoever". See page 138.

Lido.—This most celebrated of bathing-places is at the edge of the lagoon, a short distance by motor-boat from Venice. The English visitor is often surprised at not being able to get down to the sea here without paying for it; and one pays different prices, according to whether one bathes from an hotel or from the large public *stabilimento* (establishment, bathing place). Each hotel, too, has its portion of sea partitioned off, the price for bathing varying according to the class of hotel.

Serenata.—Lit.: "serenade". Each evening during the season a concert is held on the Grand Canal. The orchestra and singers go out in a large, flat-bottomed boat lit up with Chinese lanterns, and the audience follow in gondolas and tie their boats to that of the concert party. At the end of each item two very agile gondoliers leap and crawl over all the boats with money-boxes to coax and smile a good collection out of the spectators.

pratico.—Besides meaning "practical", also means "acquainted with", as: *Non sono practico di queste parti* = I don't know these parts (or: "I'm a stranger here").

si erano acquistati.—Lit. = they had acquired for themselves.

fecero pagar cari . . .—Note that there is no single verb in Italian for "to charge"; it is rendered by *far pagare* = to make to pay.

Trenta con lòde.—Lit. = thirty with praise. The usual expression for "full marks and distinction" in Italian schools and universities, as the maximum is generally thirty in most examinations.

basilica.—The name (taken from the Greek) given to Roman law court buildings and subsequently applied to early Christian churches, which in their oblong shape with nave, colonnade and apse, resembled them.

cristallerie e . . . pizzi.—Glass-blowing and lace-making are two of the chief industries of Venice today.

Venga.—Present subjunctive of *venire*, used as an imperative: "Let him come."

Cullandosi al—lit. = cradling, rocking, lulling oneself by . . . *i.e.* being lulled by. Note the preposition used in Italian.

Exercise 27

1. È un ragazzo sfrontato; mi stava guardando tutt'il tempo.
2. Non ha pagato ancora quel biglietto?

3. Non mi permette di vedere quei libri; ha chiuso a chiave la porta della sua camera.
4. Che cosa pensa di quell'uomo? È bugiardo; non crede a ciò che dice.
5. La bottiglia di vino è sulla tavola nella sala da pranzo; quella nuova cameriera dai capelli rossi l'ha lasciata lí.
6. Venezia era una della piú grandi e una delle piú importanti città del medioevo. Costruita sopra un arcipelago di centoventi isole in una laguna al nord del mare adriatico, era destinata a diventare una potenza marittima. I veneziani erano un popolo pratico e intraprendente. Acquistarono il monopolio del commercio del sale e fecero pagar caro quel prodotto. Ai tempi delle crociate seppero approfittare dell'occasione per arricchirsi e per estendere il loro potere nel Mediterraneo orientale, e le loro navi trasportarono migliaia dei fedeli che facevano guerra ai turchi. Nei viaggi di ritorno in patria quelle stesse navi venivano cariche di marmi e mosaici ricchissimi, i quali quella gente marinara adoperarono per abbellire la loro città. I bei monumenti ed edifici (or: *edifizi*) veneziani che ammiriamo oggi attestano il forte sentimento patriottico che animava i figli di questa famosa repubblica marittima del medioevo.

Translation XIII

At Venice the life of the town revolves around St. Mark's Square, or to be more precise round the little café tables there; at Milan the vital centre is the Cathedral Square, with the adjacent Victor Emanuel arcade, which also has its little tables, full at all hours of the day. The arcade, the traditional rendezvous of the Milanese, is enormous. You enter from the Cathedral Square, going through a majestic archway, and when you have gone the whole length you come out into the Scala Square, where the famous theatre of that name is to be found. Throughout its length the arcade is flanked by smart shops and numerous cafés, and I certainly have passed many pleasant hours there with friends at one of the little tables, watching and criticizing the people passing, and eating the ices, which really are delicious.

One day, after a visit to the convent of the church of Santa Maria delle Grazie (Saint Mary of the Graces) with two American tourists to see the famous "Last Supper" by Leonardo da Vinci, I came back to the arcade to rest awhile.

I sat down at my usual table, ordered my vermouth from the waiter, and settled myself to watch the passers-by. I had only a few days' holiday left, and I was thinking that I ought to go to the theatre, at least once. I called the waiter, who was already quite an old friend, for he had helped and advised me so many times, and I asked him for a newspaper so that I could see what was on at the theatres (lit.: the theatre column).

"With pleasure, sir," he replied. "The newspaper boy will go past any minute with the *Evening Post*, and I'll buy it for you myself. But as for theatres, I'm afraid that there'll be very little just now, as it is out of the season. The majority of the theatres are closed and the actors away on holiday. But there are plenty of cinemas. Wouldn't you like to see some good film?" But I already knew that there was not anything special at the cinemas.

While I was waiting for the newspaper boy I bought writing-paper and stamps from the waiter, and there at my little table I wrote home to England to let them know the date I was going back. I was putting the stamps—worth seventy lire— (*da* here stands for "of the value of") on my letter when the waiter returned with the paper. He had already looked at it, and he handed it to me saying: "There is one thing that perhaps may suit you, sir. Do you like music?" On my replying in the affirmative, he went on: "There's a special performance for charity of the lovely opera by Puccini, 'Madam Butterfly'—you must know it, sir—and there's a very good tenor and a Japanese girl singer with a divine voice. It's really worth hearing. But it's being given in a small theatre, a bit away from the centre of town, near to where I live."

"Very good, then, Beppino," I replied—for that was the good man's name—"if it's near your home, come with me tonight and hear 'Madam Butterfly', will you?"

Notes

ci si entra.—The conjunctive pronouns and adverbs (except *ne*) precede *si* when it is used impersonally as here. *mi si dice =* they tell me; *lo si fa così =* it is done like that; but when the *si* is reflexive meaning "to himself", "to herself", etc., it is an indirect pronoun, and therefore precedes the direct *lo, la, li,* etc. *se lo mise in testa =* she put it on her head (lit. = to herself she put in head).

Teatro della Scala.—One of the most famous opera houses in the world; founded in 1778, it holds nearly 3,000 people. It is the height of ambition of every Italian singer (and

singers of other countries too) to be well received by the Scala
audience.

pensavo che sarei dovuto andare.—A compound conditional
tense where we use the simple conditional. See page 146. For
the use of the auxiliary, see page 148.

gran che.—Idiomatic use of *che* as a noun. The phrase
means: "a great deal", "anything particular", "anything
special".

comprai.—One can often buy writing materials and stamps
in the cafés in Italy and write letters at the tables there.
Stamps may also be bought—as well as at the post office—at
any shop that sells salt and tobacco; for these two commodities
are government monopolies, and require a special licence—
which also applies to stamps.

ai miei.—The possessive adjective is used in the plural without any noun to mean "people", "parents", "relations".

bravo.—Note the difference in meaning in this adjective
when it precedes and when it follows its noun. In the first case
it means "good", "worthy"; in the second, "clever", "capable",
"efficient".

Exercise 28

1. Mi dia di quella carta da scrivere, per favore, voglio scrivere
   ai miei a casa.
2. Vuole che voi tutti ve ne andiate subito; non può vedere
   nessuno.
3. Dubito che vengano ora. È tanto tardi.
4. È contento che Lei lo sappia ora; ma non osava dirglielo lui
   stesso.
5. Sa Lei se siano partiti o no?
6. È il piú cattivo ragazzo che io conosca.
7. Non c'è nessuno qui che sappia suonare il pianoforte?
8. Milano è una delle piú grandi città d'Italia, con piú di un
   milione di abitanti. È la città piú importante dell'Italia
   settentrionale, e il maggior centro industriale, commerciale
   e bancario di tutta la penisola. Quando sono a Milano
   vado ogni giorno (or: *tutti i giorni*) alla Galleria Vittorio
   Emanuele, tradizionale luogo di ritrovo dei milanesi, dove
   ci sono negozi eleganti e numerosissimi caffè. Mi siedo a
   uno dei tavolini, chiedo un vermut o un caffè al cameriere,
   e mentre sto bevendo guardo passare la folla. Alcuni
   vengono qui per passeggiare su e giú, altri per chiacchierare, altri per incontrare degli amici e altri per discutere
   gli affari; ma tutti ci vengono nella speranza di avere (or:

trovare) un momento di pace e di tregua dal rumore e dal movimento della grande città industriale moderna.

Translation XIV

"Thank you, sir; you are too kind," continued Beppino. "Today, as it just so happens, I'm free, and if you really would like . . ."

So it ended by Beppino coming to the theatre with me, and not only Beppino, but the whole of his large and charming family: his wife, sister, brother, grandfather and four children. But what good-hearted folk! They simply would not let me pay for the tickets, not even for my own, in spite of all my protests. And what a crowd! Rarely in my life have I seen such enthusiasm. We could not reserve seats, there were so many people; in fact (*anzi* = on the contrary), we had to form a queue. But as soon as the doors were opened there was a surge forward (*pigia* = pushing), and with shouts and laughter everyone scrambled to get in first, and I felt myself being carried up the stairs and to a good seat in the gallery. Beppino lost sight of some of his family, but he did not seem to mind; his wife was a bit worried, however, for she had lost a shoe, but luckily it turned up later.

I shall never forget that Italian audience. They were very critical, even severely so; one singer whom they did not like they hissed unmercifully (*senza complimenti* = lit.: without compliments, without any regard to his feelings, without standing on ceremony), and they would not let him go on. They all knew the opera note for note, and they joined in singing the most well-known airs; which was somewhat irritating for me. But when the singer was really good, or if a piece was very well played, the whole audience sat rapt and quiet, as if they were all holding their breath, right up to the very last note, and then there was a storm of applause and shouts of encore that never seemed to be going to end. One of that good tenor's songs got seven encores. And the poor man, to satisfy them, came back and sang it seven times!

As can well be imagined, it was very late when we came out of the theatre; two of the children were already fast asleep, and we were all very tired, but very happy. I had to hurry on to the hotel to pack my suitcase, for I was leaving the following day. They all came with me to the tram, and after many a handshake and cries of "goodbye" and "come back soon", at last I left those delightful people.

Notes

fini per.—*finire per* = to finish by; this expression in English is followed by the present participle; the Italian equivalent takes the infinitive.

la moglie, la sorella.—The article is preferred to the possessive adjective, for it is quite clear whose wife, etc., is meant.

fare la coda.—to form a queue. *Coda* = tail.

preoccuparsene = to worry about it; *preoccuparsi* takes *di* before its object.

le arie . . . le cantava.—The repetition emphasizes *arie*.

bis = a second time. The Italians shout *bis* in the theatre where we use the French *encore*.

Exercise 29

1. Ero contento che fossero partiti (or: *che se ne fossero andati*).
2. Credevo che voi tutti foste in Italia.
3. Non l'avesse mai veduta!
4. Benché non fosse stata lei che avesse rotto lo specchio veneziano, continuò a piangere.
5. Tua moglie ti chiese dove fossi stato ieri sera?
6. No, entrai senza che lei mi vedesse.
7. Caro Giovanni, Sai dove sono venuto a passare le vacanze? Mio padre ha sempre voluto che io vedessi l'Italia, e ora finalmente eccomi qua! Ho visitato diverse città famose: Pisa, Firenze, Siena, Venezia e adesso sto a Milano, dove ho incontrato alcuni miei amici italiani. Ieri m'accompagnarono al teatro per sentire l'opera. Tutti cantarono molto bene; ma ciò che m'interessava di piú era il pubblico italiano. Che entusiasmo! Avessi visto! Quante volte "bis"! Un tenore molto bravo dovette tornare a cantare sette volte una sua canzone che piacque molto. Sette volte! D'altra parte che fischi, che grida quando c'era uno che non sapeva cantare bene! Peccato che tu non fossi stato con me! Avremmo riso tanto insieme.

    Non rispondere a questa; forse dovrò partire per l'Inghilterra fra poco. E scusami questa lettera tanto breve; avrò mille cose da raccontarti; e almeno non ti puoi lagnare che non ti abbia scritto. I meii saluti ai tuoi. Ciao! Tuo Carlo.

Translation XV

The following morning I left for Como, in the company of some Americans who were going on to Paris. By express Como is only one hour from Milan, and I arrived there before ten. After making a tour of the town, I decided to take the funicular up to Brunate, a little village on a hill to the east from where there is a fine view of the lake. While sitting on a seat to look at the view I got out my map to find my bearings. The town of Como stretched out below me with its bay and its hills, and beyond it opened out the plain of Lombardy. In front of me and to the right was the lake with its high, steep mountains, and far, far away on the horizon the majestic peaks of the Alps were shining in the sun. "Now I'm in the country of Don Abbondio and Lucia," I thought, remembering the famous novel. "Lecco must be beyond those mountains to the east, on the other branch of the lake." I looked at my map again, thinking, "Instead of staying in Como, I should really like a quieter place on the lake, somewhere a bit out of the way. Let's look again." My finger followed the steamer route: "Como, Cernobbio, Cadenabbia, Bellagio . . . there's a lovely sunny place (lit. = smiling) on a promontory where the three branches of the lake meet; yes, that will do. There are five or six hotels, none very large. All the better." I went down again to Como, took my bag out of the cloakroom, and embarked on the steamer for Bellagio.

"Good evening," I said to the hotel proprietor, who was lounging about in his doorway. "Have you a room free?"

"This way, sir," and giving my suitcase to a porter who came forward, I followed him into the hall (lit.: "he preceded me").

The hotel was small, but white and clean; it had a lovely garden at the front, with a balcony and pergola which stretched down to the shores of the lake.

"Are you staying long?" the proprietor asked me.

"No, only three or four days."

"Then I can offer you a very nice room, with a terrace and view of the lake, 2,000 lire a day, inclusive; plus the tourist tax and the 10 per cent service. There is, too, a smaller one, without terrace, and with a view over the mountains for 1,800 lire. They are both fine spacious (airy) rooms, with hot and cold water. Do you wish to see them, sir?"

"Thank you." And although it was a bit dearer than I would have liked, I let myself be tempted by the lovely view, and chose the room with the balcony.

But everything comes to an end. The last day of my holidays arrived. I bathed for the last time in those cool waters, and went for a last trip in a boat with the old boatman, Antonio. The morning of my departure I got up early, and when I had packed my case I ordered my coffee to be brought up to the terrace. While I had breakfast (lit.: "while I was eating") I watched the fishing-boats pass with their tawny red sails. Then suddenly I saw my old friend Antonio, and he left his oars and stood up, waving his cap in the air and calling out to me: "Goodbye, sir; a pleasant journey to you. Remember Antonio, and come back again soon."

"Why, of course," I thought as I went on board the steamer for Como, the first stage of my return journey. "Why of course, dear old Antonio, I will always remember you; and as for coming back again soon, why, yes, I can certainly promise you that: I shall come back again to your lovely country at the first possible opportunity."

Notes

col direttissimo.—To travel by train is: *viaggiare col treno*; by car = *coll'automobile, colla macchina* (also *nell'automobile, nella macchina*); also *coll'autobus, con la bicicletta.*

Don Abbondio . . . Lucia.—Two of the principal characters in the historical novel *I promessi sposi* (The Betrothed) by Alessandro Manzoni (1785–1873), one of the greatest figures in Italian literature. The scene of this novel is the country around the lake of Como, particularly near Lecco, a small town at the end of the arm of the lake pointing due south. The extract on page 40 is from this novel (very slightly modified).

i tre rami.—The shape of the lake should be seen on the map. It has three distinct arms meeting at one point. Como, at the end of the arm pointing south-west is a small industrial town, chiefly important for the manufacture of silk; and Bellagio is on the promontory where the three arms meet.

Si accomodi.—We have already used *accomodarsi* for "to seat oneself"; and it is also used in the imperative—*si accomodi*—for many other expressions, such as "This way, please"; "Make yourself at home"; and "Do just as you wish".

imbarcarsi = to embark. *Sbarcare* = to disembark. *S impure* at the beginning of a word is sometimes a shortened form of *dis-*, and therefore negatives the meaning of the word: *coprire* = to cover; *scoprire* = to uncover, discover; *comodo* = comfortable; *scomodo* = uncomfortable.

tassa di soggiorno = a tax levied by the Italian Government on all tourists and visitors. Italians on holiday at hotels and boarding-houses are also required to pay this tax, which varies according to the locality and to the class of hotel.

ArrivederLa—lit.: "to the seeing you again", "au revoir". Note the change of pronoun with the different forms of address: *arrivederti, arrivedervi*; also *arrivederci* is often used.

Exercise 30

1. Dissero che sarebbero venuti alle tre, ma sono le tre e mezzo e non sono ancora arrivati.
2. Se andate al teatro, non tornate tanto tardi come l'altra volta (or: *se va . . . non torni*; or: *se vai . . . non torna*).
3. Se avessi quel libro, studierei.
4. Se avessi avuto quel libro, avrei studiato.
5. Se avrò quel libro, studierò.
6. Se avesse domandato a me dov'era quella chiesa, gli avrei detto subito (or: *Se mi domandava a me dove era . . . gli dicevo . . .*).
7. Sarebbe dovuto venire piú presto se avesse voluto vedermi.
8. Se non fossi arrivato a Como troppo tardi per prendere il piroscafo per Bellagio, non avrei conosciuto Antonio. Quel vecchio barcaiuolo dagli occhi azzurri e dalla barba bianca, con quello strano berretto rosso, stava oziando sul molo quando io ci arrivai correndo, con la valigia in mano, proprio in tempo per veder partire il piroscafo. —Che rabbia! Chi sa quanto tempo dovrò aspettare? — pensai. —Mi dispiace che abbia perduto il piroscafo, Signore, vorrebbe andare in barca?— mi chiese quel vecchio, avvicinandosi a me. —Grazie— risposi, —ma è un po' troppo lontano per andarci con una barca a remi.— —Ma, ho un motoscafo, Signore.— —No, grazie, temo che quello mi costi troppo.— —Ma, Signore, Lei vuol andare a Bellagio, e ci voglio andare anch'io; lí c'è la mia casa, e la moglie e i bambini mi aspettano per la cena. Andiamo insieme; se mi vuol pagare, mi paghi il prezzo del biglietto del piroscafo; se non mi vuol pagare, non importa (*non fa niente*); ci vado lo stesso.— E cosí finii per andare con Antonio e per fare la conoscenza di uno degli uomini piú simpatici che abbia mai incontrato.

APPENDIX

ADDITIONAL NOTES ON PRONUNCIATION, ACCENTS AND SYLLABICATION

Pronunciation

The Vowels e and o.—As dictionaries do not always indicate whether *e* and *o* in stressed syllables have the open or close sound, the following notes will be of use:

e is *open* in the following cases:

1. In the diphthong *iɛ*: piɛde, ciɛlo.
2. When followed by another vowel: idɛa.
3. In words of more than two syllables that end in *-ɛro*: sevɛro.
4. When the stressed *e* is in the third from the last syllable: mɛdico, sɛcolo.
5. In the endings: *-ɛndo* and *-ɛnte*, and when *e* is followed by two or more consonants, *except* in the following endings, which are all *close*: -egno, -emmo, -enna, -esco, -etto, -evole, -ezza, and -mente.

Final *e* when stressed is *close*, except in: caffè, tè, ahimè ("alas"), cioè ("that is") and è ("is").

o is *open*:

1. In the diphthong *uɔ*: uɔmo, buɔno.
2. When followed by another vowel: pɔi (except noi and voi).
3. When it is in the third syllable from the end: pɔvero, mɔnaco.
4. When it is followed by a double consonant: dɔnna, fɔlla.
5. When it is a final vowel: comprɔ.
6. When it is followed by one or more consonants and the diphthongs *-ia* or *-io*: prɔprio.

The Consonants s and z.—Again, the *voiced* and *unvoiced* sounds are not distinguished in all dictionaries: the following will be helpful:

s is *unvoiced* (like the *s* in *taste*):

1. When followed by *c*, *f*, *p*, *q*, *t* (all voiceless consonants): aspettare.
2. When at the beginning of a word and followed by a vowel: sabato.
3. When it is double: tassa.

s is *voiced* (like the *s* in *rose*):

1. When followed by the voiced consonants: *b*, *d*, *g*, *l*, *m*, *n*, *r*, *v*: ṣbaglio, ṣmemorato.
2. When it comes between vowels: rọṣa, viṣo. There are, however, many exceptions to this rule; we may quote those which have appeared in this book: casa, cọsa, cosí, mese, risa, Pisa, inglese—in all these words the *s* is *unvoiced*, although it comes between two vowels.

z is *unvoiced* (pronounced like *ts*) when it is followed by *-ia*, *-ie*, or *-io*; grazie, azione.

z is *voiced* (pronounced like *dz*):

1. In verbs ending in *-izzare* which have more than four syllables in the infinitive: analiẓẓare (= to analyse).
2. In words derived from Greek, Hebrew or Arabic: aẓẓurro.
3. In words which begin with *z*: ẓelo (= zeal). But there are some exceptions to this rule; among them we may note: zio, zia, zoppo (all of which we have used in this book), and we may add two other useful words: zucchero (= sugar) and zuppa (= soup). In all these words, the *z* is *unvoiced*, although it is the initial letter.

Accents

In addition to the rules for the written accent, given on pp. 17–18, we must also note that there are some words which take an accent occasionally, when it is necessary to avoid confusion between words of more than one syllable, which are spelt alike, but have different meanings. These are either words which are exactly alike in form, but have a different syllable stressed, as: ancóra = again, àncora = anchor; or they are alike in form, but one has a *close e* or *o*, and the other an *open* vowel: légge = law, lègge = he reads; cólto = cultivated, còlto = gathered. It must be emphasized that such words have the accent *only* when their meaning is not clear from the context; which is not very often.

Some writers put an acute accent on the *i* of words ending in *-io* and *-ia*, when the *i* is stressed, as: signoría, scintillío, gridío, to ensure the correct pronunciation of the word; also in reading

you will find that parts of verbs taking the conjunctive pronouns after them often have an accent, as: dàtegliene, dàglielo,
fàllo (= do it).

Syllabication

The method of dividing words into syllables differs from that
used in English:

1. Every syllable, as far as possible, begins with a consonant:
   lu-ne-dí; ge-ne-ra-le.
2. Two vowels together forming a diphthong are one syllable,
   a hiatus forms two syllables: buo-no, piε-de, vi-a,
   pa-u-ra.
3. Double consonants are separated: vac-ca, gat-to.
4. Two consonants, of which the first is *l*, *m*, *n*, or *r*, are
   separated: ac-cεn-to, per-ché.
5. Any other two consonants are counted in the following
   syllable: fi-glia, giu-gno.
6. When three consonants come together, provided the first
   one is not *s*, the first is counted in the preceding
   syllable, and the other two in the following one: com-
   pra-re, com-plε-to.
7. If *s* is the first of the three consonants, all three belong to
   the following syllable: co-strin-ge-re, e-stre-mi-tà.

LIST OF COMMON IRREGULAR VERBS

Forms not listed below are regular. When an infinitive is
contracted, the original form is given in brackets, to indicate
the stem to which the endings are added for the regular parts
(present participle, imperfect indicative and imperfect subjunctive—see page 86).

Abbreviations: *fut.*: = future; *impve.* = imperative; *past
def.* = past definite; *past part.* = past participle; *pres. ind.* =
present indicative; *pres. sub.* = present subjunctive; *imp. sub.*
= imperfect subjunctive.

Verbs conjugated with *essere* are marked *; verbs which
sometimes take *essere* and sometimes *avere* are preceded by a †.

All the irregular verbs which appear in this book are included. For easy consultation the two auxiliary verbs, *avere*
and *essere*, are given together at the end of this list, on p. 220.

*accorgersi = to notice; *past. def.* accorsi, accorgesti, etc.; *past part.* accorto.

aggiungere = to add; see giungere.

*andare = to go; *pres. ind.* vado, vai, va, andiamo, andate, vanno; *fut.* andrò; *pres. sub.* vada, andiamo, andiate, vadano; *impve.* va', andiamo, andate.

*apparire = to appear; *pres. ind.* appaio or apparisco, appari or apparisci, appare or apparisce, appariamo, apparite, appaiono or appariscono; *past def.* apparsi or apparvi or apparii, apparisti, etc.; *past part.* apparso or apparito; *pres. sub.* appaia or apparisca, etc.; *impve.* appari or apparisci, appariamo, apparite.

appartenere = to belong; see tenere.

aprire = to open; *past def.* apersi or aprii, apristi, etc.; *past part.* aperto.

aspergere = to sprinkle; see spargere.

bere (bevere) = to drink; *pres. ind.* bevo; *past def.* bevvi, or bevei or bevetti, bevesti, etc.; *past part.* bevuto; *fut.* berrò or beverò; *pres. sub.* beva; *impve.* bevi, beviamo, bevete.

*cadere = to fall; *past def.* caddi, cadesti, etc.; *fut.* cadrò.

chiedere = to ask; *pres. ind.* chiedo or chieggo, chiedi, chiede, chiediamo, chiedete, chiedono or chieggono; *past def.* chiesi, chiedesti, etc.; *past part.* chiesto; *pres. sub.* chieda or chiegga; *impve.* chiedi, chiediamo, chiedete.

chiudere = to close; *past def.* chiusi, chiudesti, etc.; *past part.* chiuso.

cingere = to gird, embrace, surround; *past def.* cinsi, cingesti, etc.; *past part.* cinto.

cogliere = to gather; *pres. ind.* colgo, cogli, coglie, cogliamo, cogliete, colgono; *past def.* colsi, cogliesti, etc.; *past part.* colto; *pres. sub.* colga; *impve.* cogli, cogliamo, cogliete.

comprendere = to understand; see prendere.

condurre (conducere) = to lead; *pres. ind.* conduco, etc.; *past def.* condussi, conducesti, etc.; *past part.* condotto; *fut.* condurrò; *pres. sub.* conduca, conduciamo, conduciate, conducano; *impve.* conduci, conduciamo, conducete.

conoscere = to know; *past def.* conobbi, conoscesti, etc.

contenere = to contain; see tenere.

*convenire = to suit, agree; see venire.

coprire = to cover; see aprire.

†correre = to run; *past def.* corsi, corresti, etc.; *past part.* corso.

costringere = to compel; see stringere.

costruire = to construct; *past def.* costrussi, costruisti, etc.;
past part. costrutto or costruito.

†crescere = to grow; *past def.* crebbi, crescesti, etc.

dare = to give; *pres. ind.* do, dai, dà, diamo, date, danno; *past
def.* diedi or detti, desti, etc.; *past part.* dato; *fut.* darò; *pres.
sub.* dia, diamo, diate, diano or dieno; *impve.* da', diamo,
date; *imp. sub.* dessi, etc.

decidere = to decide; *past def.* decisi, decidesti, etc.; *past part.*
deciso.

*dipendere = to depend; see spendere.

dire (dicere) = to say; *pres. ind.* dico, dici, dice, diciamo, dite,
dicono; *past def.* dissi, dicesti, etc.; *past part.* detto; *fut.*
dirò; *pres. sub.* dica, diciamo, diciate, dicano; *impve.* di',
diciamo, dite.

*dirigersi = to direct oneself; *past def.* diressi, dirigesti, etc.;
past part. diretto.

discutere = to discuss; *past def.* discussi, discutesti, etc.; *past
part.* discusso.

dispiacere = to displease; see piacere.

disporre = to dispose; see porre.

distinguere = to distinguish; *past def.* distinsi, distinguesti,
etc.; *past part.* distinto.

*divenire = to become; see venire.

dovere = to owe, to have to, to be obliged to; *pres. ind.*
devo or debbo, devi, deve, dobbiamo, dovete, devono or
debbono; *fut.* dovrò; *pres. sub.* deva or debba, dobbiamo,
dobbiate, devano or debbano.

emettere = to emit; see mettere.

esporre = to expose; see porre.

estendere = to extend; see spendere.

fare (facere) = to do, to make; *pres. ind.* faccio or fo, fai, fa,
facciamo, fate, fanno; *past def.* feci, facesti, etc.; *past part.*
fatto; *fut.* farò; *pres. sub.* faccia, facciamo, facciate, facciano;
impve. fa', facciamo, fate.

†giungere = to arrive, to join; *past def.* giunsi, giungesti, etc.;
past part. giunto.

intendere = to intend, understand; see spendere.

invadere = to invade; *past def.* invasi, invadesti, etc.; *past
part.* invaso.

leggere = to read; *past def.* lessi, leggesti, etc.; *past part.* letto.

mettere = to put; *past def.* misi or messi, mettesti, etc.; *past
part.* messo.

*morire = to die; *pres. ind.* muoio, muori, muore, moriamo,
morite, muoiono; *past part.* morto; *fut.* morirò or morrò;

pres. sub. muoia, moriamo, moriate, muoiano; *impve.* muori, moriamo, morite.

muovere = to move; *pres. ind.* muovo or movo, muovi or movi, muove or move, moviamo, movete, muovono or movono; *past def.* mossi, movesti, etc.; *past part.* mosso; *pres. sub.* muova or mova, moviamo, moviate, muovano or movano; *impve.* muovi or movi, moviamo, movete.

*nascere = to be born; *past def.* nacqui, nascesti, etc.; *past part.* nato.

offrire = to offer; see aprire.

*parere = to seem; *pres. ind.* paio, pari, pare, paiamo, parete, paiono; *past def.* parvi or parsi, paresti, etc.; *past part.* parso; *fut.* parrò; *pres. sub.* paia, paiamo, pariate, paiano.

perdere = to lose; *past def.* persi or perdei or perdetti, perdesti, etc.; *past part.* perso or perduto.

permettere = to permit; see mettere.

piacere = to please; *pres. ind.* piaccio, piaci, piace, piacciamo, piacete, piacciono; *past def.* piacqui, piacesti, etc.; *pres. sub.* piaccia, piacciamo, piacciate, piacciano; *impve.* piaci, piacciamo, piacete.

piangere = to cry; *past def.* piansi, piangesti, etc.; *past part.* pianto.

†piovere = to rain (impersonal); *past def.* piovve.

porgere = to present, offer; *past def.* porsi, porgesti, etc.; *past part.* porto.

porre (ponere) = to put; *pres. ind.* pongo, poni, pone, poniamo, ponete, pongono; *past def.* posi, ponesti, etc.; *past part.* posto; *fut.* porrò; *pres. sub.* ponga, poniamo, poniate, pongano; *impve.* poni, poniamo, ponete.

†potere = to be able; *pres. ind.* posso, puoi, può, possiamo, potete, possono; *fut.* potrò; *pres. sub.* possa, possiamo, possiate, possano.

prendere = to take; *past def.* presi, predesti, etc.; *past part.* preso.

promettere = to promise; see mettere.

proteggere = to protect; *past def.* protessi, proteggesti, etc.; *past part.* protetto.

†raggiungere = to reach, overtake; see giungere.

riaprire = to open again; see aprire.

riconoscere = to recognize; see conoscere.

ridere = to laugh; *past def.* risi, ridesti, etc.; *past part.* riso.

*rimanere = to remain; *pres. ind.* rimango, rimani, rimane, rimaniamo, rimanete, rimangono; *past def.* rimasi, rimanesti, etc.; *past part.* rimasto; *fut.* rimarrò; *pres. sub.* rimanga,

rimaniamo rimaniate, rimangano; *impve.* rimani, rimaniamo, rimanete.

riprendere = to retake, to continue; see prendere.

rispondere = to reply; *past def.* risposi, rispondesti, etc.; *past
part.* risposto.

*riuscire = to succeed; see uscire.

rompere = to break; *past def.* ruppi, rompesti, etc.; *past part.*
rotto.

†salire = to ascend; *pres. ind.* salgo, sali, sale, saliamo, salite,
salgono; *pres. sub.* salga, saliamo, saliate, salgano; *impve.*
sali, saliamo, salite.

sapere = to know; *pres. ind.* so, sai, sa, sappiamo, sapete,
sanno; *past def.* seppi, sapesti, etc.; *fut.* saprò; *pres. sub.*
sappia, sappiamo, sappiate, sappiano; *impve.* sappi, sappiamo, sappiate.

scegliere = to choose; *pres. ind.* scelgo, scegli, sceglie,
scegliamo, scegliete, scelgono; *past def.* scelsi, scegliesti,
etc.; *past part.* scelto; *pres. sub.* scelga, scegliamo, scegliate,
scelgano; *impve.* scegli, scegliamo, scegliete.

*scendere = to descend; *past def.* scesi, scendesti, etc.; *past
part.* sceso.

sciogliere = to untie, loosen; *pres. ind.* sciolgo, sciogli, scioglie,
sciogliamo, sciogliete, sciolgono; *past def.* sciolsi, sciogliesti,
etc.; *past part.* sciolto; *pres. sub.* sciolga, sciogliamo,
sciogliate, sciolgano; *impve.* sciogli, sciogliamo, sciogliete.

scoprire = to discover; see aprire.

†scorrere = to flow; see correre.

scrivere = to write; *past def.* scrissi, scrivesti, etc.; *past part.*
scritto.

sedere = to sit; *pres. ind.* siedo or seggo, siedi, siede, sediamo,
sedete, siedono or seggono; *pres. sub.* sieda or segga, sediamo,
sediate, siedano or seggano; *impve.* siedi, sediamo, sedete.

soggiungere = to add; see giungere.

*sorgere = to arise; *past def.* sorsi, sorgesti, etc.; *past part.*
sorto.

sorprendere = to surprise; see prendere.

spargere = to scatter, shed; *past def.* sparsi, spargesti, etc.;
past part. sparso.

spendere = to spend; *past def.* spesi, spendesti, etc.; *past part.*
speso.

spingere = to push; *past def.* spinsi, spingesti; *past part.*
spinto.

*stare = to stand, to be; *pres. ind.* sto, stai, sta, stiamo, state,
stanno; *past def.* stetti, stesti, etc.; *pres. sub.* stia, stiamo,

stiate, stiano; *fut.* starò; *impve.* sta', stiamo, state; *imp. sub.* stessi, etc.

*stendersi = to stretch oneself; *past def.* stesi, stendesti, etc.; *past part.* steso.

stringere = to bind fast, hold; *past def.* strinsi, stringesti, etc.; *past part.* stretto.

*succedere = to happen; *past def.* successi or succedei or succedetti, succedesti, etc.; *past part.* successo or succeduto.

svolgere = to unfold; see volgere.

tacere = to be silent; *pres. ind.* taccio, taci, tace, taciamo, tacete, tacciono; *past def.* tacqui, tacesti, etc.; *pres. sub.* taccia, taciamo, taciate, tacciano; *impve.* taci, taciamo, tacete.

tenere = to hold; *pres. ind.* tengo, tieni, tiene, teniamo, tenete, tengono; *past def.* tenni, tenesti, etc.; *fut.* terrò; *pres. sub.* tenga, teniamo, teniate, tengano; *impve.* tieni, teniamo, tenete.

togliere = to take off, from; see sciogliere.

tradurre = to translate; see condurre.

trarre (traere) = to draw, pull; *pres. ind.* traggo, trai, trae, traiamo, traete, traggono; *past def.* trassi, traesti, etc.; *past part.* tratto; *fut.* trarrò; *pres. sub.* tragga, traiamo, traiate, traggano; *impve.* trai, traiamo, traete.

trasmettere = to transmit; see mettere.

trattenere = to hold back; see tenere.

udire = to hear; *pres. ind.* odo, odi, ode, udiamo, udite, odono; *pres. sub.* oda, udiamo, udiate, odano; *impve.* odi, udiamo, udite.

*uscire = to go out; *pres. ind.* esco, esci, esce, usciamo, uscite, escono; *pres. sub.* esca, usciamo, usciate, escano; *impve.* esci, usciamo, uscite.

*valere = to be worth; *pres. ind.* valgo, vali, vale, valiamo, valete, valgono; *past def.* valsi, valesti, etc.; *past part.* valso; *fut.* varrò; *pres. sub.* valga, valiamo, valiate, valgano.

vedere = to see; *past def.* vidi, vedesti, etc.; *past part.* visto or veduto; *fut.* vedrò.

*venire = to come; *pres. ind.* vengo, vieni, viene, veniamo, venite, vengono; *past def.* venni, venisti, etc.; *past part.* venuto; *fut.* verrò; *pres. sub.* venga, veniamo, veniate, vengano; *impve.* vieni, veniamo, venite.

vincere = to win; *past def.* vinsi, vincesti, etc.; *past part.* vinto.

*vivere = to live; *past def.* vissi, vivesti, etc.; *past part.* vissuto.

†volere = to wish; *pres. ind.* voglio, vuoi, vuole, vogliamo, volete, vogliono; *past def.* volli, volesti, etc.; *fut.* vorrò; *pres. sub.* voglia, vogliamo, vogliate, vogliano; *impve.* vogli, vogliamo, vogliate.

volgere = to turn; *past def.* volsi, volgesti, etc.; *past part.* volto.

Auxiliary Verbs

avere = to have; *pres. ind.* ho, hai, ha, abbiamo, avete, hanno; *past def.* ebbi, avesti, ebbe, avemmo, aveste, ebbero; *fut.* avrò; *pres. sub.* abbia, abbiamo, abbiate, abbiano; *impve.* abbi, abbiamo, abbiate.

essere = to be; *pres. ind.* sono, sei, è, siamo, siete, sono; *past def.* fui, fosti, fu, fummo, foste, furono; *imp. ind.* ero, eri, era, eravamo, eravate, erano; *fut.* sarò; *pres. sub.* sia, siamo, siate, siano; *imp. sub.* fossi, fossi, fosse, fossimo, foste, fossero; *impve.* sii, siamo, siate; *past part.* stato.

VOCABULARY

Numbers, days, months, seasons (pages 16–17, 95, and 98–99); articles (pages 19–20, 24–25), and personal pronouns (pages 22–23, 58, and 67), are not included in this vocabulary; nor are proper nouns, nor nouns which are the same in spelling and meaning in both languages.

Nouns ending in -o are masculine, with the one exception of *la mano*; those ending in -a are feminine unless otherwise stated; the gender of other nouns is indicated. Verbs are regular unless otherwise indicated, and where there might be uncertainty as to the stress in the present indicative, or as to the pronunciation of an *e* or an *o*, the first person is appended in brackets. Verbs conjugated with *essere* are marked *, and those which may take either auxiliary are marked †. The preposition most commonly used after a verb or adjective is shown in brackets after the word.

A

abbastanza, *enough*
abbondante (di), *abundant in*
abbozzare (abbozzo), *to outline, sketch*
abete (m.), *fir*
abitante (m.), *inhabitant*
abitare (abito), *to inhabit*
abito, *coat, suit*
abituarsi (abituo), *to accustom oneself to*
abitudine (f.), *habit*
accanto, *at the side of, next to*
accelerato, *stopping train, slow train*
accento, *accent*
*accomodarsi (accomodo), *to seat oneself, to make oneself comfortable*
accompagnare, *to accompany*
accontentare, *to satisfy*
accordo, *accord, chord*

*accorgersi (di) (irreg.), *to notice*
acqua, *water*
acquistare, *to acquire*
acre, *sour, harsh*
acuto, *acute, shrill*
adatto (a), *fit for*
addio!, *goodbye !*
*addormentarsi (addormento), *to fall asleep*
adesso, *now*
adoperare (adopero), *to use*
adornare (di), *to decorate with*
*affacciarsi (affaccio), *to show one's face at (window, door)*
affittare, *to hire*
aggiogare (aggiogo), *to yoke*
aggiungere (irreg.), *to add*
*aggrapparsi, *to cling*
agitare (agito), *to wave*
ahimè!, *alas !*

221

aiutare, *to help*
alba, *dawn*
albergo, *hotel*
albero, *tree*
alcuno, *some, any*
*allargarsi, *to widen*
allato, a lato, *at the side*
allegro, *merry*
allora, *then*
almeno, *at least*
alquanto, *somewhat*
altare (m.), *altar*
altezza, *height*
alto, *high, tall*
altrettanto, *equally, the same to you*
altro, *other*
altrui, *other, others*
*alzarsi, *to get up*
amante (m. and f.), *lover*
amare, *to love, like*
ameno, *pleasing, delightful*
amica, *friend* (f.)
amico, *friend* (m.)
amministrativo, *administrative*
ammirare, *to admire*
analizzare, *to analyse*
anche, *also, even*
ancora, *again*
àncora, *anchor*
*andare (irreg.), *to go*
    andar bene, *to suit, to be all right*
    andar a genio, *to please, to suit one's taste*
andata, *going,* see biglietto
anello, *ring*
angolo, *angle, corner*
anima, *soul, spirit*
animato, *animated*
anno, *year*
annoiare (annoio), *to annoy, bore*

annunciare (annuncio), *to announce*
ansioso, *worried*
antichità, *antiquity, antiquities*
antico, *ancient*
antiquario, *antiquarian, antique dealer*
anzi, *on the contrary*
apparecchiare (apparecchio), *to prepare, lay* (*table*)
*apparire (irreg.) (either 1st or 2nd group), *to appear*
appartenere (irreg.), *to belong*
appena, *hardly*
appena che, *as soon as*
appetito, *appetite*
applauso, *applause*
appoggiare (appoggio), *to support*
approfittare (di), *to profit by, take advantage of*
appunto, per l'appunto, *precisely*
aprire (irreg.) (2nd group), *to open*
arancia, *orange*
arazzo, *tapestry*
arcata, *arcade*
argento, *silver*
aria, *air*
arioso, *airy*
armadio, *cupboard, wardrobe*
armonia, *harmony*
armonioso, *harmonious*
armonizzare, *harmonize*
arrestare, *to arrest*
*arrestarsi, *to stop*
*arricchirsi (1st group), *to enrich*
*arrivare, *to arrive*
arrivederci!, *goodbye !*
arrosto, *roast*
arte (f.), *art*
articolo, *article*

artista (m. and f.), *artist*
artistico, *artistic*
ascensore (m.), *lift*
asciugamano (m.), *towel*
ascoltare (ascolto), *to listen*
aspergere (irreg.), *to sprinkle*
aspettare (aspetto), *to wait for, expect*
assai, *very*
assalto, *assault*
assenza, *absence*
attenzione (f.), *attention*
attore (m.), *actor*
†attraversare (attraverso), *to cross*

austero, *austere*
autobus (m.), *bus*
automobile (m.), *motor car*
autorimessa (f.), *garage*
autostrada (f.), *motor road, main road*
avanti, *in front*
avanti che, *before*
avere (irreg.), *to have*
*avviarsi, *to start out*
*avvicinarsi, *to draw near*
avvocato, *lawyer*
azione (f.), *action*
azzurro, *blue*

B

bacheca, *show case*
bagaglio, *luggage*
*bagnarsi, *to bath, bathe*
bagno, *bath*
baia, *bay*
balcone (m.), *balcony*
ballare, *to dance*
balneare, *of baths, bathing*
balzare, *to jump*
bambino, -a, *baby*
banca, *bank*
bancario, *banking*
banco, *bench*
bandiera, *banner*
baracca, *hut, tent, stall*
barba, *beard*
barbarico, *barbarian*
barbaro, *barbarian*
barca, *boat*
  barca a remi, *rowing boat*
  barca a vela, *sailing boat*
barcaiuolo, *boatman*
basso, *low, short (of stature)*
  bassorilievo, *low relief*
*bastare, *to suffice*
battere, *to beat*

battesimo, *baptism*
battezzare, *to baptize*
battistero, *baptistry*
baule (m.), *trunk*
beato, *perfectly happy*
bellezza, *beauty*
bellino, *pretty*
bello, *beautiful, fine*
beltà, *beauty*
benché, *although*
bene, *well*
  benissimo, *very well*
beneficenza, *charity*
bere (irreg.), *to drink*
berretto, *cap*
bestia, *beast*
biancheggiare (biancheggio), *to whiten*
bianco, *white*
bibita, *drink*
biblioteca, *library*
bicchiere (m.), *glass, tumbler*
biglietto, *ticket*
  biglietto di andata e ritorno, *return ticket*
bimbo, -a, *child*

binario, *railway track*
biondo, *blonde*
bis!, *encore!*
biscotto, *biscuit*
*bisognare, *to need*
bisogno, *need*
bollo, *stamp, seal*
bontà, *goodness*
bordo, *board*
  a bordo, *on board*
borgo, *suburb, village*
borsa, *purse*
bottega, *shop*
bottiglia, *bottle*
braccetto, *arm*
  a braccetto, *arm in arm*

bravo!, *well done!*
bravo, *good, capable*
breve, *short*
briciola, *crumb*
brillare, *to shine*
bronzo, *bronze*
bruscamente, *brusquely, suddenly*
brutto, *ugly*
bue (m.), *ox*
bugia, *untruth*
bugiardo, *liar*
buono, *good*
burlone, *one who jokes*
burro, *butter*

C

*cadere (irreg.), *to fall*
caffè (m.), *café, coffee*
calca, *crowd*
caldo, *warm, hot*
calma, *calm* (noun)
calmo, *calm* (adj.)
calvo, *bald*
calza, *stocking*
calzino, *sock*
camera, *bedroom*
cameriere, -a, *servant maid (waiter, waitress)*
camicia, *shirt*
†camminare, *to walk*
cammino, *way*
campagna, *country*
campana, *bell*
campanello, *little bell, door bell*
campanile (m.), *belfry*
campo, *field*
canale (m.), *canal*
candido, *pure white, shining*
cane (m.), *dog*
cantante (m. and f.), *singer*
cantare, *to sing*

cantarellare (cantarello), *to hum*
cantonata, *corner*
cantoría, *choir stall*
capelli (m. pl.), *hair*
capire (1st group), *to understand*
capitale (f.), *capital*
capitano, *captain*
capitolo, *chapter*
capo, *head*
capolavoro, *masterpiece*
capostazione (m.), *station master*
cappello, *hat*
cappotto, *cloak, overcoat*
carabiniere, *carabineer, policeman*
caramella, *sweet*
carattere (m.), *character*
carbone (m.), *coal*
caricare (carico), *to load*
carico, *load*
carne (f.), *meat*
caro, *dear*

carro, *cart*
carrozza, *carriage*
carrozza-letti, *sleeping car*
carta, *paper*
  carta da scrivere, *writing paper*
  carta geografica, *map*
cartolina, *post card*
casa, *house, home*
*cascare, *to fall*
cascatella, *little waterfall*
casella, *pigeon hole*
caso, *case, chance*
cassetto, *drawer*
castagno, *chestnut tree*
cattivo, *bad*
causa, *cause*
cava, *quarry*
cavalla, *mare*
cavalletta, *locust*
cavallo, *horse*
celebrare (celebro), *to celebrate*
celebre, *famous*
celeste, *pale blue*
cena, *supper*
cenare, *to have supper*
centesimo, *centime*
centrale, *central*
centro, *centre*
cercare, *to look for*
cerchia, *circle*
certamente, *certainly*
certo, *sure, certain*
cesta, *basket*
cestino, *little basket*
ché, *because*
che, *who, which, that*
  gran che, *of special interest*
che!, *what!, what a!*
che? che cosa?, *what?*
che . . . non, *than*
checché, *whatever*
chi, *who, whom, he who, he whom*

chi?, *who?, whom?*
chiacchierare (chiacchiero), *to chatter, gossip*
chiamare, *to call*
chiaro, *clear, light*
chiave (f.), *key*
chicchessia, *whoever, whosoever*
chiedere (irreg.), *to ask*
chiesa, *church*
chilometro, *kilometre*
chiudere (irreg.), *to close*
chiunque, *whoever*
ci (adv.), *here, there*
ciao!, *goodbye, so long*
ciascuno, *each*
cicala, *cricket*
cicerone (m.), *guide*
cieco, *blind*
cielo, *sky*
ciglio, *eyelash*
cima, *top, summit*
cimitero, *cemetery*
cingere (irreg.), *to surround*
cintura, *belt*
ciò, *that, this*
  cioè, *that is*
cioccolata, *chocolate*
cipresso, *cypress*
circolare, *circular*
circondare, *to surround*
circostante, *surrounding*
città, *town*
cittadina, *small town*
coda, *tail*
cogliere (irreg.), *to gather*
colà, *there*
colazione (f.), *lunch*
  prima colazione, *breakfast*
collana, *necklace*
colle (m.), *hill*
colletto, *collar*
collezione (f.), *collection*
collina, *hill*

colonia, *colony*

colonico, *farming, of the farmer*
   casa colonica, *farm house*

colonna, *column*

colore (m.), *colour*

colorito, *complexion*

colpevole, *guilty*

colpire (1st group), *to strike*

colpo, *blow*

coltello, *knife*

coltivare (coltivo), *to cultivate*

coltivazione (f.), *cultivation*

colto, *cultivated, educated*

colui, colui che, *he, he who*

comandare, *to command*

comare (f.), *god-mother, neighbour*

come, *as, like, how*

come!, *what!*

come?, *how?*

†cominciare (comincio) (a), *to begin*

commercio, *trade*

commesso viaggiatore, *commercial traveller*

commissionario, *representative*

comodo, *comfortable*

compagnia, *company*

compagno, -a, *companion*

compiere (compio), *to complete, fulfil*

compleanno, *birthday*

completo, *full*

complimento, *compliment*

compositore (m.), *composer*

comprare (compro), *to buy*

comprendere (irreg.), *to understand*

con, *with*

concerto, *concert*

conchiglia, *shell*

concorso, *competition*

condurre (irreg.), *to lead*

confessare, *to confess*

conico, *conical*

conoscenza, *acquaintance*

conoscere (irreg.), *to know, be acquainted with*

conquistare, *to conquer*

consigliare (consiglio), *to advise*

consistere (di, in), *to consist*

console (m.), *consul*

consultare, *to consult*

contadino, -a, *peasant*

contemplare (contemplo), *to contemplate, look at*

contenere (irreg.), *to contain*

contento (di), *contented with, pleased to*

contiguo, *adjacent*

continuare (a), *to continue*

continuo, *continual*

conto, *account, bill*

contorno, *outline, garnish (of dish for the table)*

contrada, *regione, quarter, ward*

contributo, *contribution*

contro, *against*

*convenire (irreg.), *to suit, to be profitable*

convento, *convent*

convertire, *to convert*

coprire (irreg.) (2nd group), *to cover*

coraggio, *courage*

coraggioso, *courageous*

corpo, *body*

†correre (irreg.), *to run*

correttamente, *correctly*

corridoio, *corridor*

corsa, *race*

corso, *course*

corteo, *procession*

cortile (m.), *yard, court*

corto, *short*

cosa, *thing*

così, *thus, so*

così . . . come, *as . . . as, so . . . as*

costà, *there*

costare, *to cost*

costeggiare (costeggio), *to coast*

costì, *there*

costringere (irreg.), *to compel*

costruire (irreg.) (1st group), *to construct*

costui, *that man*

costume (m.), *habit*

cravatta, *tie*

credere, *to believe, think*

†crescere (irreg.), *to grow*

crisi (f.), *crisis*

cristalleria, *glass ware*

Cristianesimo, *Christianity*

Cristiano, *Christian*

criticare (critico), *to criticize*

critico, *critical*

crocefisso, *crucifix*

crociata, *crusade*

cucchiaio, *spoon*

cucina, *kitchen*

cui, *whom, which*

il cui, *whose*

cullare, *to rock*

cuoco, -a, *cook*

cuoio, *leather*

cuore (m.), *heart*

cuscino, *cushion, pl. seats in carriage, car or train*

D

da, *by, with, from*

dappertutto, *everywhere*

dapprima, *at first*

dare (irreg.), *to give*

dare luogo a, *to give place to*

dare retta a, *to pay attention to*

data, *date*

datare, *to date*

davanti a, *in front of*

davvero, *indeed*

decadenza, *decline*

decidere (di) (irreg.), *to decide*

*decidersi (a, di) (irreg.), *to decide*

declivio, *slope*

decorazione (f.), *decoration*

degno, *worthy*

denaro, *money*

dentista (m.), *dentist*

dentro, *in, within*

deposito, *deposit, cloakroom*

desiderare (desidero), *to desire*

destinare (destino), *to destine*

destra, *right hand*

deviazione (f.), *deviation*

di, *of*

dì, *day (poetical)*

dialetto, *dialect*

diamine!, *heavens!*

dichiarare (dichiaro), *to declare*

dietro, *behind*

difficile, *difficult*

difficoltà, *difficulty*

dimenticare (dimentico), *to forget*

dio mio!, *Good Lord!*

*dipendere (da) (irreg.), *to depend on*

dire (irreg.), *to say*

diretto, *direct*

*dirigersi (irreg.), *to direct oneself*

diritto (noun and adj.), *right* (noun); *straight* (adj.)

discepolo, *follower*

discutere (irreg.), *to discuss*

disegno, *design*

disoccupato, *unemployed*
disonore (m.), *dishonour*
disordine (m.), *disorder*
*dispiacere (irreg.), *to displease*
disporre (irreg.), *to dispose, arrange*
disposizione (f.), *disposal*
distanza, *distance*
distinguere (irreg.), *to distinguish*
dito, *finger*
*divenire (irreg.), *to become*
diventare (divento), *to become*
diverso, *different*
divertente, *amusing*
divertimento, *enjoyment*
*divertirsi (2nd group), *to enjoy oneself*
divinamente, *divinely*
divino, *divine*
dogana, *Customs office*
doganiere (m.), *Customs officer*

dolce, *sweet* (adj. and noun)
domanda, *question*
domandare, *to ask*
domani, *tomorrow*
domenicale, *of Sunday*
dominare (domino), *to dominate*
donna, *woman*
dopo, *afterwards, after*
dopo che, *after*
dormire (2nd group), *to sleep*
dottore (m.), *doctor*
dove, *where*
†dovere (irreg.), *to owe, to have to*
dovunque, *everywhere*
dozzina, *dozen*
dubbio, *doubt*
dubitare (dubito), *to doubt*
duca (m.), *duke*
dunque, *then, therefore*
duomo, *dome, cathedral*

E

e, ed, *and*
eccellente, *excellent*
eccetto, *except*
ecco, *here is* (*are*), *there is* (*are*)
eco (m. or f.), *echo*
edifizio, *building*
effetto, *effect*
elegante, *elegant*
eleganza, *elegance*
elemento, *element*
emettere (irreg.), *emit*
enorme, *enormous*
*entrare (in), *to enter*
entrata, *entrance*
entro, *within*
entusiasmo, *enthusiasm*

epoca, *epoch*
equestre, *equestrian*
erba, *grass*
esecuzione (f.), *execution*
esercitarsi (esercito), *to practise, exercise*
esitare (esito), *to hesitate*
esperimento, *experiment*
esporre (irreg.), *to expose, exhibit*
*essere (irreg.), *to be*
est (m.), *east*
estate (f.), *summer*
estendere (irreg.), *to extend*
esterno, *exterior*
estivo, *of summer*
estremità, *extremity, end*

F

fa, *ago*
fabbrica, *building*
fabbricare, *to build*
facchino, *porter*
faccia, *face*
  di faccia, *opposite*
facciata. *façade, front*
facile, *easy*
fame (f.), *hunger*
famiglia, *family*
famoso, *famous*
fanciulletta, *little girl*
fantastico, *fantastic*
fantino, *jockey*
fare (irreg.), *to make, to do*
  fare caldo, freddo, bel tempo, *to be hot, cold, fine weather*
  fare caso di, *to take notice of*
farmacia, *chemist's shop*
farsi avanti, *to come forward*
fascino, *fascination*
favore, *favour*
  per favore, *please*
fazzoletto, *handkerchief*
felice, *happy*
feriale, giorno feriale, *ordinary day, week day*
fermaglio, *brooch*
fermare, *fermarsi, *to stop*
ferrato, *of iron*
  strada ferrata, *railway lines*
ferrovia, *railway*
festa, *holiday, festival*
festivo, *festive*
festone (m.), *festoon*
fetta, *slice*
  fettona, *large slice*
fiaccheraio, *cab driver*
fiancheggiare (fiancheggio), *to flank*
fiaschettino, *little bottle*

fiasco, *bottle, flask*
fico, *fig*
fidarsi (di), *to trust in*
fieno, *hay*
figlia, *daughter*
figlio, *son*
figurarsi (figuro), *to imagine*
fila, *line, file*
finalmente, *finally*
finché, *until*
fine (f.), *end*
finestra, *window*
  finestrino, *little window*
  finestrone, *large window*
†finire (1st group), *to finish*
fino a, *until, up to*
fioraio, *florist*
fiore (m.), *flower*
fiorentino, *Florentine*
fiorito, *in flower*
firma, *signature*
firmare, *to sign*
fischiare (fischio), *to whistle*
fischio, *whistle*
fissare, *to fix*
fisso, *fixed, fixedly*
fiume (m.), *river*
foglio, *sheet of paper*
folla, *crowd*
fondare, *to found*
fondo, *bottom*
  in fondo a, *at the bottom of*
fontana, *fountain*
fonte (m. and f.), *font* (m.); *fount* (f.)
forchetta, *fork*
forestiere, *foreigner*
forma, *shape*
formaggio, *cheese*
fornaio, *baker*
fornire (di) (1st group), *to furnish, supply with*

forse, *perhaps*
forte, *strong*
fortezza, *fortress*
fortunato, *lucky*
forza, *strength*
  a forza di, *by dint of*
fra, *among, within*
francese, *French*
franco, *franc*
francobollo, *stamp*
fratello, *brother*
freddo, *cold*
fregio (m.), *frieze*
frenetico, *frenzied*
fresco, *cool*

fretta, *haste*
frontiera, *frontier*
fronte (f.), *forehead, front*
  di fronte, *opposite*
frutta, *dessert*
frutto, *fruit*
fumo, *smoke*
funicolare (f.), *funicular rail-*
  way
fuoco, *fire*
fuorché, *except*
fuori, *outside, outside of*
  fuori di mano, *out of the way,*
    off the track
furbo, *cunning*

G

galleria, *arcade, gallery*
gamba, *leg*
gatto, *cat*
gelare (gelo), *to freeze*
gelatiere, *ice cream seller*
gelato, *ice cream*
generale, *general*
generalmente, *generally*
genio, *genius, character, taste*
  (see andare)
gente (f.), *people*
gentile, *kind*
gesso, *chalk*
ghiaccio, *ice*
ghiro, *dormouse*
già, *already*
giacca, *coat, jacket*
giacchetta, *jacket*
giallo, *yellow*
giapponese, *Japanese*
giardino, *garden*
gigante (m.), *giant*
ginocchio, *knee*
gioia, *joy*
gioiello, *jewel*
giornalaio, *newspaper seller*

giornale, *newspaper*
giorno, *day*
giovane, *young, youth*
giovanotto, *youth, young man*
giro, *tour*
gita, *excursion*
giú, *down*
giudice (m.), *judge*
†giungere (irreg.), *to arrive, to*
  join
giusto, *right, just*
godere, *to enjoy*
golfo, *gulf*
gondola, *gondola*
gondoliere (m.), *gondolier*
gonna, *skirt*
gotico, *gothic*
gradevole, *pleasant*
grande, *large, great*
grandinare (grandina) (im-
  pers.), *to hail*
grandioso, *grandiose*
grano, *corn, grain*
granturco, *maize*
grasso, *fat*
grave (m.), *weight*

grazie, *thanks*
greco, *Greek*
gridare, *to shout*
gridìo, *shouting*
grido, *shout*
grigio, *grey*
grosso, *large*
gruccia (f.), *clothes-hanger, crutch*

gruppo, *group*
guancia, *cheek*
guanciale (m.), *pillow*
guardare, *to look at*
guardia (f.), *guard*
guerra, *war*
guida (f.), *guide, guide book*
gusto, *taste*

H

ha, *he has*

hanno, *they have*

I

ieri, *yesterday*
illuminare (illumino), *to illumine*
*imbarcarsi, *to embark*
*immaginarsi (immagino), *to imagine to oneself*
immensamente, *immensely*
imparare, *to learn*
impetuoso, *impetuous*
impiegato, *clerk*
importanza, *importance*
importare (importo), *to matter*
impressionante, *impressive*
in, *in, to*
*incamminarsi, *to start on the way*
inchiostro, *ink*
incontrare (incontro), *to meet*
indicare (indico), *to indicate*
indicazione (f.), *indication*
indietro, *behind*
indifferente, *indifferent*
indirizzo, *address*
indovinare, *to guess*
industriale, *industrial*
infatidire (1st group), *to annoy, irritate*
inferiore, *inferior, lower*

informazione (f.), *information*
inglese, *English*
ingombrare (ingombro), *to crowd around, to get in the way*
iniziare (inizio), *to begin*
*innalzarsi, *to tower up, rise up*
innocenti, *foundlings* (lit.: *innocent ones*)
*inoltrare, *to go on, forward*
inondare, *to inundate, to pervade, to fill*
insegnare, *to teach*
insetto, *insect*
insieme, *together*
integro, *honest, upright*
intelligente, *intelligent*
intendere (irreg.), *to understand, to intend, to hear*
*intendersi (di), *to be expert, practised in*
intenzione (f.), *intention*
interessante, *interesting*
*interessarsi (a, di), *to be interested in*
intermedio, *intermediate*
interminabile, *unceasing*
interno, *interior*

intimo, *intimate*
intorno, *around*
   intorno a, *round* (prep.)
intraprendente, *enterprising*
invadere (irreg.), *to invade*
invasione (f.), *invasion*
*invecchiare (invecchio), *to become old*

invece, *on the other hand, instead*
   invece di, *instead of*
invitare, *to invite*
isola, *island*
isolato, *isolated*
italiano, *Italian*
itinerario, *route*

L

là, *there*
   al di là di, *beyond* (prep.)
labbro, *lip*
laggiú, *down there*
*lagnarsi (di), *to complain*
lago, *lake*
laguna, *lagoon*
lambire (either 1st or 2nd group), *to lap, lick*
lampada, *lamp*
lampeggiare (lampeggio), *to lighten*
larghezza, *width, generosity*
largo, *wide*
lasciare, *to let, leave*
lato, *side*
latte (m.), *milk*
*lavarsi, *to wash oneself*
lavorare (lavoro), *to work*
lavoro, *work*
legare (lego), *to bind*
legge (f.), *law*
leggere (irreg.), *to read*
leggiadria, *beauty, grace, elegance*
legno, *wood*
lento, *slow*

lenzuolo, *sheet*
lettera, *letter*
letto, *bed*
*levarsi, *to get up, to rise up*
lezione (f.), *lesson*
liberare (libero), *to free*
libero, *free*
libro, *book*
limpido, *clear, limpid*
linea, *line*
lingua, *tongue, language*
livello, *level*
lode (f.), *praise*
loggiata, *series of loggias*
lombardo, *of Lombardy*
lontananza, *distance*
lontano, *far*
loppio, *small maple*
luce (f.), *light*
luminoso, *bright, light*
luna, *moon*
lunghezza, *length*
lungo, *long*
luogo, *place*
lupa, *she-wolf*
lupo, *wolf*

M

ma, *but*
macchina, *machine, engine, car*
macchinista (m.), *engine driver*

madre (f.), *mother*
maestà, *majesty*
maestoso, *majestic*

maestro *or* maestro, *master*

maggiore, *older, larger, greater*

magnifico, *magnificent*

magro, *thin*

mai, *ever, never*

male, *bad, badly*

malgrado, *in spite of*

mancanza, *lack*

mancare, *to lack*

mancia, *tip (money)*

mandare, *to send*

mangiare (mangio), *to eat*

mangiatoia, *manger*

maniera, *manner, way*

mano (f.), *hand*

*maravigliarsi (di) or meravi-
gliarsi, *to be surprised at*

marciapiede (m.), *pavement*

mare (m.), *sea*

marinaro, *seafaring*

marino, *of the navy, of the sea*

marittimo, *maritime*

marmo, *marble*

marmoreo, *marble* (adj.)

mattina, mattino, *morning*

maturo, *mature*

medico, *doctor*

medioevale, *mediaeval*

medioevo, *middle ages*

meglio, *better*

mela, *apple*

melanconico, *melancholy*

membro (pl. membri), *member*

membro (pl. membra), *limb*

meno, *less*

 a meno che . . . non, *unless*

mensola, *bracket*

mente (f.), *mind*

mentre, *while*

meraviglioso   (maraviglioso),
wonderful

mercante (m.), *merchant*

mercato, *market*

merce (f.), *merchandise*

merenda, *lunch, picnic*

meridionale, *southern*

merlato, *battlemented*

merlo, *battlement*

mese (m.), *month*

metà, *half* (noun)

metro, *metre*

mettere (irreg.), *to put*

mezzanotte (f.), *midnight*

mezzo, *half* (adj.)

 in mezzo a, di, *in the middle
of*

mezzogiorno, *midday*

miglio, *mile*

minore, *less, smaller, younger*

minuto, *minute*

mio, *my*

mirabile, *wonderful*

miracolo, *miracle*

miriade (f.), *myriad*

misero, *wretched*

misterioso, *mysterious*

misto, *mixed*

mite, *gentle, soft*

mobile (m.), *piece of furniture*

moderno, *modern*

modo, *way*

 di modo che, *in such a way
that*

moglie (f.), *wife*

mole (f.), *mass*

molo, *jetty*

molto, *much, very*

momento, *moment*

 a momenti, *any moment*

monaco, *monk*

monastero, *monastery*

mondo, *world*

monolitico, *monolithic*

monopolio, *monopoly*

montagna, *mountain*

monte (m.), *mountain*

monumento, *monumento*

*morire (irreg.), *to die*

mormorio, *murmur*
mortaretto, *small gun, mortar*
morte (f.), *death*
mosaico, *mosaic*
mostrare, *to show*
moto, *movement*
motoscafo, *motor boat*
movimento, *movement*

mulo, *mule*
muovere (irreg.), *to move*
muretto, *little wall*
muro, *wall*
museo, *museum*
musica, *music*
musicale, *musical*
*mutarsi, *to change oneself*

N

narrare, *to relate*
*nascere, *to be born*
naso, *nose*
natalizio, *of one's birth*
naturale, *natural*
naturalmente, *naturally*
navata, *nave*
nave (f.), *ship*
ne, *of it, some, any*
né . . . né, *neither, nor*
nebbia, *mist, fog*
necessario, *necessary*
negare, *to deny*
negozio, *shop*
nemica, *enemy*
neppure, *not even*
nero, *black*
nervoso, *nervous*
nessuno, *none, no one, nobody*
nevicare (impers.) (nevica), *to snow*

niente, *nothing*
noleggiare (noleggio), *to hire*
nome (m.), *name*
non, *not*
  non . . . che, *only*
  non ostante che, *in spite of the fact that*
nondimeno, *nevertheless*
nonno, *grandfather*
nord, *north*
nostro, *our*
nota, *note*
notare (noto), *to note*
notte (f.), *night*
novella, *short story*
nudo, *bare*
nulla, *nothing*
numero, *number*
numeroso, *numerous*
nuovo, *new*
  di nuovo, *again*

O

o, *or*
occasione (f.), *opportunity*
occhiali (m. pl.), *spectacles*
occhiata, *glance*
occhio, *eye*
*occuparsi (di) (occupo), *to occupy oneself with, to be busy with*

occupato, *busy, engaged*
offrire (irreg.) (2nd group), *to offer*
oggetto, *object*
oggi, *today*
ogni, *every, each*
  ogni tanto, *every now and then*

ognuno, *each one, every one*
olmo, *elm*
oltre, *beyond, besides*
ombra, *shade*
onestà, *honesty*
opinione (f.), *opinion*
opera, *work, opera*
opposto, *opposite*
oppure, *or*
ora, *hour, now*
  or ora, *just now*
oramai, *now, now finally*
orchestra, *orchestra*
ordine (m.), *order*
orecchini (m. pl.), *ear-rings*
orecchio, *ear*
orefice (m.), *goldsmith*
oretta, *short hour, about an hour*
organo, *organ*

orientarsi, *to find one's direction*
oriente (m.), *east*
originale, *original*
orizzonte (m.), *horizon*
ornato, *ornate*
  ornatissimo, *very ornate*
orologio, *clock*
osare, *to dare*
oscillazione (f.), *swing*
oscuro, *dark*
ospedale (m.), *hospital*
ospite (m. and f.), *host, guest*
osservare (osservo), *to observe*
osso, *bone*
ottagonale, *octagonal*
ottimo, *very good, best*
ovest (m.), *west*
oziare (ozio), *to idle, lounge about*

P

pacco, *parcel*
pace (f.), *peace*
padre (m.), *father*
paesaggio, *scenery, landscape*
paese (m.), *country, region*
pagare, *to pay*
paglia, *straw*
paio, *pair*
paladino (noun and adj.), *champion*
palazzo, *palace*
panca, *bench*
pane (m.), *bread*
panino, *roll of bread*
panno, *cloth*
panorama (m.), *view*
paradiso, *paradise*
parco, *park*
parecchio, *much*, pl. *several*
parentesi, *parenthesis*
  fra parentesi, *by the way*

*parere (irreg.), *to seem*
parlare, *to speak*
parola, *word*
parte (f.), *part*
partecipare (partecipo), *to take part in*
partenza, *departure*
*partire (2nd group), *to depart*
pascolo, *pasture*
passante (m. and f.), *passer-by*
passaporto, *passport*
passare, *to pass*
passeggiare (passeggio), *to walk*
passeggiata, *walk*
passo, *step, pace*
pasto, *meal*
patria, *fatherland*
paura, *fear*
pausa, *pause*
pazzo, *mad*

peccato, *pity*
  che peccato!, *what a pity!*
pecora, *sheep*
peggio, *very bad, worse*
pellicola, *film*
pena, *trouble*
pendere, *to hang*
pendice (f.), *slope*
pendolo, *pendulum*
penisola, *peninsula*
penna, *pen*
pensare (penso), *to think*
pensiero, *thought*
pensione (f.), *pension, boarding house*
per, *for, through*
  per favore, *please*
  per quanto, *however*
pera, *pear*
perché, *why?, because*
percorso, *route*
perdere (irreg.), *to lose*
perdonare (perdono), *to pardon*
perfetto, *perfect*
perfino, *even*
periodo, *period*
permettere (di) (irreg.), *to allow*
però, *however*
persin, persino, *even*
persona, *person*
personaggio, *character, figure*
pesca, *fishing*
pesce (m.), *fish*
pessimo, *very bad, worst*
pezzo, *piece*
piacere (m.), *pleasure*
  per piacere, *please*
†piacere (irreg.), *to please*
piangere (irreg.), *to weep*
pianista (m. and f.), *pianist*
piano (adj.), *quiet, soft, flat, level*

piano (n.), *floor, storey*
  piano superiore, *upper floor*
  pianterreno, *ground floor*
pianoforte (m.), *piano*
pianta, *plant, plan*
pianura, *plain* (noun)
piattino, *saucer*
piatto, *plate*
piazza, *square*
piazzale, *large square, open space*
piccione (m.), *pigeon*
piccolo, *small*
piede (m.), *foot*
  a piedi, *on foot*
piemontese, *Piedmontese*
pieno, *full*
pietra, *stone*
pigia pigia (m.) (pigiare = to press), *crowd, mob*
pigliare, *to catch*
pigro, *lazy*
pineta, *pine wood*
pino, *pine*
pio, *pious*
pioggia, *rain*
†piovere (irreg.), *to rain*
piroscafo, *steamer*
pisano, *Pisan*
pittore (m.), *painter*
pittoresco, *picturesque*
pittura, *painting*
piú, *more*
piuttosto, *rather*
pizzo, *lace*
poco, *a little, few*
  un po' di, *a little*
poesia, *poetry, short poem*
poeta, *poet*
poggiare (poggio), *to lean*
poggio, *small hill, mound*
poi, *then, afterward*
polizia, *police*
poliziotto, *policeman*

pollo, *chicken*

pomeriggio, *afternoon*

ponte (m.), *bridge*

porco, *pig*

porgere (irreg.), *to hand, give*

porre (irreg.), *to put*

porta, *door*

portacenere (m.), *ash tray*

portamonete (m.), *purse*

portare (porto), *to bring, carry, wear*

portiere, *door keeper*

porto, *port*

posare (poso), *to alight, to settle*

posizione (f.), *position*

possibile, *possible*

possibilissimo, *quite possible*

posta, *post office*

postino, *postman*

posto, *place, seat*

potente, *powerful*

potenza, *power*

potere (irreg.), *to be able*

potere (n., m.), *power*

povero, *poor*

pozzo, *well*

pranzare, *to dine*

pranzo, *dinner*

praticare (pratico), *to practise, to frequent*

pratico, *practical, practised, acquainted with*

prato, *meadow*

precedere, *to precede*

*precipitarsi (precipito), *to hurl oneself, to rush*

precipizio, *precipice*

precisamente, *exactly*

predominare (predomino), *to prevail, to dominate*

preferire (1st group), *to prefer*

pregare, *to pray*

preghiera, *prayer*

premere, *to press*

premio, *prize*

prendere (irreg.), *to take*

prenotare (prenoto), *to reserve*

*preoccuparsi (preoccupo), *to trouble oneself*

preparare, *to prepare*

presentare (presento), *to present, introduce*

presto, *early, soon*

prete (m.), *priest*

prezzo, *price*

prima che (conj.), *before*

prima di (prep.), *before*

principale, *principal*

principio, *beginning, principle*

privo, *deprived*

prodotto, *product*

professore (m.), *professor*

profeta (m.), *prophet*

profondamente, *deeply*

profondità, *depth*

profondo, *deep*

profugo, *refugee*

profumatamente, *very generously* (lit.: *with perfumes*)

profumo, *perfume*

progetto, *plan*

proibire (1st group), *to forbid*

promettere (irreg.), *to promise*

promontorio, *promontory*

prontamente, *promptly*

pronto, *ready*

proporzione (f.), *proportion*

proprietario, *proprietor*

proprio, *own, just*

prosciutto, *ham*

proseguire (2nd group), *to carry on, continue*

prossimo, *next*

proteggere (irreg.), *to protect*

protesta, *protest*

provare (provo), *to try*

provincia, *province*
pubblico (adj. and n.), *public, audience*
pulire (1st group), *to polish, clean*

pulpito, *pulpit*
purché, *provided that*
pure, *also, yet*
puro, *pure*
putto, *child, baby*

Q

qua, *here*
quadrato, *squared, square*
quadro, *picture*
qualche, *some, any*
qualchecosa, *something, anything*
qualcuno, *someone, anyone*
quale, *which?*
  il quale, *which* (rel. pro.)
qualsiasi, *whatever*
qualunque, *whatever*
quando, *when*

quanto, *how much*
  in quanto a, *with regard to*
quarto, *quarter*
quasi, *almost*
quegli, *that man*
quello, *that*
  quel che, quello che, *that which, what*
questi, *this man*
questo, *this*
qui, *here*
quindi, *then, therefore*

R

rabbia, *anger, rage*
raccomandare (raccomando), *to recommend, register*
raccomandato, *registered*
raccontare (racconto), *to relate*
radio (f.), *wireless*
ragazza, *girl*
ragazzo, *boy*
raggiungere (irreg.), *to reach*
ragione (f.), *reason*
rallentare (rallento), *to slow down*
ramo, *branch*
rapido (adj.), *rapid*
rapido (noun), *express train*
rapimento, *rapture*
rappresentare (rappresento), *to represent*
rauco, *hoarse*
re (m.), *king*

recita, *recitation, performance*
regalare (regalo), *to give a present*
regalino, *small present*
registrare (registro), *to register*
regola, *rule, order*
regolare (regolo), *to regulate*
regolarmente, *regularly*
relazione (f.), *connection*
religioso, *religious*
remo, *oar*
repubblica, *republic*
resistere, *to resist*
respiro, *breath*
ressa, *crowd*
*restare, *to stay, remain*
rete (f.), *net, luggage rack*
reticella, *little net, luggage rack*
retta, *attention* (see dare)
riaprire (2nd group) (irreg.), *to open again*

ricevere, *to receive*

ricevuta, *receipt*

richiamare (richiamo), *to call*

riconoscere (irreg.), *to recognize*

*ricordarsi (di) (ricordo), *to remember*

ridere (irreg.), *to laugh*

riduzione (f.), *reduction*

rientrare (in), *to enter again*

rifiutare (di) (rififuto), *to refuse*

rimandare, *to postpone*

*rimanere (irreg.), *to remain*

rio, *stream, river*

ripartire (2nd group), *to depart again*

ripetere, *to repeat*

ripido, *steep*

riportare (riporto), *to bring back, report*

*riposarsi (riposo), *to rest*

riprendere (irreg.), *to continue, take up again*

risaltare (risalto), *to stand out in relief*

riservare (riservo), *to reserve*

riso, *laugh*

rispettare (rispetto), *respect*

rispondere (irreg.), *to reply*

risposta, *reply*

ristorante (m.), *restaurant*

ritirare (ritiro), *to draw back*

ritmo, *rhythm*

ritrovo, *meeting place*

*riuscire (irreg.), *to succeed*

riva, *bank, shore*

rivista, *review, magazine*

roccioso, *rocky*

romanico, *romanesque*

romano, *Roman*

romantico, *romantic*

romanzo, *novel*

rompere (irreg.), *to break*

rondine (f.), *swallow*

rosa, *rose*

rosario, *rosary*

rosso, *red*

rossiccio, *ruddy, tawny*

rotondo, *round*

*rovesciarsi (rovescio), *to turn upside down, inside out*

rubrica, *section, column of newspaper*

rullio, *rolling, beating (drums)*

ruminare (rumino), *to chew the cud*

rumore (m.), *noise*

S

sabbia, *sand*

sacrificare (sacrifico), *to sacrifice*

sala, *room*

    sala da pranzo, *dining room*

    sala d'aspetto, *waiting room*

    sala di scrittura, *writing room*

salame (m.), *sausage meat*

saldo, *solid*

sale (m.), *salt*

*salire (irreg.), *to go up*

salotto, *drawing room*

salsiccia, *sausage*

saltare, *to jump*

salterellare (salterello), *to keep on giving little jumps*

salubre, *healthy, health-giving*

salutare (saluto), *to greet*

santo, *holy*

    campo santo, *cemetery*

sapere (irreg.), *to know*

sasso, *stone, rock*

sbagliare, *to mistake*

sbaglio, *mistake*
sboccare (sbocco), *to have its mouth in, to empty into, open into*
scaffale (m.), *bookcase*
scala, *stair, stairway*
scaletta, *ladder*
scalino, *stair*
scarpa, *shoe*
scarrozzare (scarrozzo), *to drive*
scarrozzata (f.), *drive, driving in a carriage*
scarso, *scarce*
scatola, *box*
scegliere (irreg.), *to choose*
scena, *scene*
*scendere (irreg.), *to go down*
scherzare (scherzo), *to joke*
sciarpa, *scarf*
scienziato, *scientist*
scintillare (scintillo), *to glitter*
scintillio, *glittering, twinkling*
sciocco, *fool*
sciogliere (irreg.), *to loosen*
scommessa, *bet*
scomodo, *uncomfortable*
scompartimento, *compartment (of railway carriage)*
scoppiare (scoppio), *to burst, explode*
scoprire (2nd group) (irreg.), *to discover*
†scorrere (irreg.), *to flow*
scorso, *last, past*
scossa, *bump, jerk*
scottare (scotto), *to be scorching hot, to burn*
scrittrice, *woman writer*
scrivania, *desk*
scrivere (irreg.), *to write*
scroscio, *splash*
scultura, *sculpture*
scuro, *dark coloured*

scusare, *to excuse*
scuola, *school*
*sdraiarsi (sdraio), *to lie down, stretch out*
se, *if*
sé, *himself*, etc.
sebbene, *although*
secolo, *century*
secondo, *second*
sede (f.), *seat*
*sedersi (irreg.), *to seat oneself*
sedia, *chair*
segnare (segno), *to mark*
seguire (2nd group), *to follow*
sella, *saddle*
*sembrare (sembro), *to seem*
semplice, *simple*
sempre, *always*
senese, *Sienese*
sensazione (f.), *sensation, feeling*
senso, *feeling*
sentimentale, *sentimental*
sentire (2nd group) (sento), *to feel, hear*
senza, *without*
separare (separo), *to separate*
sera, *evening*
serale, *of the evening*
sereno, *clear, bright, serene*
serie (f.), *series*
servire (2nd group) (servo), *to serve*
servizio, *service*
seta, *silk*
sete (f.), *thirst*
settentrionale, *northern*
settimana, *week*
sfrontato, *cheeky*
sfruttare, *to exploit*
sguardo, *glance*
si, *himself*, etc.
sí, *yes*
siccome, *as, because*

sicuro, *safe, certain*

sigaretta, *cigarette*

sigaro, *cigar*

significato, *meaning*

signora, *lady, madam, Mrs.*

signore, *gentleman, sir, Mr.*

signoria, *lordship, authority, council of magistrates*

signorina, *young lady, Miss*

silenzio, *silence*

simpatico, *nice, likeable, charming*

sinceramente, *sincerely*

sincerità, *sincerity*

sincero, *sincere*

singolare, *strange*

sipario, *curtain*

smemorato, *forgetful*

soave, *suave, soft, gentle*

sobrio, *sober*

soddisfatto (di), *satisfied with*

soggiorno, *stay*

soglia, *threshold*

solamente, *only*

soldato, *soldier*

sole (m.), *sun*

solenne, *solemn*

solitario, *solitary*

solito, *usual*

  di solito, *usually*

solo, *only, alone*

soltanto, *only*

soma, *burden*

sommità, *summit*

sonno, *sleep*

sopra, *above*

soprabito, *overcoat*

soprattutto, *above all, especially*

sorella, *sister*

*sorgere (irreg.), *to rise*

sorprendere (irreg.), *to surprise*

sorpresa, *surprise*

sorridente, *smiling*

sorriso, *smile*

sotto, *under*

spagnuolo, *Spanish*

spalla, *shoulder*

spargere (irreg.), *to scatter*

spazio, *space*

specchio, *mirror*

speciale, *special*

  specialmente, *specially*

spedire (1st group), *to send, forward*

spendere (irreg.), *to spend*

speranza, *hope*

sperare (spero), *to hope*

spesso, *often, thick*

spessore, *thickness*

spettacolo, *spectacle, sight*

spettro, *ghost*

spiaggia, *shore, beach*

spillo, *pin*

spingere (irreg.), *to push*

spinta, *push*

sposare (sposo), *to marry*

sposo, *bridegroom*

squillo, *ring (bell), blast (trumpet)*

squisito, *exquisite*

staccare, *to detach*

stagione (f.), *season*

stamane, stamani, stamattina, *this morning*

stanco, *tired*

stanotte (f.), *tonight, last night*

stanza, *room*

  stanza da bagno, *bathroom*

*stare (irreg.), *to be, to stand*

  stare per, *to be about to, on the point of*

stasera, *this evening, tonight*

stato, *state*

statua, *statue*

statuetta, *small statue*

stazione (f.), *station*

*stendersi (irreg.), *to stretch oneself, extend*
stesso, *the same, self*
stile (m.), *style*
stipendio, *salary*
storia, *story, history*
storico, *historian*
strada, *street*
   straducola, *back street, alley*
straordinario, *extraordinary*
strapiombare (strapiombo), *to lean from the vertical, to be out of the plumb line*
stretta di mano, *handshake*
stringere (irreg.), *to grasp, press*

studente (m.), *student*
studiare, *to study*
studio, *study*
su, *on*
subito, *straight away*
*succedere (irreg.), *to happen*
suggerire (1st group), *to suggest*
suo, *his*
suonare (suono), *to sound, ring*
superiore, *upper, superior*
svariare, *to vary*
*svegliarsi (sveglio), *to awake*
sventolio, *fluttering, waving*
*svolgersi (irreg.), *to turn*

T

tabacco, *tobacco*
tacere (irreg.), *to be silent*
tamburo, *drum*
tanto, *so much*
   tanto . . . quanto, *as . . . as, so . . . as, as much . . . as, so much . . . as*
tappa, *stage, stopping place*
tappeto, *carpet*
tardare, *to delay*
tardi, *late*
tasca, *pocket*
tassa, *tax, fee*
tavola, *table*
tavolino, *small table*
tazza, *cup*
tè, *tea*
teatrale, *theatrical*
teatro, *theatre*
tegola, *tile, slate*
telefonare (telefono), *to telephone*
telefono, *telephone*
telegramma (m.), *telegram*
temere, *to fear*

tempesta, *storm*
tempo, *time, weather*
tenda, *tent*
tenere (irreg.), *to hold*
tenore (m.), *tenor*
tentare, *to try*
tentazione (f.), *temptation*
termine (m.), *term, period*
terra, *land, earth*
terrazza, *terrace*
terreno, *ground, earth*
testa, *head*
Testamento, *Testament*
tetto, *roof*
tiglio, *lime*
timidamente, *timidly*
tipico, *typical*
tirare, *to throw, to draw*
toccare, *to touch*
togliere (irreg.), *to take off*
tomba, *tomb*
tondo (adj. and n.), *round, plate, plaque*
tonnellata, *ton*
topografico, *topographical*

torchietto, *flare, torch*
*tornare (torno), *to return*
toro, *bull*
torre (f.), *tower*
torrente (m.), *torrent*
tovaglia, *table cloth*
tovagliolino, *small serviette, bib*
tovagliolo, *serviette*
tra, *between, among*
tradizionale, *traditional*
tradizione (f.), *tradition*
tradurre (irreg.), *translate*
tralcio, *tendril*
tramontare, *to set (sun)*
tranquillamente, *calmly*
tranquillità, *tranquillity*
trarre (irreg.), *to draw, drag*
trasalire (1st group), *to start, shiver*
trasformazione (f.), *transformation*
trasmettere (irreg.), *to transmit*
trasportare (trasporto), *to transport*

trattenere (irreg.), *to hold back*
tratto, *period, interval*
  a un tratto, *suddenly*
  a tratti, *at intervals*
†traversare (traverso), *to cross*
tregua, *respite*
tremendo, *tremendous*
treno, *train*
  treno merci, *goods train*
  treno omnibus, *slow stopping train*
tributario, *tributary*
tromba, *trumpet*
tronco, *trunk*
troppo, *too, too much*
trovare (trovo), *to find*
truppa, *troup*
*tuonare, *to thunder*
turco, *Turk*
turismo, *touring, travelling*
turista, *tourist*
  turistico, *of the tourist*
tuttavia, *nevertheless*
tutto, *all, whole*

U

uccello, *bird*
udire (irreg.), *to hear*
ufficio, uffizio, *office*
uliveto, *olive grove*
ulivo, *olive*
ultimo, *last*
unico, *only, unique*
uniforme (m.), *uniform*

uomo, *man*
uovo, *egg*
urlo, *shout*
usare, *to use*
*uscire (irreg.), *to go out*
uscita, *exit*
utile, *useful*
uva (collective noun), *grapes*

V

vacanza, *holiday*
vacca, *cow*
*valere (irreg.), *to be worth*
valevole, *valid*

valigia, *suitcase*
valle (f.), *valley*
valore (m.), *value*
vapore (m.), *steam*

vaporetto, *steamer*

vaporino, *steamer*

vassoio, *tray*

vecchio (adj. and n.), *old, old man*

vedere (irreg.), *to see*

veduta, *view*

vegetazione (f.), *vegetation*

vela, *sail*

veloce, *quick, quickly*

velocemente, *quickly*

vendere, *to sell*

venditore (m.), *seller*

veneziano, *Venetian*

*venire (irreg.), *to come*

ventaglio, *fan*

venticello, *breeze*

vento, *wind*

verde, *green*

vermut, *vermouth*

vero, *true*

verso, *towards*

verticale, *vertical*

vestibolo, *hall*

vestire (2nd group) (di) (vesto), *to dress*

vestito, *dress, suit*

vetrina, *shop window*

vetro, *glass*

vi (adv.), *here, there*

via, *road, way*

viaggiare (viaggio), *to travel*

viaggiatore (m.), *traveller*

viaggio, *journey*

viale (m.), *avenue*

vicino, *near, neighbour*

vicolo, *alley*

vigna, *vineyard*

vigneto, *vineyard*

villaggio, *village*

villeggiare (villeggio), *to holiday in the country*

villeggiatura, *stay in the country, country-seat*

villino, *small villa, cottage*

vincere (irreg.), *to conquer*

vincitore (m.), *conqueror, winner*

vincitrice (f.), *conqueror, winner*

vino, *wine*

violino, *violin*

virtú, *virtue*

visione (f.), *sight*

visita, *visit*

visitare (visito), *to visit*

visitatore (m.), *visitor*

viso, *face*

visto, *visa*

vitale, *vital*

vite (f.), *vine*

vitello, *veal*

vittima, *victim*

viva!, *long live !*

vivace, *vivacious*

vivere (irreg.), *to live*

vivo, *lively, bright*

voce (f.), *voice*

volare, *to fly*

volentieri, *willingly*

†volere (irreg.), *to wish, want*

volgere (irreg.), *to turn*

volo, *flight*

volta, *turn*

qualchevolta, *sometimes*

*voltarsi (volto), *to turn round*

volto, *face*

voluntario, *volunteer*

votare, *to vote*

Z

zɛlo, *zeal*
zɛro, *zero, nought, nothing*
zia, *aunt*
zio, *uncle*

zɔppo, *lame*
zucchero, *sugar*
zuppa, *soup*

INDEX

The numbers refer to pages

a, 20, 132–133; before an infinitive, 126; before names of towns, 132, 172; combined with article, 31; idiomatic uses, 47, 132–133

-a, nouns ending in, 20, 25, 68, 69; plurals in, 70

abbreviations, 214

absolute construction, use of past participle in, 179

absolute superlative: adjectives, 92–93; adverbs, 104, 186

accent, 17–18, 213–214; stress, 12–13; written, 17–18, 213–214

active voice, 53–54

address: direct, 58–61; modes of, 28–29; polite pronoun in, 28–29

adjectival clauses, 137–138

adjectival function of present participle, 183–184

adjectives: agreement, 25–26, 193; comparison, 90–93; demonstrative, 42–43, 111–112; gender and number of, 25–26, 29; in **-e,** 29; in **-io,** 51; in **-o,** 25–26; indefinite, 32–33, 112–114; interrogative, 46–47; irregular, 37–38; position of, 26, 36–38; possessive, 44–46; preceded by **di,** 188; prepositions following, 131, 172, 186; used as adverb, 104; used as noun, 44, 183–184, 206; verbal, 183–184

adverbial clauses: second past perfect in, 56; subjunctive in, 142–143

adverbs: adjectives in place of, 104; comparison, 104; conjunctive, 64; formation of, 103; of manner, 103–104; of place, 103; of quantity, 103; position of, 103

age, 96

alcuno, 32

alphabet, 11

altrui, 114

andare, 215; as auxiliary in passive, 107; in progressive tense, 179

any: adjective, 32–33; pronoun, 59

apostrophe: with conjunctive pronoun, 59, 61; with definite article, 24–25; with indefinite article, 19–20

article, see: definite, indefinite; repeated before each noun, 21

auxiliary verbs: see **avere, andare, essere, restare, rimanere, venire;** in compound tenses, 52–56; irregular forms, 220; past participle with, 53; semi-auxiliaries, 125–126, 173; with **dovere** and infinitive, 147–148; with impersonal verbs, 108; with the passive voice, 54, 107; with reflexive verbs, 54, 73; with transitive and intransitive verbs, 53–54

avere, 220; idiomatic phrases with, 96, 172; past participle with, 54; used as auxiliary, 52–56

belief, verbs expressing, 136

bello, 37

buono, 37–38; comparison, 93
by, 31; with passive voice, 107; with present participle, 65

-ca, nouns and adjectives in, 69
can, 83, 125, 173; see **sapere,** 100
capitals, 17, 22, 30
cardinal numbers, 16–17, 95; uses, 95–96; with possessive, 46
-care, verbs ending in, 104
century, 99
-cere, verbs ending in, 105
che: conjunction *(than),* 90–91; interjection, 43; interrogative adjective and pronoun, 46–47; relative pronoun, 71–73; used as a noun, 206
ci: adverb, 64, 107, 191; and position of, 64, 205; pronoun, 58–61; and position of, 59–61, 63–64; reflexive pronoun, 73–74
-cia, nouns and adjectives in, 104–105
-ciare, verbs ending in, 104–105
ciò, 18, 112
clauses: main, subjunctive in, 135–136, 141; subordinate: adjectival, 137–138; adverbial, 142–143; conditional, 146–147; depending on impersonal verb, 108; expressing indirect question or statement, 143–144; translated by Italian present participle, 65; use of second past perfect tense in, 56
close vowels, 13–14, 212
-co, nouns and adjectives ending in, 68–69, 197
codesto, 43
collective numerals, 99
colui, 112
combined letters, 16
command, verbs of, 127, 136
comparative, *see* comparison
comparison: adjectives, 90–93, irregular, 93; adverbs, 104, irregular, 104; than-clause, 142; translation of "than", 67, 90–92; use of disjunctive pronouns in, 67
compound tenses, 52–56, 79–80; agreement of past participle in, 54; uses, 56
con, combined with article, 31
conditional, 48–49, 79–80; contracted stem in formation of, 86–87; uses, 50
conditional clauses, 146–147
conditional perfect, 53–55, 80; uses, 56, 206
conjugations: first and second, 21–22; third, 27–28; irregular verbs, 214–220; regular verbs, 77–81
conjunctions: requiring subjunctive, 142–143, 172; with second past perfect, 56
conjunctive adverbs, 64
conjunctive pronouns, 57–61, 63–64; changes in forms, 63–64; direct becoming indirect, 125–126; elision of, 59, 61; position of, 59–64, 125–126, 173, 205; with dependent infinitive, 125–126, 173; with **ecco,** 62

conoscere, 100

consonants, 14–17; double, 15; groups of, 16; **s** and **z**, 212–213

contraction: of prepositions, 31; of infinitive stem, 48–49; of infinitive form, 84, 86–87

costui, 112

da: combined with article, 31; before an infinitive, 126, 183, 193; idiomatic uses, 47, 118, 131–132, 188, 193

dare, 86–87, 216

dates, 96

days of week, 17

definite article, 24–26; combined with prepositions, 31–33; in expressions of time, 51; in place of possessive, 118, 208; omission of, 45, 117–118, 172; various uses of, 47, 116–118; with infinitive as verbal noun, 124–125; with possessives, 44–46

demonstrative: adjectives, 42–43, 111–112; adverbs (of place), 103; pronouns, 111–112

dependent infinitive, 125–127

di: after certain adjectives, 130, 186; after comparatives, 90; after superlatives, 92; combined with article, 31; idiomatic uses, 129, 130, 132; partitive, 32; possession, 27; preceding an adjective, 188; preceding an infinitive, 126–127; *than,* 90

diphthongs, 14

dire, 87, 216

disjunctive pronouns, 67–68; in comparisons, 90–92; in exclamations, 68; in place of possessive, 45; objects of verbs, 67–68; subjects of verb, 22–23, 28–29; various uses, 67–68

do, auxiliary, translation of: interrogative sentences, 23; negative sentences, 33

double consonants, 15

double negation, 33

doubt, verbs of, with subjunctive, 136, 142–143, 146–147

dovere, 83, 216; followed by infinitive, 125, 147–148, 173; translating "ought", 147–148

e, close, open, 13–14, 212

ecco, 62

elision: with article, 19–20, 24–25; with conjunctive pronoun, 59, 61

-errimo, superlative in, 92

essere, 220; as auxiliary, 53–56; impersonal construction, 74, 108; past participle with, 53–56; with impersonal verbs, 108–109; with passive voice, 107

exclamations, 43; disjunctive pronouns in, 68; omission of indefinitive article, 118

fare, 86, 87, 216; idiomatic phrases with, 108, 180; position of pronoun objects with, 125–126; with dependent infinitive, 125–126, 183

fear, verbs expressing, 137

first conjugation, 21–22, 76–81; irregular verbs of, 86–87, 215–216, 218; orthographic changes in, 104–105
former, 112
fractions, 99
future, 48–49, 77, 78, 80; contracted stem in, 86–87; of probability, 50; uses of, 49–50
future perfect, 53–56, 80; English rendered by simple future, 109; uses of, 56

-ga, nouns and adjectives ending in, 69
-gare, verbs ending in, 104
gender, 19–20, 25–26, 29, 42, 68–70; masculines in **-a,** 68; nouns of two genders, 68
-gere, verbs ending in, 105
gerund, or present participle, 64–65; forming progressive tenses, 65
-gia, nouns and adjectives ending in, 69–70
-giare, verbs ending in, 104–105
-go, nouns and adjectives ending in, 68–69
grande, 37, 38; comparative of, 93

have, see **avere;** have to, *see* **dovere**
he who, 72–73
hiatus, 14
hope, verbs expressing, 137
hours, 51, 100
however, 113–114, 138

-iare, verbs ending in, 105
if: conditional sentences, 146–147; followed by the future, 49–50; rendered by present participle, 65
imperative, 59–60, 79; irregular forms of, 87; negative, 60–61; polite form, 59–61, 136; with conjunctive pronouns, 60–61
imperfect indicative, 40–42, 78; of auxiliary verbs, 42, 220; idiomatic use, 109; in conditional sentences, 147; use of, 35, 40–42
imperfect subjunctive, 79; of **essere,** 140, 220; in conditional clauses, 146–147; sequence of tenses, 141–144
impersonal construction, with reflexive, 74–75
impersonal verbs, 107–108; auxiliary with, 108; idiomatic uses of, 173, 176, 191, 197
in: after a superlative, 92; combined with article, 31; idiomatic uses of, 132; omission of, 176; rendered by **a,** 132, 172; by **di,** 132; by **fra,** 133; with the present participle, 65
indefinite adjectives, 32–33, 112–114; followed by the subjunctive, 114, 138
indefinite antecedent of relative pronoun, 138
indefinite article, 19–20; omission of, 118; uses of, 118; with the possessive, 46
indefinite pronouns, 33, 112–114; followed by the subjunctive, 114, 138
independent clauses, subjunctive in, 136, 141

indicative mood, *see* tenses
indirect object, conjunctive pronoun as, 58–61, 63–64; position, 59–61, 63–64
indirect question or statement, with subjunctive, 143–144
infinitive, 21, 77; contracted, 86–87; governed by a preposition, 126–127, 179; imperative negative, 60–61; translating English past participle, 125; verbal noun, 91, 124–125, 202; with conjunctive pronouns, 61, 125–126, 173; with semi-auxiliary verbs, 125, 173; without preposition, 125–126
-ing, English, rendered by: present participle, 64–65; verbal adjective, 183–184; verbal noun, 91, 124–126
interrogative: adjectives and pronouns, 46–47; sentences, 23; subjunctive following, 137, 143
intransitive verbs, 53–54
invariable nouns, 42
-io, nouns and adjectives ending in, 50–51
irregular comparison: adjectives, 101; adverbs, 114
irregular plural of nouns, 68–70
irregular verbs, 83, 85–88, 214–220; moods and tenses having irregularities, 86–88; irregular past definite, 86–88; regular forms of, 86
-isc-, in third conjugation: imperative, 60; present indicative, 27–28, 78; present subjunctive, 79
-issimo: adjectival suffix, 121; adverbial, 186
-ista, nouns ending in, 68
it, subject of impersonal verbs, 107–108
it is I, it is you, etc., 73

know, **sapere** and **conoscere**, 100

lasciare, with dependent infinitive, 125, 183
latter, 112
Lei, in polite address, 28–29
letters: alphabet, 11; capitals, 17, 22, 30; combined, 15–16; consonants, 14–17, 212–213; vowels, 11–15, 212
loro: conjunctive pronoun, 58–61, 63; disjunctive, 67; position, 60–63
Loro, in polite address, 28–29, 58–61

manner, adverbs of, 102–104; adjectives used as, 104
may, see **potere**
measurements, 96
modal auxiliary, *see* semi-auxiliary
months, 17
moods, *see* conditional, imperative, indicative, infinitive, participle, subjunctive, tenses
must, see **dovere**

ne: adverb, 64; pronoun, 59, 63–64
né, conjunction, 33
negative: double, 33; expressions, 32–33; sentences, 32–33; subjunctive following, 137, 143

nessuno, niente, 33; subjunctive following, 137
non, 27, 32–33; double negative, 33
noun clauses, 136–137, 141, 143
nouns: see gender, plural; change of gender in plural, 70; endings in
   -a, 19–20, 25, 68; in **-ca, -ga, -cia, -gia, -co, -go,** 68–70; in **-e,** 29;
   in **-io,** 50; in **-o,** 19, 25; in apposition, 118; in comparisons, 90–91;
   infinitive as noun, 91, 124–125; invariable in plural, 42; irregular
   plurals, 68–70; of two genders, 68
nulla, *see* **niente**
number, *see* plural
numerals, *see* cardinal, collective, fractions, ordinal; in comparisons,
   90

o, close, open, 13–14, 212
objects, direct, indirect, *see* conjunctive, disjunctive pronouns
omission of articles, 45, 117–118, 172
on: in dates, 96; omission of, 96, 176; with present participle, 65
one, impersonal, 74–75, 205
only, requiring subjunctive, 137
open vowels, 13–14, 212
opinion, verbs expressing, 136
ordinal numbers, 98–99
orthographic changes in verbs, 104–105
osare, with dependent infinitive, 125
ought, see **dovere,** 83, 125, 147–148, 173

participle, past, 52–56, 77–80; absolute construction with, 179;
   agreement of, 53–54, 61; position of conjunctive pronouns with, 61
participle, perfect, 64, 80
participle, present, 64–65: English rendered in Italian, 64–65, 91,
   124–125, 183–184; in progressive tense, 65, 179; position of conjunctive pronouns with, 61, 63; uses of, 64–65; verbal adjective,
   183–184
partitive, 32
passive voice, 107; auxiliaries used with, 53–54, 107; reflexive in
   place of, 74
past definite, 35–36, 78; of auxiliary verbs, 36, 220; irregular, 86–88;
   use, 35–36
past participle, *see* participle
past perfect and second past perfect, 53–56, 80; uses, 56
past perfect subjunctive, 80; in conditional clauses, 147; in independent sentences, 141; in subordinate clauses, 141
past subjunctive, *see* imperfect subjunctive
people, one, they, impersonal, 74–75, 205
per, combined with article, 31
perfect, *see* past perfect, present perfect
perfect infinitive, 80
perfect participle, *see* participle
personal pronouns, *see* conjunctive, disjunctive
place, adverbs of: conjunctive, 64; demonstrative, 103

plural of adjectives: in -ca, -ga, -cia, -gia, -co, -go, 68–70; in -e, 29; in -io, 50; in -o, 25–26; irregular forms, 37–38
plural of definite article, 24–25
plural of nouns: in -a (feminine), 25–26; in -a (masculine), 68; in -ca, -ga, -cia, -gia, -co, -go, 68–70; in -e, 29; in -io, 50–51; in -o, 19–20, 25–26; invariable, 42; irregular, 68–70; with change of gender, 70
plural of pronouns, see conjunctive, disjunctive; subject pronouns, 22–23
polite pronoun, 28–29, 58–61
porre, 86–87, 217
position: of adjectives, 26, 36–38; form and meaning of adjective altered by, 36–38; of pronouns, 59–61, 63–64; of pronouns with dependent infinitive, 125–126, 173; of pronouns with impersonal **si,** 205
possession, see **di,** 27
possessive adjectives and pronouns, 44–46; definite article omitted with, 45–46; omission of, 179, 208; plural used to denote kindred, 206; preceded by definite article, 44–46; reflexive in place of, 74
potere, 83–84, 217; as semi-auxiliary, 125, 173
prepositional phrases, 131, 200
prepositions: combined with definite article, 31–32; governing an infinitive, 125–127, 200; idiomatic uses, 129–133; omitted in Italian where required in English, 129–130; required after certain verbs, 129–130, 184; required in Italian where omitted in English, 129; simple, 131–133; translated by an adverb of place, 184; with certain adjectives, 131
present indicative: auxiliary verbs, 28–29, 220; irregular verbs, 214–220; regular, 77–78; idiomatic use of, 109; progressive tense, 65
present participle, see participle
present perfect, 35, 80; use, 53–56
present perfect subjunctive, 80; use, 140–143
present subjunctive, 79; uses, 135–138, 140–143; as imperative, 59–61
probability, future of, 49–50
progressive tenses, 65, 179
pronouns, see address, conjunctive, demonstrative, disjunctive, indefinite, polite, possessive, reciprocal, reflexive, relative, subject; in comparisons, 90–92; as direct objects, 58–61, 63–64; as indirect objects, 58–61, 63–64
pronunciation, 11–18, 212–213; close and open è and ò, 13, 212; consonants, 14–16; diphthongs, 13–14; double consonants, 15, 212–213; groups of consonants, 16, 212–213; triphthongs, 14; two or more vowels together, 13–14; vowels, 11–14, 212

qualche, 32, 113
qualunque, 114; followed by subjunctive, 138
quello, forms of, 43

reciprocal pronouns, *one another, each other,* 59
reflexive pronouns, 58; in place of possessive, 74; position of object pronouns with, 205; uses, 73–75, 200

reflexive verbs, 73–75; auxiliary with, 73; impersonal construction, 74–75; indefinite **si** for first person plural, 200; in place of possessive, 74; position of object pronouns with, 205; translating the English passive, 74

regular forms in irregular verbs, 86–87

relative clauses, requiring subjunctive, 136–138, 141–143

relative pronouns, 71–73; subjunctive after, 136–138

relative superlative: adjectives, 92–93; adverbs, 104; subjunctive after, 137

restare, rimanere, as auxiliaries, 107

s: unvoiced, voiced, 15, 212–213; impure, 20, 25

santo, forms of, 37

sapere, 218; meanings, 100; with dependent infinitive, 125

second conjugation, 22, 77–80; irregular verbs of, 83, 87–88, 214–220

second past perfect, 53–56, 80; use, 56

semi-auxiliary verbs, 125, 147–148

sentire, with infinitive, 125

sequence of tenses, 140–143

si, *see* reflexive pronouns; position of, with pronoun objects, 205

simple tenses, conjugated, 77–79

some: adjective, 32; pronoun, 59

stare, 218; idiomatic uses, 179; in progressive tenses, 65

stem, of verbs, 21–22; infinitive as, 48–49; in irregular verbs, 86–88

stress, 12, 17–18, 213–214

su: combined with article, 31–32; idiomatic use, 100, 188

subject pronouns, 22–23, omission of, 22

subjunctive: conjugation of tenses of auxiliary verbs, 136, 140, 220; of irregular verbs, 86, 214–220; of regular verbs, 79–80

subjunctive, uses of: after impersonal verbs, 108; as imperative, 59–61, 136; in adjectival clauses, 137–138; in adverbial clauses, 142–143; in conditional clauses, 146–147; in indirect questions and statements, 143; in main clauses, 136, 141; in noun clauses, 136–138; sequence of tenses in, 140–143. Also see: conjunctions requiring subjunctive

subordinate clauses, *see* clauses

suffixes, 120–122, 188

superlative: of adjectives, absolute, irregular, relative, 92–93; of adverbs, absolute, irregular, relative, 104

syllabication, 214

tenses: conjugation of auxiliary verbs, 220; compound, 79–80; simple, 77–79

tenses: idiomatic uses of, 109; irregular forms, 86–87, 214–220; regular forms, 77–81; sequence of, 140–143

than, translation of, 90–91; *than*-clause, 91, 142

third conjugation, 27–28; irregular verbs of, 214–220; regular, 77–81

through, with present participle, 65

time: conjunctions of, with second past perfect, 56; conjunctions of, taking the subjunctive, 142–143; expressions of, 51, 100

titles, article with, 117
transitive verbs, with auxiliary, 53–54
triphthongs, 14

udire, 219; with dependent infinitive, 125
uno: article, 19–20; numeral, 95; pronoun, 112–114

vedere, 219; with dependent infinitive, 125
venire, 219; as auxiliary, 107
verbs, *see* auxiliary, conjugations, imperative, indicative, infinitive,
   intransitive, irregular, orthographic changes in, reflexive, regular,
   stem, subjunctive, transitive
verbal: adjective, 183; noun, 124–127
vi: adverb, 64; conjunctive pronoun, 58–61, 63–64; reflexive pronoun, 73–75
voice, *see* active, passive
volere, 83, 220; as semi-auxiliary verb, 125, 173; impersonal use, 107,
   191
vowels, 11–14, 212

weather, expressions of, 107–108, 180
whatever, whoever, etc., followed by the subjunctive, 114, 138
written accent, 17–18, 213–214

z, unvoiced and voiced, 15, 212–213